G　　U　　I　　D　　E

Reporting on Controls at a Service Organization

Relevant to Security, Availability, Processing Integrity, Confidentiality, or Privacy (SOC 2℠)

WITH CONFORMING CHANGES AS OF
MARCH 1, 2012

Preface

About AICPA Guides

This AICPA Guide has been developed by the AICPA SOC 2^{SM} Guide Working Group comprised of members of the AICPA Assurance Services Executive Committee's Trust/Data Integrity Task Force and the AICPA Information Technology Executive Committee's Privacy Task Force and Cloud Computing Task Force to assist CPAs in performing examinations under AT section 101, *Attest Engagements* (AICPA, *Professional Standards*), to report on a service organization's controls over its system relevant to security, availability, processing integrity, confidentiality, or privacy. The Auditing Standards Board (ASB) has found the descriptions of attestation standards, procedures, and practices in this guide to be consistent with existing standards covered by Rule 202, *Compliance With Standards* (AICPA, *Professional Standards*, ET sec. 202 par. .01), and Rule 203, *Accounting Principles* (AICPA, *Professional Standards*, ET sec. 203 par. .01).

Attestation guidance included in an AICPA guide is recognized as an attestation interpretation as defined in AT section 50, *SSAE Hierarchy* (AICPA, *Professional Standards*). Attestation interpretations are recommendations on the application of Statements on Standards for Attestation Engagements (SSAEs) in specific circumstances, including engagements for entities in specialized industries. Attestation interpretations are issued under the authority of the ASB. The members of the ASB have found the attestation guidance in this guide to be consistent with existing SSAEs.

A practitioner[1] should be aware of and consider attestation interpretations applicable to his or her attestation engagement. If a practitioner does not apply the attestation guidance included in an applicable attestation interpretive publication, the practitioner should be prepared to explain how he or she complied with the SSAE provisions addressed by such attestation guidance.

Purpose and Applicability

This guide has been prepared to assist CPAs engaged to examine and report on a service organization's controls over one or more of the following:

- The security of a service organization's system
- The availability of a service organization's system
- The processing integrity of a service organization's system
- The confidentiality of the information that the service organization's system processes or maintains for user entities
- The privacy of personal information that the service organization collects, uses, retains, discloses, and disposes of for user entities

The engagement described in this guide is based on the requirements and guidance established in AT section 101. SSAEs are also known as the attestation standards. The attestation standards enable a practitioner to report on

---

[1] In the attestation standards, a CPA performing an attestation engagement ordinarily is referred to as a *practitioner*. Statement on Standards for Attestation Engagements No. 16, *Reporting on Controls at a Service Organization* (AICPA, *Professional Standards*, AT sec. 801), uses the term *service auditor*, rather than *practitioner*, to refer to a CPA reporting on controls at a service organization, as does this guide.

subject matter other than financial statements. AT section 101 provides a framework for all attestation engagements.

A practitioner may be engaged to examine and report on controls at a service organization related to various types of subject matter (for example, controls that affect user entities' financial reporting or the privacy of information processed for user entities' customers). The applicable attestation standard for such engagements may vary, depending on the subject matter. To make practitioners aware of the various professional standards and guides available to them for examining and reporting on controls at a service organization and to help practitioners select the appropriate standard or guide for a particular engagement, the AICPA has introduced the term *service organization controls (SOC) reports*. The following are designations for three such engagements and the source of the guidance for performing and reporting on them:

- SOC 1[SM]: SSAE No. 16, *Reporting on Controls at a Service Organization* (AICPA, *Professional Standards*, AT sec. 801), and the AICPA Guide *Service Organizations: Applying SSAE No. 16,* Reporting on Controls at a Service Organization *(SOC 1[SM])*

- SOC 2[SM]: AT section 101 and the AICPA Guide *Reporting on Controls at a Service Organization Relevant to Security, Availability, Processing Integrity, Confidentiality, or Privacy (SOC 2[SM])*

- SOC 3[SM]: AT section 101 and appendix C, "Practitioner's Guidance in Scoping and Reporting Issues," of TSP section 100, *Trust Services Principles, Criteria, and Illustrations for Security, Availability, Processing Integrity, Confidentiality, and Privacy* (AICPA, *Technical Practice Aids*), which discusses issues related to SOC 3 engagement planning, performance, and reporting

This guide focuses on SOC 2 engagements. Paragraph 1.24 of this guide includes a table that compares features of the three engagements.

Recognition

Darrel R. Schubert
Chair, ASB

William Titera
Chair, ASEC

Auditing Standards Board (2010–2011)

Darrel R. Schubert, *Chair*
Ernest F. Baugh, Jr.
Brian R. Bluhm
Robert E. Chevalier
Samuel K. Cotterell
James R. Dalkin
David D. Duree
Edwin G. Jolicoeur
David M. Morris
Kenneth R. Odom
Thomas A. Ratcliffe
Brian R. Richson
Thomas M. Stemlar
Mark H. Taylor
Kim L. Tredinnick
H. Steven Vogel

Phil D. Wedemeyer
Kurtis Wolff
Megan F. Zietsman

Assurance Services Executive Committee (2010–2011)

William Titera, *Chair*
Alan Anderson
Suzanne Christensen
Sean Denham
Robert Dohrer
Glenn Galfond
Theresa Grafenstine
Charles E. Harris
Fain McDaniel
Leslie Murphy
Donny Shimamoto
Glenn Stastny
Leslie Thompson
Miklos Vasarhelyi

SOC 2^{SM} Guide Working Group

Chris Halterman, *Chair*
Gary Baker
Efrim Boritz
Sheri Fedokovitz
Everett Johnson
Audrey Katcher
Kevin Knight
Chris Kradjan
John Lainhart
Rena Mears
David Palmer
Thomas Patterson
Doron Rotman
Don Sheehy
Curtis Stewarts
Steve Ursillo Jr.

AICPA Staff

Charles E. Landes
Vice President
Professional Standards

Amy Pawlicki
Director
Business Reporting, Assurance and Advisory Services & XBRL

Judith Sherinsky
Senior Technical Manager
Audit and Attest Standards

Erin Mackler
Senior Manager
Business Reporting, Assurance and Advisory Services

Diana Krupica
Technical Manager
Accounting and Auditing Publications

Guidance Considered in This Edition

This edition of the guide has been modified by the AICPA staff to include certain changes necessary due to the issuance of authoritative guidance since the guide was originally issued, and other revisions as deemed appropriate. Authoritative guidance issued through March 1, 2012, has been considered in the development of this edition of the guide. This includes relevant guidance issued up to and including the following:

- SSAE No. 17, *Reporting on Compiled Prospective Financial Statements When the Practitioner's Independence is Impaired* (AICPA, *Professional Standards*, AT sec. 301)
- Interpretation No. 1, "Reporting Under Section 112 of the Federal Deposit Insurance Corporation Improvement Act," of AT section 501, *An Examination of an Entity's Internal Control Over Financial Reporting That Is Integrated With an Audit of Its Financial Statements* (AICPA, *Professional Standards*, AT sec. 9501 par. .01–.07)

Users of this guide should consider guidance issued subsequent to those items listed previously to determine their effect on entities covered by this guide. In determining the applicability of recently issued guidance, its effective date should also be considered.

The changes made to this edition of the guide are identified in the schedule of changes appendix. The changes do not include all those that might be considered necessary if the guide were subjected to a comprehensive review and revision.

AICPA.org Website

The AICPA encourages you to visit its website at www.aicpa.org, and the new Financial Reporting Center at www.aicpa.org/frc. Included in the Financial Reporting Center is a resource center covering SOC reporting. For more information, visit www.aicpa.org/soc.

The Financial Reporting Center was created to support members in the execution of high-quality financial reporting. Whether you are a financial statement preparer or a member in public practice, this center provides exclusive member-only resources for the entire financial reporting process, and provides timely and relevant news, guidance and examples supporting the financial reporting process, including accounting, preparing financial statements and performing compilation, review, audit, attest or assurance and advisory engagements. Certain content on the AICPA's websites referenced in this guide may be restricted to AICPA members only.

Select Recent Developments Significant to This Guide

ASB's Clarity Project

Although this guide is an attestation guide, the following information on the ASB Clarity Project has been included to alert users that the auditing standards references herein will be updated for clarity in the next edition. To address concerns over the clarity, length, and complexity of its standards, the ASB has made a significant effort to clarify the Statements on Auditing Standards (SASs). The ASB established clarity drafting conventions and undertook to redraft all of its SASs in accordance with those conventions, which include the following:

- Establishing objectives for each clarified SAS
- Including a definitions section, where relevant, in each clarified SAS
- Separating requirements from application and other explanatory material
- Numbering application and other explanatory material paragraphs using an A- prefix and presenting them in a separate section that follows the requirements section
- Using formatting techniques, such as bulleted lists, to enhance readability
- Including, when appropriate, special considerations relevant to audits of smaller, less complex entities within the text of the clarified SAS
- Including, when appropriate, special considerations relevant to audits of governmental entities within the text of the clarified SAS

In addition, as the ASB redrafted standards for clarity, it also converged the standards with the International Standards on Auditing (ISA), issued by the International Auditing and Assurance Standards Board. As part of redrafting the standards, they now specify more clearly the objectives of the auditor and the requirements which the auditor has to comply with when conducting an audit in accordance with generally accepted auditing standards (GAAS).

With the release of SAS Nos. 117–120 and Nos. 122–125, the project is near completion. As of the date of this guide, the only SASs remaining to be clarified are

- SAS No. 59, *The Auditor's Consideration of an Entity's Ability to Continue as a Going Concern* (AICPA, *Professional Standards*, AU sec. 341), as amended; and
- SAS No. 65, *The Auditor's Consideration of the Internal Audit Function in an Audit of Financial Statements* (AICPA, *Professional Standards*, AU sec. 322).

Note that SAS No. 122 withdraws SAS No. 26, *Association With Financial Statements*, as amended, from *Professional Standards*.

SAS Nos. 122–125 will be effective for audits of financial statements for periods ending on or after December 15, 2012. Refer to individual AU-C sections for specific effective date language. Early adoption is not permitted.

As part of the Clarity Project, the resulting clarified auditing standards are numbered based on equivalent ISAs and are located in "AU-C" sections within AICPA *Professional Standards*. This is a change from the "AU" section numbers where the extant standards are located. "AU-C" is a temporary identifier being used to avoid confusion with references to existing "AU" sections, which remain effective through 2013. The "AU-C" identifier will revert to "AU" in 2014, by which time the clarified auditing standards become fully effective for all engagements. Note that AU-C section numbers for clarified SASs with no equivalent ISAs have been assigned new numbers. The ASB believes that this recodification structure will aid firms and practitioners that use both ISAs and GAAS.

All auditing interpretations corresponding to a SAS have been considered in the development of a clarified SAS and incorporated accordingly, and have been withdrawn by the ASB except for certain interpretations that the ASB has retained and revised to reflect the issuance of SAS No. 122. A listing of the retained interpretations can be found in AU-C exhibit B, *Retained Interpretations*. The effective date of the revised interpretations aligns with the effective date of the corresponding clarified SAS.

This AICPA Guide will be fully conformed to the clarified auditing standards in a subsequent edition. In the interim, readers are encouraged to refer to appendix F, "Guidance Updates—Clarified Auditing Standards," of this guide for information on the changes to the extant auditing standards found to be substantive (that is, likely to affect the firms' audit methodology and engagements because they contain substantive or other changes) or primarily clarifying (that is, intended to explicitly state what may have been implicit in the extant standards). See also appendix G, "Mapping and Summarization of Changes—Clarified Auditing Standards." This appendix cross references extant AU sections with AU-C sections and indicates the nature of changes made in the clarified standard.

TABLE OF CONTENTS

Contents

Chapter 1

Introduction and Background

> This chapter explains the relationship between a service organization and its user entities, provides examples of service organizations, identifies the criteria that are used to evaluate the design and operating effectiveness of controls at a service organization, explains the difference between a type 1 and type 2 service auditor's report, and presents three reporting options for CPAs reporting on controls at a service organization.

1.01 Many entities function more efficiently and profitably by outsourcing tasks or entire functions to other organizations that have the personnel, expertise, equipment, or technology to accomplish these tasks or functions. This guide focuses on organizations that collect, process, transmit, store, organize, maintain, or dispose of information for other entities. In this guide, an organization or segment of an organization that operates information systems and provides services to other entities is known as a *service organization*, and entities that use the services of service organizations are known as *user entities*. Examples of the services provided by such service organizations are as follows:

- *Cloud computing.* Providing on-demand network access to a shared pool of configurable computing resources (for example, networks, servers, storage, applications, and services). (Additional information about cloud computing is presented in appendix E, "Service Auditor Considerations in Performing SOC 2^{SM} or SOC 3^{SM} Engagements for Cloud Computing Service Organizations," of this guide.)

- *Managed security.* Managing access to networks and computing systems for user entities (for example, granting access to a system and preventing, or detecting and mitigating, system intrusion).

- *Customer support.* Providing customers of user entities with online or telephonic postsales support and service management. Examples of these services are warranty inquiries and investigating and responding to customer complaints.

- *Sales force automation.* Providing and maintaining software to automate business tasks for user entities that have a sales force. Examples of such tasks are order processing, information sharing, order tracking, contact management, customer management, sales forecast analysis, and employee performance evaluation.

- *Health care claims management and processing.* Providing medical providers, employers, and insured parties of employers with systems that enable medical records and related health insurance claims to be processed securely and confidentially.

- *Enterprise IT outsourcing services.* Managing, operating, and maintaining user entities' IT data centers, infrastructure, and application systems and related functions that support IT activities, such as network, production, security, change management, hardware, and environmental control activities.

1.02 Management of a user entity is responsible for assessing and addressing risks faced by the user entity related to financial reporting, compliance with laws and regulations, and the efficiency and effectiveness of operations. When a user entity engages a service organization to perform key processes or functions, the user entity exposes itself to additional risks related to the service organization's system. Although management of a user entity can delegate tasks or functions to a service organization, the responsibility for the product or service provided to customers of the user entity cannot be delegated. Management of the user entity is usually held responsible by those charged with governance (for example, the board of directors); customers; shareholders; regulators; and other affected parties for establishing effective internal control over outsourced functions.

1.03 To assess and address the risks associated with an outsourced service, management of the user entity needs information about the service organization's controls[1] over the system through which the services are provided. When assessing controls at a service organization that may be relevant to and affect the services provided to user entities, management of a user entity may ask the service organization for a CPA's report on the design and operating effectiveness of controls over the service organization's system that may be relevant to the security, availability, or processing integrity of the system (security, availability, processing integrity) or the confidentiality or privacy of the information processed for user entities (confidentiality or privacy).

1.04 Footnote 1 of TSP section 100, *Trust Services Principles, Criteria, and Illustrations for Security, Availability, Processing Integrity, Confidentiality, and Privacy* (AICPA, *Technical Practice Aids*), contains the following definition of a system:

> A *system* consists of five key components organized to achieve a specified objective. The five components are categorized as follows:
>
> - *Infrastructure.* The physical and hardware components of a system (facilities, equipment, and networks)
> - *Software.* The programs and operating software of a system (systems, applications, and utilities)
> - *People.* The personnel involved in the operation and use of a system (developers, operators, users, and managers)
> - *Procedures.* The programmed and manual procedures involved in the operation of a system (automated and manual)
> - *Data.* The information used and supported by a system (transaction streams, files, databases, and tables)

1.05 TSP section 100 provides criteria for evaluating and reporting on controls related to security, availability, processing integrity, confidentiality, and privacy. In TSP section 100, these five attributes of a system are known as *principles*, and they are defined in paragraph .10 of TSP section 100 as follows:

> a. *Security.* The system is protected against unauthorized access (both physical and logical).
>
> b. *Availability.* The system is available for operation and use as committed or agreed.
>
> c. *Processing integrity.* System processing is complete, accurate, timely, and authorized.

---

[1] In this guide, *controls* are policies and procedures that enable an entity to meet specified criteria.

d. *Confidentiality*. Information designated as confidential is protected as committed or agreed.

e. *Privacy*. Personal information[2] is collected, used, retained, disclosed, and destroyed[3] in conformity with the commitments in the entity's privacy notice[4] and with criteria set forth in generally accepted privacy principles (GAPP) issued by the AICPA and CICA.[5] [The criteria in GAPP are the same as the criteria for the privacy principle in TSP section 100.]

1.06 The primary focus of this guide is on examining and reporting on a description of a service organization's system and the suitability of the design and operating effectiveness of its controls relevant to security, availability, processing integrity, confidentiality, or privacy. Paragraphs 1.08–.09 describe two related engagements and are included here to provide context and background for the engagement that is the primary focus of this guide.

1.07 Statements on Standards for Attestation Engagements (SSAEs)— also known as the attestation standards—enable a CPA to report on subject matter other than financial statements. Most of the attestation standards address specific subject matter, such as reporting on an entity's compliance with laws and regulations or on a financial forecast or projection. AT section 101, *Attest Engagements* (AICPA, *Professional Standards*), however, provides a framework for performing and reporting on all attestation engagements.

Service Organization Controls 3 Engagements in Accordance With AT Section 101 Using the Trust Services Criteria

1.08 The implementation guidance in TSP section 100 for performing and reporting on an examination engagement using the trust services criteria is based on AT section 101. A practitioner may report on one or more of the five

---

[2] Personal information is information that is about or can be related to an identifiable individual.

[3] Collection, use, retention, disclosure, and disposal or anonymization are the aspects of the personal information life cycle.

[4] Entities that collect personal information generally establish and document their policies regarding the nature of the information they collect and how that information will be used, retained, disclosed, and disposed of or anonymized. These policies and the entity's commitment to adhere to them when included in a written communication to individuals about whom personal information is collected (sometimes referred to as data subjects) are referred to as a privacy notice. A privacy notice also includes information about such matters as the purpose of collecting the information; the choices individuals have related to their personal information; the security of such information; and how individuals can contact the entity with inquiries, complaints, and disputes related to their personal information. When a user entity collects personal information from individuals, it typically provides a privacy notice to those individuals.

When a service organization is involved in any of the phases of the personal information life cycle, it may or may not be responsible for providing a privacy notice to the individuals about whom information is collected. If the user entity is responsible for providing the privacy notice, the service organization provides a statement of privacy practices to the user entities that includes the same types of policies and commitments as would be included in a privacy notice, but the statement is written from the perspective of the service organization communicating its privacy-related policies and commitments to the user entities. The statement of privacy practices provides a basis for the user entities to prepare a privacy notice to be sent to individuals or for ensuring that the service organization has appropriate practices for meeting the existing privacy commitments of user entities.

[5] The criteria for the content of a statement of privacy practices are set forth in paragraph 1.35e of this guide.

trust services principles (principles). In the examination report included in TSP section 100, the practitioner expresses an opinion on whether the service organization maintained effective controls over its system, based on the criteria in TSP section 100 that are applicable to the principle(s) being reported on. In this guide, the examination engagement described in TSP section 100 is known as a *service organization controls (SOC) 3^{SM} engagement*, and the resulting report is known as a *SOC 3 report*. Although a SOC 3 report is designed to meet the needs of a broad range of users, it does not contain a detailed description of the service auditor's tests of the operating effectiveness of controls and the results of those tests, which may be necessary for a particular user to determine how it is affected by those controls. Appendix C, "Practitioner Guidance on Scoping and Reporting Issues," of TSP section 100 discusses issues related to SOC 3 engagement planning, performance, and reporting.

SOC 1^{SM} Engagements in Accordance With SSAE No. 16

1.09 SSAE No. 16, *Reporting on Controls at a Service Organization* (AICPA, *Professional Standards*, AT sec. 801),[6] establishes the requirements and guidance for a CPA examining and reporting on a service organization's description of its system and its controls that are likely to be relevant to user entities' internal control over financial reporting. Service organizations frequently receive requests from user entities for these reports because they are needed by the auditors of the user entities' financial statements (user auditors) to obtain information about controls at the service organization that may affect assertions in the user entities' financial statements. In this guide, an engagement performed under SSAE No. 16 is known as a *SOC 1 engagement*, and a report on that engagement is known as a *SOC 1 report*. SOC 1 reports are intended solely for the information and use of existing user entities (for example, existing customers of the service organization); their financial statement auditors; and management of the service organization.

SOC 2^{SM} Engagements in Accordance With AT Section 101 and the AICPA Guide *Reporting on Controls at a Service Organization Relevant to Security, Availability, Processing Integrity, Confidentiality, or Privacy (SOC 2^{SM})*, Using the Trust Services Criteria

1.10 This guide provides performance and reporting guidance based on AT section 101 for an examination of a service organization's description of its system and controls that are likely to be relevant to the security, availability, or processing integrity of a service organization's system or the confidentiality or privacy of the information processed by the system. In this guide, such an engagement is known as a *SOC 2 engagement*, and a report on such an

---

[6] AU section 324, *Service Organizations* (AICPA, *Professional Standards*), addresses the user auditor's responsibility for obtaining sufficient appropriate audit evidence in an audit of the financial statements of a user entity. Prior to the issuance of Statement on Standards for Attestation Engagements (SSAE) No. 16, *Reporting on Controls at a Service Organization* (AICPA, *Professional Standards*, AT sec. 801), the applicable requirements and guidance for both service auditors and user auditors was included in AU section 324. The requirements and guidance for service auditors was moved to SSAE No. 16. The requirements and guidance for user auditors is retained in AU section 324. When AU-C section 402, *Audit Considerations Relating to an Entity Using a Service Organization* (AICPA, *Professional Standards*), becomes effective, it will replace the guidance for user auditors currently in AU section 324. AU-C section 402 is effective for audits of financial statements for periods ending on or after December 15, 2012.

engagement is known as a *SOC 2 report*. Similar to a SOC 3 engagement, it uses the criteria in TSP section 100 to evaluate the design and operating effectiveness of the service organization's controls. Unlike a SOC 3 engagement, a practitioner's SOC 2 report includes a detailed description of the service auditor's tests of controls and the results of those tests. Although SSAE No. 16 is intended only for reporting on controls at a service organization that are likely to be relevant to user entities' internal control over financial reporting, paragraph .02 of AT section 801 indicates that the guidance in SSAE No. 16 may be helpful to a practitioner[7] performing an engagement under AT section 101 to report on a service organization's controls other than those that are likely to be relevant to user entities' internal control over financial reporting. Much of the guidance is this guide is modeled after SSAE No. 16.

Criteria for a SOC 2 Engagement: Description Criteria and Trust Services Criteria

1.11 A service auditor may be engaged to report on a description of a service organization's system and the suitability of the design and operating effectiveness of controls relevant to one or more of the trust services principles listed in paragraph 1.05. The decision about which principles the description will address is usually made by management of the service organization and is often based on input from users.

1.12 In this guide, the criteria used to evaluate the fairness of the presentation of management's description of the service organization's system are known as the *description criteria*, and they are identified in paragraphs 1.34–.35. The criteria in TSP section 100 that are applicable to the principle(s) being reported on and that are used to evaluate the suitability of the design and operating effectiveness of the service organization's controls are known as the *applicable trust services criteria*. In a SOC 2 report, the service auditor expresses an opinion on the following:

- Whether the description of the service organization's system is fairly presented, based on the description criteria in paragraphs 1.34–.35

- Whether the controls are suitably designed to provide reasonable assurance that the applicable trust services criteria would be met if the controls operated effectively

- In type 2 reports (described in paragraph 1.17*a*), whether the controls were operating effectively to meet the applicable trust services criteria

- In engagements to report on the privacy principle, whether the service organization complied with the commitments in its statement of privacy practices

1.13 In evaluating the fairness of the presentation of management's description of the service organization's system, the service auditor should determine whether the description meets all of the description criteria in paragraphs 1.34–.35. Paragraph .23 of AT section 101 requires that criteria be available to users. Because the criteria in paragraphs 1.34–.35 may not be readily available to report users, management of the service organization should include in its assertion all of the description criteria in paragraphs

---

[7] In the attestation standards, a CPA performing an attestation engagement ordinarily is referred to as a *practitioner*. SSAE No. 16 uses the term *service auditor*, rather than *practitioner*, to refer to a CPA reporting on controls at a service organization, as does this guide.

1.34–.35. Although all of the criteria should be included in management's assertion, certain description criteria may not be pertinent to a particular service organization or system. For example, the criterion in paragraph 1.34a(v) would not be pertinent to a service organization that does not prepare and deliver reports or other information to user entities or other parties, and the criterion in paragraph 1.34a(vii)(2) would not be applicable to a service organization that does not use a subservice organization. If certain description criteria are not pertinent to a service organization, report users generally find it useful if management presents all of the description criteria and indicates which criteria are not pertinent to the service organization and the reasons therefore. Management may do so either in its system description or in a note to the specific description criteria.

1.14 To meet the criteria in paragraph 1.34a(vii), the service auditor should determine that all of the applicable trust services criteria have been included in management's description. For example, if a service auditor is reporting on the design and operating effectiveness of controls at a service organization relevant to the security of user entities' information, the service auditor should determine that all of the criteria in the set of trust services criteria related to security have been included in the description. The applicable trust services criteria for each principle are presented in appendix B, "Trust Services Principles and Criteria for Security, Availability, Processing Integrity, Confidentiality, and Privacy," of this guide.

1.15 If the description includes one or more applicable trust services criteria that are not addressed by controls, the description should include an explanation of why the criteria are not addressed by controls. The absence of controls to meet one or more applicable trust services criteria is appropriate if the criteria are not pertinent to the system that is the subject of the engagement. For example, consider an engagement that addresses the privacy principle in which the user entities, rather than the service organization, collect personal information from individuals. In those circumstances, it would be appropriate for the service organization's description to include a criteria related to the collection of personal information, exclude controls that address that criterion, and include an explanation of why those controls are not included in the description. However, the fact that a service organization has a policy or procedure to address certain applicable trust services criteria does not serve as justification for omitting those criteria. For example, in a report that addresses the privacy principle, it would not be appropriate for a service organization to omit criteria related to the disclosure of personal information to third parties because the service organization's policies forbid such disclosure.

1.16 Unlike SSAE No. 16, the primary users of SOC 2 reports generally are not user auditors but, rather, management of the service organization and management of the user entities. SOC 2 reports are intended to assist management of the user entities in carrying out their responsibility for monitoring the services provided by a service organization. For example, controls at a service organization that provides Internet-based storage of a user entity's backup of proprietary information and trade secrets is unlikely to be of significance to the user entity's financial statement auditor. However, management of the user entity may be particularly concerned about the security and confidentiality of the backed-up information. SOC 2 reports also may be useful to a user entity's internal auditors or practitioners reporting on a user entity's security, availability, processing integrity, confidentiality, or privacy. For example, a practitioner may be reporting on the privacy of the personal information of customers of a user entity and on the user entity's compliance with the commitments in its privacy notice. The practitioner may use a SOC 2 report that addresses the privacy principle that has been provided by the user entity's service organization as part of the evidence needed to report on the privacy of the user entity's customers' personal information.

Content of Type 1 and Type 2 SOC 2 Reports

1.17 This guide provides for the following two types[8] of SOC 2 reports:

    a. Report on management's description of a service organization's system and the suitability of the design and operating effectiveness of controls (referred to in this guide as a *type 2 report*). This is a report that includes the following:

        i. Management's description of the service organization's system

        ii. A written assertion by management of the service organization[9] about whether, in all material respects

            (1) management's description of the service organization's system fairly presents the service organization's system that was designed and implemented throughout the specified period, based on the criteria in management's assertion (which are the criteria in paragraphs 1.34–.35).[10]

            (2) the controls stated in management's description of the service organization's system were suitably designed throughout the specified period to meet the applicable trust services criteria

---

[8] SSAE No. 16 provides for the same two types of reports, but the subject matter is controls that may be relevant to user entities' internal control over financial reporting.

[9] Paragraph .09 of AT section 101, *Attest Engagements* (AICPA, *Professional Standards*), indicates that a practitioner should ordinarily obtain a written assertion in an examination or a review engagement. Paragraph .58 of AT section 101 states, in part

> If a written assertion cannot be obtained from the responsible party, the practitioner should consider the effects on his or her ability to obtain sufficient evidence to form a conclusion about the subject matter. When the practitioner's client is the responsible party, a failure to obtain a written assertion should result in the practitioner concluding that a scope limitation exists [footnote omitted].

In evaluating the effect of the service auditor's inability to obtain a written assertion from management of the service organization, the service auditor should consider the following guidance in AT section 101:

> **.73** Restrictions on the scope of an engagement, whether imposed by the client or by such other circumstances as the timing of the work or the inability to obtain sufficient evidence, may require the practitioner to qualify the assurance provided, to disclaim any assurance, or to withdraw from the engagement. For example, if the practitioner's client is the responsible party, a failure to obtain a written assertion should result in the practitioner concluding that a scope limitation exists. (See paragraph .58.)

> **.74** The practitioner's decision to provide a qualified opinion, to disclaim an opinion, or to withdraw because of a scope limitation in an examination engagement depends on an assessment of the effect of the omitted procedure(s) on his or her ability to express assurance. This assessment will be affected by the nature and magnitude of the potential effects of the matters in question, and by their significance to the subject matter or the assertion. If the potential effects are pervasive to the subject matter or the assertion, a disclaimer or withdrawal is more likely to be appropriate. When restrictions that significantly limit the scope of the engagement are imposed by the client or the responsible party, the practitioner generally should disclaim an opinion or withdraw from the engagement. The reasons for a qualification or disclaimer should be described in the practitioner's report.

[10] These criteria are also included in appendix A, "Information for Management of a Service Organization," of this guide.

(3) the controls stated in management's description of the service organization's system operated effectively throughout the specified period to meet the applicable trust services criteria

(4) when the service organization's description of the system addresses the privacy principle, management of the service organization complied with the commitments in its statement of privacy practices throughout the specified period

   iii. A service auditor's report that

(1) expresses an opinion on the matters in (a)(ii)(1)–(4) when the report covers the privacy principle

(2) includes a description of the service auditor's tests of controls and the results thereof, and when the report addresses the privacy principle, a description of the service auditor's tests of the service organization's compliance with the commitments in its statement of privacy practices and the results thereof

   b. Report on management's description of a service organization's system and the suitability of the design of controls (referred to as a *type 1 report*). This is a report that includes the following:

   i. Management's description of the service organization's system

   ii. A written assertion by management of the service organization[11] about whether, in all material respects and based on suitable criteria

(1) management's description of the service organization's system fairly presents the service organization's system that was designed and implemented as of a specified date, based on the criteria in paragraphs 1.34–.35

(2) the controls stated in the description were suitably designed to meet the applicable trust services criteria as of a specified date

   iii. A service auditor's report that expresses an opinion on the matters in (b)(ii)(1)–(2)

In both a type 1 and type 2 engagement, to clearly communicate that management is responsible for the description of the service organization's system; the suitability of the design of the controls; and in a type 2 report, the operating effectiveness of the controls, management's written assertion is attached to the description of the service organization's system. When the report addresses the privacy principle, the statement of privacy practices should be included in, or attached to, the description.[12]

---

[11] See footnote 9.

[12] The criteria for a service organization's statement of privacy practices are presented in paragraph 1.35e and in appendix A of this guide. In a type 1 and type 2 report, the service auditor's opinion on the fairness of the presentation of the description of the service organization's system also addresses the fairness of the presentation of the service organization's statement of privacy practices.

Difference Between SOC 2 and SOC 3 Reports

1.18 Although SOC 2 and SOC 3 reports address similar subject matter and use the same criteria (the criteria in TSP section 100), a SOC 2 report differs from a SOC 3 report in that a SOC 2 report provides report users with the following report components that are not included in a SOC 3 report:

- A description of the service organization's system prepared by management of the service organization. In a SOC 3 report, management provides a description of the service organization's system and its boundaries, which typically is less detailed than the description in a SOC 2 report. Also, in a SOC 3 engagement, the practitioner does not express an opinion on the fairness of the presentation of the description.

- In a type 2 report, a description of the service auditor's tests of the operating effectiveness of the service organization's controls and the results of those tests

- In a type 2 report that addresses the privacy principle, a description of the service auditor's tests of the service organization's compliance with the commitments in its statement of privacy practices and the results of those tests

1.19 Another significant difference between a SOC 2 and SOC 3 report is that use of a SOC 2 report usually is intended for specified parties who are knowledgeable about the following:

- The nature of the service provided by the service organization

- How the service organization's system interacts with user entities, subservice organizations,[13] and other parties

- Internal control and its limitations

- The applicable trust services criteria, the risks that may prevent those criteria from being met, and how controls address those risks

- Complementary user-entity controls and how they interact with related controls at the service organization to meet the applicable trust services criteria

A SOC 3 report, however, ordinarily is a general-use report, which means that management of the service organization may provide the report to anyone. For that reason, management of a service organization may consider engaging a service auditor to perform and report on a SOC 2 and SOC 3 engagement to meet the governance needs of existing customers and market the service organization's services to prospective customers, which is a permitted use of a SOC 3 report.

1.20 The work performed in a SOC 2 engagement may enable a service auditor to report on a SOC 3 engagement, as well. However, because a SOC 3 engagement requires that all the applicable trust services criteria (all of the

---

(footnote continued)

In a type 2 report, the service auditor expresses an opinion on the service organization's compliance with the commitments in its statement of privacy practices. In a type 1 report, the service auditor does not express such an opinion.

[13] In this guide, *subservice organization* is defined as a service organization used by another service organization to perform services related to the trust services principles. If a service organization uses a subservice organization, the description of the service organization's system may either (*a*) include the subservice organization's services, using the inclusive method, or (*b*) exclude the subservice organization's services, using the carve-out method.

criteria for the principle being reporting on) be met in order for the practitioner to issue an unqualified opinion, certain conditions would preclude the service auditor from issuing an unqualified SOC 3 opinion. The following are examples of such situations:

- An engagement in which the service organization has carved out subservice organizations from its system description. Under TSP section 100, the scope of the engagement would need to include all subservice organizations for which controls would need to be operating effectively to meet the applicable trust services criteria.[14]

- An engagement in which complementary user-entity controls are significant to achieving the applicable trust services criteria. (See paragraph 1.21 for a discussion of complementary user-entity controls.) An example would be a service organization that provides managed security services to user entities that require the user entities to implement authentication procedures. Because the criteria cannot be entirely met by procedures implemented at the service organization, an unqualified opinion could not be issued.

1.21 In many cases, the applicable trust services criteria stated in the description cannot be met by implementing controls at a service organization alone and may require that user entities implement certain controls (complementary user-entity controls). If the implementation of complementary user-entity controls is necessary to meet specified applicable trust services criteria, the description should separately identify those complementary user-entity controls, along with the criteria that cannot be met by the service organization's controls alone. An example of a complementary user-entity control is a system designed with the assumption that user entities will have an authorized employee approve the accuracy of data prior to its submission to the service organization for processing.

1.22 A SOC 2 engagement is not intended to supersede or replace a SOC 3 engagement. In many instances, the detail in a description of a service organization's system and in the service auditor's description of tests of controls is not needed by report users. In that case, a SOC 3 engagement may be a better option.

Trust Services Criteria for SOC 2 and SOC 3 Engagements and Control Objectives for SOC 1 Engagements

1.23 In SOC 2 and SOC 3 engagements, the criteria used to evaluate whether controls were suitably designed or operating effectively are the applicable trust services criteria. Accordingly, in every SOC 2 and SOC 3 engagement that addresses the same principle(s), the criteria will be the same (the applicable trust services criteria). However, in a SOC 1 engagement, the service auditor evaluates whether the service organization's controls were suitably

[14] In order for a practitioner to issue an unqualified practitioner's report for a service organization controls (SOC) 3 engagement, all of the criteria in TSP section 100, *Trust Services Principles, Criteria, and Illustrations for Security, Availability, Processing Integrity, Confidentiality, and Privacy* (AICPA, *Technical Practice Aids*), that are applicable to the principle(s) being reported on (applicable trust services criteria) must be met. If a service organization engages a practitioner to perform a SOC 3 engagement in which subservice organizations have been carved out of the engagement and one or more controls necessary to meet one or more of the criteria have been carved out (excluded from the scope of the engagement), the service auditor will be unable to issue an unqualified practitioner's report.

designed or operating effectively by determining whether the control objectives specified by management of the service organization were achieved.[15] SSAE No. 16 requires that the control objectives for a SOC 1 report be reasonable in the circumstances. Although most service organizations providing like services will have similar control objectives, in order for control objectives to be reasonable in the circumstances, they should reflect features of the particular service organization, such as the nature of the services provided and the industries in which the user entities operate. Accordingly, in SOC 1 engagements, not all service organizations will have the same control objectives.

Combining SOC 1 and SOC 2 Reports Not Permitted

1.24 A service organization's controls may be relevant to a user entity's internal control over financial reporting and also to the trust services principles. This guide is not intended to permit a SOC 2 report to be issued that combines reporting on a service organization's controls relevant to user entities' internal control over financial reporting with reporting on controls relevant to the trust services principles. A service organization may engage a service auditor to separately perform an engagement that addresses a service organization's controls related to user entities' internal control over financial reporting. If a service auditor is engaged to perform both a SOC 1 and SOC 2 engagement, certain testing performed in either engagement may provide evidence for the other engagement.

---

[15] SSAE No. 16 defines control objectives as the aim or purpose of specified controls at the service organization.

Comparison of SOC 1, SOC 2, and SOC 3 Engagements and Related Reports

1.25 The following table identifies differences between SOC 1, SOC 2, and SOC 3 reports:

	Service Organizational Controls (SOC) 1 Reports	SOC 2 Reports	SOC 3 Reports
Under what professional standard and implementation guidance is the engagement performed?	Statement on Standards for Attestation Engagements (SSAE) No. 16, *Reporting on Controls at a Service Organization* (AICPA, *Professional Standards*, AT sec. 801). The AICPA Guide *Service Organizations: Applying SSAE No. 16, Reporting on Controls at a Service Organization (SOC 1^{SM}).*	AT section 101, *Attest Engagements* (AICPA, *Professional Standards*). The AICPA Guide *Reporting on Controls at a Service Organization Relevant to Security, Availability, Processing Integrity, Confidentiality, or Privacy (SOC 2^{SM}).*	AT section 101. Appendix C, "Practitioner Guidance on Scoping and Reporting Issues," of TSP section 100, *Trust Services Principles, Criteria, and Illustrations for Security, Availability, Processing Integrity, Confidentiality, and Privacy* (AICPA, *Technical Practice Aids*).
What are the criteria for the engagement?	Paragraph 14 of SSAE No. 16 contains the minimum criteria for the description of the service organization's system. Paragraph 15 of SSAE No. 16 provides the criteria for evaluating the suitability of the design of controls.	Paragraphs 1.34–.35 of the AICPA Guide *Reporting on Controls at a Service Organization Relevant to Security, Availability, Processing Integrity, Confidentiality, or Privacy (SOC 2^{SM})* contain the criteria for the description of the service	TSP section 100 contains the criteria for evaluating the design and operating effectiveness of controls, as well as the criteria for evaluating the content of a privacy notice.

	Service Organizational Controls (SOC) 1 Reports	SOC 2 Reports	SOC 3 Reports
	Paragraph 16 of SSAE No. 16 contains the criteria for evaluating the operating effectiveness of controls.	organization's system. TSP section 100 contains the criteria for evaluating the design and operating effectiveness of controls, as well as the criteria for evaluating the content of a privacy notice.	
What is the subject matter of the engagement?	Controls at a service organization relevant to user entities' internal control over financial reporting.	Controls at a service organization relevant to security, availability, processing integrity, confidentiality, or privacy. If the report addresses the privacy principle, the service organization's compliance with the commitments in its statement of privacy practices.	Controls at a service organization relevant to security, availability, processing integrity, confidentiality, or privacy. If the report addresses the privacy principle, the service organization's compliance with the commitments in its privacy notice.[16]
What is the purpose of the report?	To provide the auditor of a user entity's financial statements with information and a CPA's opinion about controls	To provide management of a service organization, user entities, and other specified parties with	To provide interested parties with a CPA's opinion about controls at the service organization relevant to

(continued)

---

[16] See the second paragraph of footnote 4 in this chapter for an explanation of the difference between a privacy notice and a statement of privacy practices.

	Service Organizational Controls (SOC) 1 Reports	SOC 2 Reports	SOC 3 Reports
	at a service organization that may be relevant to a user entity's internal control over financial reporting. It enables the user auditor to perform risk assessment procedures and, if a type 2 report is provided, to use the report as audit evidence that controls at the service organization are operating effectively.	information and a CPA's opinion about controls at the service organization relevant to security, availability, processing integrity, confidentiality, or privacy. A type 2 report that addresses the privacy principle also provides information and a CPA's opinion about the service organization's compliance with the commitments in its statement of privacy practices.	security, availability, processing integrity, confidentiality, or privacy. A report that addresses the privacy principle also provides a CPA's opinion about the service organization's compliance with the commitments in its privacy notice.
What are the components of the report?	A description of the service organization's system. A written assertion by management of the service organization regarding the description of the service organization's system; the suitability of the design of	A description of the service organization's system. A written assertion by management of the service organization regarding the description of the service organization's system; the suitability of the design of	A description of the system and its boundaries[17] or, in the case of a report that addresses the privacy principle, a copy of the service organization's privacy notice. A written assertion by management of the service organization

---

[17] These descriptions are typically less detailed than the descriptions in SOC 1 or SOC 2 reports and are not covered by the practitioner's opinion.

	Service Organizational Controls (SOC) 1 Reports	SOC 2 Reports	SOC 3 Reports
	the controls; and in a type 2 report, the operating effectiveness of the controls in achieving the specified control objectives. A service auditor's report that contains an opinion on the fairness of the presentation of the description of the service organization's system; the suitability of the design of the controls to achieve specified control objectives; and in a type 2 report, the operating effectiveness of those controls. In a type 2 report, a description of the service auditor's tests of the controls and the results of the tests.	the controls; and in a type 2 report, the operating effectiveness of the controls in meeting the applicable trust services criteria. If the report addresses the privacy principle, the assertion also covers the service organization's compliance with the commitments in its statement of privacy practices. A service auditor's report that contains an opinion on the fairness of the presentation of the description of the service organization's system; the suitability of the design of the controls to meet the applicable trust services criteria; and in a type 2 report, the operating effectiveness of those controls. If the report	regarding the effectiveness of controls in meeting the applicable trust services criteria and, if the report addresses the privacy principle, compliance with the commitments in the service organization's privacy notice. A service auditor's report on whether the entity maintained effective controls over its system as it relates to the principle being reported on (that is, security, availability, processing integrity, confidentiality, or privacy), based on the applicable trust services criteria. If the report addresses the privacy principle, the service auditor's opinion on whether the service

(continued)

	Service Organizational Controls (SOC) 1 Reports	SOC 2 Reports	SOC 3 Reports
		addresses the privacy principle, the service auditor's opinion on whether the service organization complied with the commitments in its statement of privacy practices. In a type 2 report, a description of the service auditor's tests of controls and the results of the tests. In a type 2 report that addresses the privacy principle, a description of the service auditor's tests of the service organization's compliance with the commitments in its statement of privacy practices and the results of those tests.	organization complied with the commitments in its privacy notice.
Who are the intended users of the report?	Management of the service organization; user entities during some or all of the period covered by the report (for type	Management of the service organization and other specified parties who have sufficient knowledge and	Anyone

	Service Organizational Controls (SOC) 1 Reports	SOC 2 Reports	SOC 3 Reports
	2 reports) and user entities as of a specified date (for type 1 reports); and auditors of the user entities' financial statements.	understanding of the following: • The nature of the service provided by the service organization • How the service organization's system interacts with user entities, subservice organizations, and other parties • Internal control and its limitations • Complementary user-entity controls and how they interact with related controls at the service organization to meet the applicable trust services criteria • The applicable trust services criteria • The risks that may threaten the achievement of the applicable trust	

	Service Organizational Controls (SOC) 1 Reports	*SOC 2 Reports*	*SOC 3 Reports*
		services criteria and how controls address those risks	

Boundaries of the System

1.26 In addition to the differences identified in the table in paragraph 1.25, SOC 1 engagements differ from SOC 2 engagements in other areas. For example, the boundaries of the systems addressed in SOC 2 engagements may be less apparent than the systems addressed in SOC 1 engagements, which address financial reporting systems or parts thereof. For that reason, the boundaries of a system addressed by a SOC 2 engagement need to be clearly understood, defined, and communicated. For example, a financial reporting system is likely to be bounded by the components of the system related to financial transaction initiation, authorization, recording, processing, and reporting. Whereas the boundaries of a system related to processing integrity (system processing is complete, accurate, timely, and authorized) may extend to other operations (for example, processes at customer call centers).

1.27 In a SOC 2 engagement that addresses the privacy principle, the system boundaries cover, at a minimum, all the system components, as they relate to the personal information life cycle, which consists of the collection, use, retention, disclosure, and disposal or anonymization of personal information, within well-defined processes and informal ad hoc procedures, such as e-mailing personal information to an actuary for retirement benefit calculations. The system boundaries would also include instances in which the personal information is combined with other information (for example, in a database or system), a process that would not otherwise cause the other information to be included in the scope of the engagement. That notwithstanding, the scope of a privacy engagement may be restricted to a business unit (online book sales) or geographical location (Canadian operations), as long as the personal information is not commingled with information from, or shared with, other business units or geographical locations.

Risks Addressed by Controls

1.28 Because of differences in the subject matter of SOC 1 and SOC 2 reports and the needs of intended report users, the risks and the controls that address those risks are likely to differ in SOC 1 and SOC 2 engagements. For example, in a SOC 1 engagement, controls over changes to application programs would typically focus on risks related to unauthorized changes to the programs that could affect the financial reporting process. In a SOC 2 engagement that addresses the processing integrity principle, controls over program changes might need to cover the risks of unauthorized changes to a much broader range of application programs (for example, customer service applications and manufacturing process control applications).

Meaning of the Term *Security*

1.29 The term *security* may be interpreted more narrowly in a SOC 1 engagement than it would be in a SOC 2 engagement. For example, security in a SOC 1 engagement generally relates to the authorization of transactions and protection of the integrity of those transactions throughout the financial reporting process. In a SOC 1 engagement, protection of such information from unauthorized read access or disclosure may not be a concern. However, in a SOC 2 engagement that addresses the privacy or confidentiality principle, the term *security* relates to the authorization of transactions and protection of the integrity of those transactions throughout the system and also protecting personal and other information from unauthorized use or disclosure from the time it is collected until the time it is disposed of. In a SOC 2 engagement that addresses the availability principle, the term *security* may also relate to the protection of the system from interruptions in processing availability.

Difference Between Privacy and Security

1.30 Some individuals consider effective privacy practices to be the same as effective information security. However, privacy encompasses a much broader set of activities beyond security that contribute to the effectiveness of a privacy program, including, for example, providing users with the following:

- Notice of the service organization's privacy commitments and practices
- Choice regarding the use and disclosure of their personal information
- Access to their personal information for review and update
- An inquiry, complaint, and dispute resolution process[18]

Type 1 or Type 2 SOC 2 Reports

1.31 Because management of a user entity is responsible for assessing risks to the user entity and establishing and maintaining controls that address those risks, management of the user entity will need information about the design and operating effectiveness of controls at the service organization that affect the service provided to the user entity. A type 1 report does not include tests of the operating effectiveness of controls and the results thereof; therefore, it is unlikely to provide users with sufficient information to assess the effectiveness of controls at the service organization that address risks related to the outsourced service. However, a type 1 report may be useful to a user entity in understanding the service organization's system and controls. The following are circumstances in which a type 1 report may be useful:

- The service organization has not been in operation for a sufficient length of time to enable the service auditor to gather sufficient appropriate evidence regarding the operating effectiveness of controls.
- The service organization has recently made significant changes to the system and related controls and does not have a sufficient history with a stable system to enable a type 2 engagement to be performed.

---

[18] A definition of *privacy* and a further description of these activities are included in generally accepted privacy principles.

Because of the limitations of a type 1 engagement, a service auditor may recommend that in such situations, a type 2 engagement covering a short period (for example, two months) be performed, rather than a type 1 engagement.

1.32 A service auditor's report may not include both a type 1 opinion for certain applicable trust services criteria and controls and a type 2 opinion for other applicable trust services criteria and controls. The service auditor is engaged to perform either a type 1 or type 2 engagement.

Contents of a SOC 2 Report

1.33 A type 2 SOC 2 report contains the service auditor's opinion about whether

- management's description of the service organization's system is fairly presented (see paragraphs 1.34–.35).
- the controls included in the description are suitably designed to meet the applicable trust services criteria stated in management's description (see paragraph 1.36).
- the controls included in the description were operating effectively to meet the applicable trust services criteria (see paragraph 1.37).
- for SOC 2 reports that address the privacy principle, management complied with the commitments in its statement of privacy practices throughout the specified period (see paragraph 1.38). (Management's statement of privacy practices should be included in, or attached to, management's description of the service organization's system.)

Criteria for Evaluating the Fairness of the Presentation of the Description

1.34 The criteria for determining whether the description of the service organization's system is fairly presented are as follows:

a. The description contains the following information:

 i. The types of services provided

 ii. The components of the system used to provide the services, which are the following:

   (1) *Infrastructure.* The physical and hardware components of a system (facilities, equipment, and networks).

   (2) *Software.* The programs and operating software of a system (systems, applications, and utilities).

   (3) *People.* The personnel involved in the operation and use of a system (developers, operators, users, and managers).

   (4) *Procedures.* The automated and manual procedures involved in the operation of a system.

   (5) *Data.* The information used and supported by a system (transaction streams, files, databases, and tables).

 iii. The boundaries or aspects of the system covered by the description

iv. How the service organization's system captures and addresses significant events and conditions[19]

v. The process used to prepare and deliver reports and other information to user entities and other parties

vi. For information provided to, or received from, subservice organizations and other parties

  (1) how the information is provided or received and the role of the subservice organizations and other parties

  (2) the procedures the service organization performs to determine that such information and its processing, maintenance, and storage are subject to appropriate controls

vii. For each principle being reported on, the related criteria in TSP section 100 (applicable trust services criteria) and the related controls designed to meet those criteria, including, as applicable, the following:

  (1) Complementary user-entity controls contemplated in the design of the service organization's system

  (2) When the inclusive method is used to present a subservice organization, controls at the subservice organization

viii. If the service organization presents the subservice organization using the carve-out method

  (1) the nature of the services provided by the subservice organization

  (2) each of the applicable trust services criteria that are intended to be met by controls at the subservice organization, alone or in combination with controls at the service organization, and the types of controls expected to be implemented at carved-out subservice organizations to meet those criteria

ix. Any applicable trust services criteria that are not addressed by a control and the reasons therefore

x. Other aspects of the service organization's control environment, risk assessment process, information and communication systems, and monitoring of controls that are relevant to the services provided and the applicable trust services criteria

xi. In the case of a type 2 report, relevant details of changes to the service organization's system during the period covered by the description

b. The description does not omit or distort information relevant to the service organization's system while acknowledging that the description is prepared to meet the common needs of a broad range of users and may not, therefore, include every aspect of the system that each individual user may consider important to its own particular needs.

1.35 If the description addresses controls over privacy, in addition to the criteria in paragraph 1.34 for determining whether the description of the

---

[19] For example, the setup of access rights for new users of the system.

service organization's system is fairly presented, the description should also include the following information:

a. The types of personal information collected from individuals or obtained from user entities or other parties[20] and how such information is collected and, if collected by user entities, how it is obtained by the service organization

b. The process for (i) identifying specific requirements in agreements with user entities and in laws and regulations applicable to the personal information and (ii) implementing controls and practices to meet those requirements

c. If the service organization presents the subservice organization using the carve-out method

   i. any aspects of the personal information life cycle for which responsibility has been delegated to the subservice organization

   ii. the types of activities the subservice organization would need to perform to comply with the service organization's privacy commitments

d. If the service organization provides the privacy notice to individuals about whom personal information is collected, used, retained, disclosed, and disposed of or anonymized, the privacy notice prepared in conformity with the relevant criteria for a privacy notice set forth in TSP section 100

e. If the user entities, rather than the service organization, are responsible for providing the privacy notice to individuals, a statement regarding how the privacy notice is communicated to individuals, that the user entities are responsible for communicating such notice to individuals, and that the service organization is responsible for communicating its privacy practices to the user entities in its statement of privacy practices, which includes the following information:

   i. A summary of the significant privacy and related security requirements common to most agreements between the service organization and its user entities and any requirements in a particular user entity's agreement that the service organization meets for all or most user entities

   ii. A summary of the significant privacy and related security requirements mandated by law, regulation, an industry, or a market that are not included in user entity agreements but the service organization meets for all or most user entities

   iii. The purposes, uses, and disclosures of personal information as permitted by user entity agreements and beyond those permitted by such agreements but not prohibited by such agreements and the service organization's commitments regarding the purpose, use, and disclosure of personal information that are prohibited by such agreements

---

[20] An example of an entity that collects personal information from user entities is a credit reporting bureau that maintains information about the creditworthiness of individuals.

iv. A statement that the information will be retained for a period no longer than necessary to fulfill the stated purposes or contractual requirements or for the period required by law or regulation, as applicable, or a statement describing other retention practices

v. A statement that the information will be disposed of in a manner that prevents loss, theft, misuse, or unauthorized access to the information

vi. If applicable, how the service organization supports any process permitted by user entities for individuals to obtain access to their information to review, update, or correct it

vii. If applicable, a description of the process to determine that personal information is accurate and complete and how the service organization implements correction processes permitted by user entities

viii. If applicable, how inquiries, complaints, and disputes from individuals (whether directly from the individual or indirectly through user entities) regarding their personal information are handled by the service organization

ix. A statement regarding the existence of a written security program and what industry or other standards it is based on

x. Other relevant information related to privacy practices deemed appropriate for user entities by the service organization

f. If the user entities, rather than the service organization, are responsible for providing the privacy notice to individuals, the service organization's statement of privacy practices.

1.36 The criterion for determining whether controls are suitably designed is that the controls identified in the description would, if operating as described, provide reasonable assurance that the applicable trust services criteria would be met.

1.37 The criterion for determining whether the controls identified in the description of the service organization's system operated effectively to meet the applicable trust services criterion is that the controls were consistently operated as designed throughout the specified period, including whether manual controls were applied by individuals who have the appropriate competence and authority.

1.38 In an engagement that addresses the privacy principle, the criterion for determining whether a service organization complied with the commitments in its statement of privacy practices is that the service organization collected, used, retained, disclosed, and disposed of or anonymized personal information in conformity with the commitments in its statement of privacy practices.

1.39 A service organization may request that the service auditor's report address additional subject matter that is not specifically covered by the criteria in this guide. An example of such subject matter is the service organization's compliance with certain criteria based on regulatory requirements (for example, security requirements under the Health Insurance Portability and Accountability Act of 1996) or compliance with performance criteria established in a service-level agreement. In order for a service auditor to report on such additional subject matter, the service organization provides the following:

- An appropriate supplemental description of the subject matter
- A description of the criteria used to measure and present the subject matter
- If the criteria are related to controls, a description of the controls intended to meet the control-related criteria
- An assertion by management regarding the additional subject matter

1.40 The service auditor should perform appropriate procedures related to the additional subject matter, in accordance with AT section 101 or AT section 601, *Compliance Attestation* (AICPA, *Professional Standards*), and the relevant guidance in this guide. The service auditor's description of the scope of the work and related opinion on the subject matter should be presented in separate paragraphs of the service auditor's report. In addition, based on the agreement with the service organization, the service auditor may include additional tests performed and detailed results of those tests in a separate attachment to the report.

Applying Certain Auditing Standards

1.41 The following AU sections relate to audits of financial statements; however, when relevant, they may be adapted and applied in performing a SOC 2 engagement:

- AU section 314, *Understanding the Entity and Its Environment and Assessing the Risks of Material Misstatement* (AICPA, *Professional Standards*)
- AU section 316, *Consideration of Fraud in a Financial Statement Audit* (AICPA, *Professional Standards*)
- AU section 322, *The Auditor's Consideration of the Internal Audit Function in an Audit of Financial Statements* (AICPA, *Professional Standards*)
- AU section 350, *Audit Sampling* (AICPA, *Professional Standards*)
- AU section 561, *Subsequent Discovery of Facts Existing at the Date of the Auditor's Report* (AICPA, *Professional Standards*)

Definitions

1.42 Definitions of the terms used in this guide are included in appendix H, "Definitions," of this guide. These definitions are similar to the definitions in SSAE No. 16; however, certain differences exist due to the difference in the subject matter addressed by SOC 1 and SOC 2 engagements.

Chapter 2

Planning a Service Auditor's Engagement

> In planning a service auditor's engagement, management of the service organization and the service auditor each have specific responsibilities. This chapter describes the matters to be considered and procedures to be performed by the service auditor in planning the engagement. Appendix A, "Information for Management of a Service Organization," of this guide identifies management's responsibilities in a service auditor's engagement.

Responsibilities of Management of a Service Organization

2.01 When undergoing an examination of a description of a service organization's system and the design and operating effectiveness of controls, as described in this guide, management of a service organization is responsible for the following:

- Preparing a description of the service organization's system.
- Providing a written assertion.
- Determining the type of engagement to be performed; which principle(s) are addressed in the engagement; the scope of the engagement; and whether any subservice organizations will be included in, or carved out of, the description and service auditor's report.
- Providing written representations at the conclusion of the engagement. When the inclusive method is used, management of the service organization and management of the subservice organization agree to provide and do provide such representations.
- Having a reasonable basis for its assertion.

Responsibilities of the Service Auditor

2.02 During planning, the service auditor is responsible for the following:

- Determining whether to accept or continue an engagement
- Reading the description of the service organization's system and obtaining an understanding of the system
- Establishing an understanding with management of the service organization, which ordinarily is documented in an engagement letter, regarding the services to be performed and the responsibilities of management and the service auditor

Engagement Acceptance and Continuance

2.03 A service auditor should accept or continue an engagement to report on controls at a service organization only if

a. the service auditor has the capabilities and competence to perform the engagement. Having relevant capabilities and competence to perform the engagement includes having

    i. adequate technical training and proficiency to perform an attestation engagement;

    ii. adequate knowledge of the subject matter;

    iii. reason to believe that the subject matter is capable of evaluation against criteria that are appropriate for the intended use;

    iv. knowledge of the service organization's industry and business;

    v. appropriate knowledge of systems and technology;

    vi. experience evaluating risks related to the suitability of the design of controls; and

    vii. experience evaluating the design of manual and IT controls related to the selected trust services principles, performing tests of such controls, and evaluating the results of the tests.

b. the service auditor is independent in mental attitude in all matters relating to the engagement and exercises due professional care in planning and performing the engagement and preparing the report.

c. the service auditor's preliminary knowledge of the engagement circumstances indicates that

    i. the criteria to be used will be suitable and available to the intended users of the report;

    ii. the service auditor will have access to sufficient and appropriate evidence to the extent necessary to conduct the engagement; and

    iii. the scope of the engagement and management's description of the service organization's system will not be so limited that they are unlikely to be useful to the intended users of the report. If the inclusive method is used, these conditions also apply with respect to the subservice organization.

2.04 Before accepting an engagement, the service auditor should consider the following:

- The integrity and reputation of management of the service organization and significant shareholders or principal owners

- The likelihood that association with the client will expose the service auditor to undue risk of damage to his or her professional reputation or financial loss or expose report users to misinformation and financial loss

2.05 The service auditor may obtain information about the matters in paragraph 2.04 by communicating with a predecessor service auditor, if any, regarding the reasons for change in service auditors, any disagreements between the predecessor auditor and service organization, and similar matters. The guidance in AU section 315, *Communications Between Predecessor and Successor Auditors* (AICPA, *Professional Standards*), may be adapted and applied for this purpose. If the predecessor service auditor has issued a service auditor's report, it is not necessary for the service auditor to review the predecessor service auditor's working papers because of the detailed nature of the report.

2.06 As stated in paragraph 2.03*b*, the service auditor should accept or continue an engagement to report on controls at a service organization only if the service auditor is independent of the service organization. Independence is required by the AICPA Code of Professional Conduct for examination engagements. Examples of relevant matters to consider when assessing independence are the scope of other services provided to the service organization, fee arrangements for all services, firm and individual financial relationships, firm business relationships, and alumni and familial relationships with the client and client personnel.

2.07 Paragraph .03 of ET section 92, *Definitions* (AICPA, *Professional Standards*), provides the following definition of a *client*: "A client is any person or entity, other than the member's employer, that engages a member or a member's firm to perform professional services or a person or entity with respect to which professional services are performed." Based on this definition, when management's description uses the inclusive method to present a subservice organization, the subservice organization would be considered a client because the service auditor has performed professional services with respect to the subservice organization. Consequently, the service auditor should be independent of the subservice organization.

2.08 The service auditor need not be independent of the users of the service organization.

2.09 Additional matters that are relevant when determining whether to accept or continue an engagement include the scope of the system being reported on, the functions performed by the system, how subservice organizations are used, how information about subservice organizations will be presented, the relevance of the trust services principle being reported on to the system, and the period covered by the report. Consideration should be given to these matters to determine whether the resulting report will be useful and not misleading to users of the report. For example, assume that management of the service organization wishes to engage the service auditor to perform a type 2 examination for a period of less than two months. In those circumstances, the service auditor should consider whether a report covering that period will be useful to users of the report, particularly if many of the controls related to the applicable trust services criteria are performed on a monthly or quarterly basis.

2.10 Another matter that the service auditor should consider when determining whether to accept or continue a service organization controls (SOC) 2 engagement is the intended users of the report. If the intended report users are unlikely to understand the nature of the engagement or the tests and results (for example, acceptable deviation rates or substantive tests versus tests of controls), a greater potential exists for the report to be misunderstood.

2.11 The service auditor may also consider whether management has realistic expectations about the engagement, particularly if it is likely that the report may require a qualification or other modification.

2.12 A service auditor may question accepting an engagement in which a service organization functions primarily as an intermediary between the user entities and subservice organization and performs few or no functions related to the service provided to user entities. If a service organization's controls do not contribute to meeting the applicable trust services criteria, a report on that service organization's controls is not likely to be useful to report users.

2.13 A service auditor ordinarily should accept or continue an engagement to report on controls at a service organization only if management of the service organization acknowledges and accepts responsibility for the following:

a. Preparing its description of the service organization's system and its assertion, including the completeness, accuracy, and method of presentation of the description and assertion

b. Providing a written assertion that will be attached to management's description of the service organization's system and provided to users

c. Having a reasonable basis for its assertion

d. Designing, implementing, and documenting controls that are suitably designed and operating effectively to provide reasonable assurance that the applicable trust services criteria are met

e. Providing the service auditor with the following:

   i. Access to all information, such as records and documentation, including service level agreements, of which management is aware that is relevant to the description of the service organization's system and the assertion

   ii. Additional information that the service auditor may request from management for the purpose of the examination engagement

   iii. Unrestricted access to personnel within the service organization from whom the service auditor determines it is necessary to obtain evidence relevant to the service auditor's engagement

2.14 In preparing for an engagement in which the inclusive method will be used to present a subservice organization, the service auditor should obtain from the service organization written acknowledgement and acceptance by the subservice organization of its responsibility for the matters in paragraph 2.13.

2.15 When the inclusive method is used, the requirements and guidance in paragraphs 2.01–.14 also apply with respect to the subservice organization. Accordingly, during planning, the service auditor determines whether it will be possible to obtain an assertion from management of the subservice organization and evidence that supports the service auditor's opinion on the subservice organization's description of its system and the suitability of the design and operating effectiveness of the subservice organization's controls, including written representations from management of the subservice organization. If the subservice organization will not provide a written assertion and appropriate written representations, the service organization will be unable to use the inclusive method but may be able to use the carve-out method. Additional guidance on the inclusive method is provided in paragraphs 3.26–.28 of this guide.

Planning to Use the Work of the Internal Audit Function

2.16 The phrase *using the work of the internal audit function* is derived from AU section 322, *The Auditor's Consideration of the Internal Audit Function in an Audit of Financial Statements* (AICPA, *Professional Standards*), and it refers to work designed and performed by the internal audit function. This includes tests of controls designed and performed by the internal audit function during the period covered by the type 2 report and the results of those tests.

This differs from work that the internal audit function performs to provide direct assistance to the service auditor, including assistance in performing tests of controls that are designed by the service auditor and performed by members of the internal audit function, under the direction, supervision, and review of the service auditor.

2.17 If the service organization has an internal audit function, the service auditor may obtain an understanding of the responsibilities and activities of the internal audit function to determine whether the work of the internal audit function is likely to be relevant to the engagement. The service auditor may obtain this understanding by making inquiries of appropriate management of the service organization and internal audit personnel. Examples of matters that may be important to this understanding are the internal audit function's

- organizational status within the service organization;
- application of, and adherence to, professional standards;
- audit plan, including the nature, timing, and extent of audit procedures; and
- access to records and whether limitations exist on the scope of the internal audit function's activities.

2.18 Work of the internal audit function that provides information or evidence about the fairness of the presentation of the description of the service organization's system, the suitability of the design of the controls, or the operating effectiveness of the controls that pertain to the trust services principle being reported on would be considered relevant to the engagement. The following are examples of information that may assist the service auditor in assessing the relevancy of that work:

- Knowledge gained from prior-year examinations related to the principle being reported on
- How management and the internal audit function assess risk related to the trust services principle being reported on and how audit resources are allocated to address those risks

2.19 Certain internal audit activities may not be relevant to a SOC 2^{SM} engagement (for example, the internal audit function's evaluation of the efficiency of certain management decision-making processes).

2.20 If, after obtaining an understanding of the internal audit function, the service auditor concludes that (*a*) the activities of the internal audit function are not relevant to the trust services principle being reported on, or (*b*) it may not be efficient to consider the work of the internal audit function, the service auditor does not need to give further consideration to the work of the internal audit function.

2.21 If the service auditor intends to use the work of the internal audit function or use internal audit personnel in a direct assistance capacity, the service auditor should determine whether the work performed by the internal audit function is likely to be adequate for the purposes of the engagement by evaluating the following:

- *a.* The objectivity and technical competence of the members of the internal audit function
- *b.* Whether the work of the internal audit function is likely to be carried out with due professional care

    c. Whether it is likely that effective communication will occur between the internal audit function and service auditor, including consideration of the effect of any constraints or restrictions placed on the internal audit function by the service organization

2.22 If the service auditor determines that the work of the internal audit function is likely to be adequate for the purposes of the engagement, the service auditor should evaluate the following factors in determining the planned effect that the work of the internal audit function will have on the nature, timing, and extent of the service auditor's procedures:

    a. The nature and scope of specific work performed or to be performed by the internal audit function

    b. The significance of that work to the service auditor's conclusions

    c. The degree of subjectivity involved in the evaluation of the evidence gathered in support of those conclusions

Materiality

2.23 When planning and performing a SOC 2 engagement, the service auditor should evaluate materiality with respect to (*a*) the fair presentation of management's description of the service organization's system; (*b*) the suitability of the design of the controls; (*c*) in a type 2 engagement, the operating effectiveness of the controls; and (*d*) in a type 2 engagement that addresses the privacy principle, the service organization's compliance with the commitments in its statement of privacy practices. The concept of materiality takes into account that the report is intended to provide information to meet the common information needs of a broad range of users who understand the manner in which the system is being used. Materiality with respect to the service organization also applies to the subservice organization.

2.24 Materiality with respect to the fair presentation of management's description of the service organization's system and with respect to the design of controls primarily includes the consideration of qualitative factors. For example, whether

- management's description of the service organization's system includes the significant aspects of system processing.

- management's description of the service organization's system omits or distorts relevant information.

- the controls have the ability, as designed, to provide reasonable assurance that the applicable trust services criteria stated in management's description of the service organization's system would be met.

2.25 Materiality with respect to the operating effectiveness of controls includes the consideration of both quantitative and qualitative factors (for example, the service auditor's tolerable rate and observed rate of deviation in the results of tests [a quantitative matter] and the nature and cause of any observed deviations [a qualitative matter]).

2.26 The concept of materiality is not applicable when disclosing in the description of tests of controls (and tests of compliance with privacy commitments, if applicable) the results of those tests for which deviations have been identified. This is because a deviation may have significance for a specific user entity beyond whether, in the opinion of the service auditor, it prevents a control from operating effectively. For example, the control to which the deviation relates may be particularly significant in preventing a certain type of error, the results of which may be material to a particular user entity but not other users.

Identifying Deviations

2.27 Before the service auditor begins tests of controls and tests of compliance, the service auditor should determine the procedures that will be performed and the circumstances under which a test result will be considered a deviation, so that all such results are reported as deviations in the description of tests of controls and tests of compliance.

Establishing an Understanding With the Client

2.28 Paragraph .46 of AT section 101, *Attest Engagements* (AICPA, *Professional Standards*), requires the practitioner to establish an understanding with the client regarding the services to be performed. That understanding should be documented in the working papers, preferably through a written communication with the client. Typically, this understanding is documented in an engagement letter. A documented understanding reduces the risk that either the service auditor or management of the service organization will misinterpret the needs or expectations of the other party. For example, it reduces the risk that management of the service organization will rely on the service auditor to protect the service organization from certain risks or perform certain management functions that are not part of the service auditor's responsibilities in a SOC 2 engagement.

2.29 The engagement letter typically includes the objectives of the engagement, a description of the services to be provided, the responsibilities of management of the service organization, the responsibilities of the service auditor, and the limitations of the engagement. Such matters as fees and timing may also be addressed in the engagement letter. If the service auditor believes that an understanding has not been established with management of the service organization, the service auditor would typically decline to accept or continue the engagement.

Chapter 3

Performing the Engagement

> This chapter identifies matters that the service auditor considers and procedures that the service auditor performs to test (*a*) the fairness of the presentation of management's description of the service organization's system; (*b*) the suitability of the design of the controls included in the description; (*c*) in a type 2 report, the operating effectiveness of the controls included in the description; and (*d*) in a type 2 service organization controls (SOC) 2 engagement that addresses the privacy principle, whether the service organization complied with the commitments in its statement of privacy practices.

Obtaining and Evaluating Evidence About Whether the Description of the System Is Fairly Presented

3.01 The service auditor should read the description of the service organization's system and perform procedures to determine whether the description is fairly presented. A description that is fairly presented should

- meet the criteria in paragraphs 1.34–.35 of this guide.
- describe the system as it was designed and implemented.
- include relevant details of changes to the system.

3.02 The procedures that the service auditor may perform to evaluate whether the description of the service organization's system is fairly presented typically include a combination of the following:

- Reading contracts and service level agreements with user entities to understand the nature and scope of the service provided by the service organization, as well as the service organization's contractual obligations to user entities
- Obtaining an understanding of the aspects of laws or regulations relevant to the services provided
- Observing the procedures performed by service organization personnel
- Reading service organization policy and procedure manuals and other documentation of the system (for example, flowcharts, narratives, and software and hardware asset management records)
- Performing walkthroughs of control activity-related policies and procedures and observing other system components
- Obtaining a list of user entities and determining how the services provided by the service organization are likely to affect the user entities (for example, determining the predominant type(s) of user entities, whether they are regulated entities, and the common types of services provided to the user entities)

- Discussing with management and other service organization personnel the content of management's assertion and the description of the service organization's system

- Reading reports of the internal audit function relevant to the principle being reported on

3.03 A conclusion that a description of a service organization's system is fairly presented does not imply that the controls included in the description are suitably designed or operating effectively to meet the applicable trust services criteria.

3.04 In determining whether the description of a service organization's system is fairly presented, the service auditor evaluates whether each control as presented provides sufficient information for users to understand how that control may affect the particular user. The description of a control generally will need to include the following information:

Relevant Information When Describing a Control	*Example*
The frequency with which the control is performed or the timing of its occurrence	Management reviews error reports on a monthly basis. On a daily basis, a departmental clerk reviews reconciling items identified in the comparison of the ABC report with the data feed from user entities.
The party responsible for performing the control	The security manager reviews... An input processing clerk compares...
The nature of the activity that is performed	The system compares the name of the user entity employee requesting access to the system with approved user information submitted by authorized user entity personnel. Service organization department managers review the list of service organization personnel who have access to the system for appropriateness of access on a monthly basis and evidence this review with a sign-off.
The subject matter to which the control is applied	Program changes are reviewed by....

3.05 In determining whether the description of the service organization's system is fairly presented, the service auditor compares his or her understanding of the service provided and the system through which it is provided with the description of the service organization's system, as they relate to the trust services principle(s) being reported on. The description is considered fairly presented if it includes the information required by paragraphs 1.34–.35 of this guide, does not omit or distort information relevant to users, and objectively describes what actually occurs at the service organization.

3.06 The description is not fairly presented if it states or implies that system elements exist that do not exist, if it states or implies that controls are being performed when they are not being performed, or if it inadvertently or intentionally omits or distorts relevant system information.

3.07 Additionally, a description that is fairly presented should not contain statements that cannot be objectively evaluated. For example, describing a service organization as being the "world's best" or "most respected in the industry" is subjective and, therefore, would not be appropriate for inclusion in a description of the service organization's system.

3.08 As part of the service auditor's evaluation of whether the description materially omits information relevant to users, the service auditor determines whether the description addresses all the major aspects of the system within the scope of the engagement. An example of an omission would be failing to include in the description significant aspects of the processing performed at another location that is included in the scope of the engagement.

3.09 A service organization may have controls that it considers to be outside the boundaries of the system, such as controls related to the conversion of new user entities to the service organization's systems. To avoid misunderstanding by users, the service auditor considers whether the description clearly delineates the boundaries of the system that are included in the scope of the engagement.

3.10 When performing a type 2 engagement, the service auditor should inquire about changes in the service organization's system, such as changes in controls that were implemented during the period covered by the service auditor's report. (If the report addresses the privacy principle, this would include changes in the service organization's privacy practices.) If the service auditor believes that the changes would be considered significant by users, the service auditor should determine whether the changes have been included in the description of the service organization's system at an appropriate level of detail, including the date the change occurred and how the system differed before and after the change. If the changes relate to privacy practices, they would be included in the description of the service organization's system or the service organization's statement of privacy practices. If management has not included such changes in the description, the service auditor should ask management to amend the description to include this information. If management refuses to include this information in the description, the service auditor considers the effect of such changes on his or her conclusions regarding the fairness of the presentation of management's description of the service organization's system and the service auditor's report.

3.11 In evaluating which aspects of the service organization's system are relevant and should be included in the description of the service organization's system, the service auditor considers the common information needs of the broad range of users for whom the report is intended.

3.12 Paragraphs 1.34–.35 of this guide present the information to be included in management's description of the service organization's system. Paragraph 1.34*a*(x) requires the description to include aspects of the service organization's internal control other than its control activities if they are relevant to meeting the applicable trust services criteria (for example, aspects of the control environment). If these aspects relate to meeting a specific criterion, they should be included in the description of the specific controls designed to meet that criterion.

Evaluating Whether Controls Have Been Implemented

3.13 To be fairly presented, the description of the service organization's system should include only controls that have been implemented. Controls that have been implemented have been placed in operation versus existing only in the description. The service auditor should determine whether the controls included in management's description of the service organization's system have been implemented by performing inquiry in combination with other procedures. Such other procedures may include observation, inspection of records and other documentation of the manner in which the service organization's system operates and controls are applied, and reperformance of the control.

3.14 The service auditor's procedures to determine whether the controls included in the description have been implemented may be similar to, and performed in conjunction with, procedures to obtain an understanding of the system and the system's boundaries. For example, when performing a walkthrough to verify the service auditor's understanding of the design of controls, the service auditor may also determine whether controls have been implemented as stated in the description of the service organization's system. Performing a walkthrough entails asking relevant members of the service organization's management and staff to describe and demonstrate their actions in performing a procedure. In performing a walkthrough, the service auditor follows a system, event, or activity from origination through the service organization's processes, including its information systems, until its final disposition, using the same documents and IT that service organization personnel use. Walkthrough procedures usually include a combination of inquiry; observation; inspection of relevant documentation (that is, corroboration); and reperformance of controls. It may be helpful to use flowcharts, questionnaires, or decision tables to facilitate understanding the design of the controls.

3.15 If the service auditor determines that certain controls identified in management's description have not been implemented, the service auditor should ask management of the service organization to delete those controls from the description. The service auditor considers only controls that have been implemented when assessing the suitability of the design and operating effectiveness of controls. Paragraph 4.22 of this guide presents an illustrative explanatory paragraph that would be added to the service auditor's report when the description includes controls that have not been implemented.

Other Information in the Description That Is Not Covered by the Service Auditor's Report

3.16 A service organization may decide to provide report users with information, other than the information required by paragraphs 1.34–.35 of this guide, that will not be covered by the service auditor's report. Examples of such information are pending changes to the system and regulatory matters. Such other information should be distinguished from the service organization's description of its system by excluding the information from the description. If the other information is attached to the description or included in a document that contains the description of the service organization's system and the service auditor's report, the other information should be differentiated from the information covered by the service auditor's report, for example, through the use of a title such as "Other Information Provided by Example Service Organization That Is Not Covered by the Service Auditor's Report."

3.17 When other information that is not covered by the service auditor's report is attached to the description or included in a document containing the description and the service auditor's report, the service auditor should apply the requirements and guidance in paragraph .92 of AT section 101, *Attest Engagements* (AICPA, *Professional Standards*), which requires the service auditor to read the other information and identify any material inconsistencies, such as an apparent misstatement of fact. Ordinarily, the service auditor would discuss such inconsistencies with management of the service organization, and if management refuses to correct the information, the service auditor should determine which of the actions described in paragraphs .92–.94 of AT section 101 are appropriate.

3.18 The service auditor may emphasize in the service auditor's report that the other information is not a part of the description of the service organization's system and is not covered by the service auditor's report. In these instances, the service auditor may include an explanatory paragraph in the report describing the other information and stating that the service auditor's report does not address the other information. Paragraph 4.27 of this guide presents an example of such a paragraph.

Materiality Relating to the Fair Presentation of the Description

3.19 The service auditor should consider materiality when evaluating the fair presentation of the description of the service organization's system. Materiality in this context primarily relates to qualitative factors, such as whether significant aspects of the system and processing have been included in the description or whether relevant information has been omitted or distorted.

3.20 The following are some examples of how the service auditor might consider materiality when evaluating whether the description of a service organization's system is fairly presented:

- Example Service Organization uses a subservice organization to perform all of its back-office functions and elects to use the carve-out method of presentation. Management's description of the service organization's system includes information about the nature of the services provided by the subservice organization and describes the service organization's monitoring and other controls that the service organization implements with respect to the processing performed by the subservice organization. In this example, the description of the service organization's system should include such information because it is likely to be relevant to users and, therefore, would be considered material to the description.

- A service auditor is reporting on Example Service Organization's controls related to the security principle. Example Service Organization uses a separate facility for its off-site storage of backup tapes. Data written to the backup tapes is encrypted, and Example Service Organization's description includes information about its controls over the encryption of the information. The description does not include information about controls over physical access to the separate facility. Controls over physical access would be intended to meet the following trust services criterion: procedures exist to restrict physical access to the defined system, including, but not limited to, facilities; backup media; and other system components, such as firewalls, routers, and servers. In this example, such an omission is not likely to be material to users because controls over the encryption of the tapes prevent unauthorized access to the information and compensate for the omission of controls over physical access to the facility.

Complementary User-Entity Controls

3.21 A service organization may design its services with the assumption that certain controls will be implemented by the user entities. If such complementary user-entity controls are necessary to meet certain applicable trust services criteria, the service auditor evaluates whether the service organization's description adequately describes the complementary user-entity controls and their importance in meeting the applicable trust services criteria to which they relate.

3.22 To evaluate whether complementary user-entity controls included in the description are adequately described, the service auditor compares the information in the description with documents such as contracts with user entities and system or procedure manuals and makes inquiries of service organization personnel to gain an understanding of the user entities' responsibilities for achieving the applicable trust services criteria and whether those responsibilities are appropriately described in the description.

3.23 For example, if the service organization manages logical security for the user entities and provides access to its system based on user-entity authorization, the following trust services criterion could not be met without the implementation of controls at the user entities because access authorization rests with them: procedures exist to restrict logical access to the defined system, including, but not limited to, registration and authorization of new users. Accordingly, in addition to describing the relevant controls performed by the service organization, the description would include information, such as the following, alerting user entities to the need for a complementary user-entity control: user entities are responsible for implementing controls over the authorization of access to the system by employees of the user entity and for communicating to the service organization user registration and access information in a timely manner.

Subservice Organizations

3.24 Management of the service organization should determine whether controls over the functions performed by an organization from which it has contracted services (a vendor) are needed to meet one of more of the trust services criteria or are otherwise relevant to the fair presentation of the description of the service organization's system. If so, the vendor is considered a subservice organization, and the service organization's description of its system should include, depending on whether the inclusive or carve-out method is used, the information set forth in paragraphs 3.26 and 3.29. For each subservice organization, the service organization determines whether to use the inclusive method of presentation, as described in paragraphs 3.26–.28, or the carve-out method of presentation, as described in paragraph 3.29. The service auditor should obtain an understanding of the significant vendors whose services affect the service organization's system and assess whether management has made an appropriate determination about whether these vendors are subservice organizations. Paragraphs 4.37–.39 of this guide present illustrative report paragraphs marked to show the changes that would be made to those paragraphs when using the carve-out method. (The illustrative report paragraphs in paragraph 4.39 of this guide show the changes that would be made to the report if the service organization uses the carve-out method, and the service auditor is disclaiming an opinion.) Paragraph 4.40 of this guide presents an illustrative report marked to show the changes that would be made to the report when the inclusive method is used.

3.25 In evaluating services provided by a vendor, the service organization should assess whether controls at the service organization alone or the service organization's monitoring of the effectiveness of controls at the vendor enable the applicable trust services criteria affected by those services to be met. Examples of monitoring the effectiveness of a vendor's controls include tests of the vendor's controls performed by the service organization's internal audit function, review and approval of vendor output, periodic visits to the vendor and assessments, and review of reports on attestation engagements that address the vendor's services and controls. In these instances, the service organization does not need to treat the vendor as a subservice organization, omits from the description information about controls at the vendor, and omits any description of the effect the vendor's controls may have on meeting the applicable trust services criteria. When a service organization has determined that its controls alone meet the applicable trust services criteria or that its monitoring of the vendor's controls is sufficient to meet the related criteria, the service auditor evaluates this determination as part of the evaluation of the suitability of the design of the controls in meeting the applicable trust services criteria and tests the operating effectiveness of such controls or the monitoring performed by the subservice organization.

3.26 For the purposes of this guide, under the inclusive method, the relevant aspects of the subservice organization's infrastructure, software, people, procedures, and data are to be considered a part of the service organization's system and would be included in the description of the service organization's system. Although these relevant aspects would be considered a part of the service organization's system, the portions of the system that are attributable to the subservice organization should be separately identified.

3.27 When the inclusive method is used, the guidance set forth in this guide also applies to the services provided by the subservice organization to the extent they affect the service organization's ability to meet the applicable trust services criteria, including the following:

- Obtaining acknowledgement and acceptance of responsibility for the matters in paragraph 2.13 of this guide from management of the subservice organization

- Obtaining an understanding of the portion of the system provided by the subservice organization

- Obtaining and evaluating evidence about the fairness of the presentation of the description for the portions of the system provided by the subservice organization

- Obtaining evidence about whether the described controls have been implemented at the subservice organization

- Evaluating the suitability of the design of controls at the subservice organization

- For a type 2 report, obtaining evidence of the operating effectiveness of controls at the subservice organization

- Obtaining evidence of the subservice organization's compliance with the privacy commitments it has made to the service organization, if applicable

- For a type 2 report, obtaining a written assertion addressing the matters in paragraph 1.17a(ii)(1)–(4) of this guide that are relevant to the services provided by the subservice organization, and for a type 1 report, the matters in paragraph 1.17b(ii)(1)–(2) of this guide

- Obtaining written representations about the matters in paragraph 3.90 that are relevant to the services provided by the subservice organization

3.28 When the inclusive method is used, the service auditor should

- evaluate whether the description of the service organization's system, including the relevant aspects of the system provided by the subservice organization, is fairly presented.

- evaluate the suitability of the design of the controls at the subservice organization.

- for a type 2 report, perform tests of the operating effectiveness of those controls.

- when the report addresses the privacy principle, test the subservice organization's compliance with the commitments in the service organization's statement of privacy practices.

3.29 If the service organization uses the carve-out method to present a subservice organization, the description of the service organization's system identifies the following:

- The nature of the services provided by the subservice organization

- If the description addresses the privacy principle, any aspects of the personal information life cycle for which responsibility has been delegated to the subservice organization, if applicable

- Each of the applicable trust services criteria that are intended to be met by controls at the subservice organization alone or in combination with controls at the service organization

- The types of controls expected to be implemented at carved-out subservice organizations that are necessary to meet the applicable trust services criteria, either alone or in combination with controls at the service organization

- If the description addresses the privacy principle, the types of activities that the subservice organization would need to perform to comply with the service organization's privacy commitments

The description of the service organization's system and the service auditor's engagement exclude all other aspects of the subservice organization's infrastructure, software, people, procedures, and data relevant to the services provided (see additional considerations in paragraphs 3.37–.39).

3.30 A service organization may use multiple subservice organizations and prepare its description using the carve-out method of presentation for one or more subservice organizations and the inclusive method of presentation for others.

3.31 Paragraph 4.23 of this guide presents an illustrative explanatory paragraph that would be added to the service auditor's report when the service

>> i. How the control was applied. (Was the control performed as designed?)

>> ii. The consistency with which the control was applied throughout the period.

>> iii. By whom or by what means the control was applied. (Is the control automated or manual? Has there been high turnover in the position, and is the control being performed by an inexperienced person?)

> *b.* determines whether the controls to be tested depend on other controls and, if so, whether it is necessary to obtain evidence supporting the operating effectiveness of those other controls.

> *c.* determines an effective method for selecting the items to be tested to meet the objectives of the procedure.

3.55 The other procedures that the service auditor should perform in combination with inquiry to obtain evidence about the operating effectiveness of controls include the following:

- Observation of the application of the control
- Inspection of documents, reports, or electronic files that contain evidence of the performance of the controls, such as system log files
- Reperformance of the control

3.56 Inquiry alone usually does not provide sufficient appropriate evidence of the operating effectiveness of controls. Some tests of controls provide more convincing evidence of the operating effectiveness of controls than others. Performing inquiry combined with inspection or reperformance ordinarily provides more convincing evidence than performing inquiry and observation.

3.57 Evidence of the operating effectiveness of controls may be lost, misplaced, or inadvertently deleted by the service organization. In such instances, the service auditor determines whether other evidence of the operating effectiveness of the control exists and whether the results of tests of the other evidence would provide sufficient appropriate evidence. If not, the service auditor should modify the report. Paragraph 4.34 of this guide presents an illustrative explanatory paragraph that would be added to the service auditor's report when a scope limitation exists that prevents the service auditor from obtaining evidence about the operating effectiveness of controls.

3.58 When information produced by the service organization's information system is provided to the service auditor as a source for testing, the service auditor should obtain evidence about the validity, completeness, and accuracy of that information. For example, the service organization might provide the service auditor with a quarterly system-generated report of user access to the system that is reviewed by management for appropriateness of access based on assigned job responsibilities. In testing management's review, the service auditor evaluates whether the report is complete and accurate, based on the user access rules for the system.

Testing Controls at an Interim Date

3.59 The service auditor may perform tests of controls at interim dates, at the end of the examination period, or after the examination period. The

- Quantitative factors, such as the tolerable rate of deviation and the observed rate of deviation. (In this guide, the *tolerable rate of deviation* is the maximum rate of deviations in the operation of the prescribed control that the service auditor is willing to accept without modifying the opinion relating to one or more applicable trust services criteria.)

- Qualitative factors (for example, the nature and cause of any identified deviations).

3.50 If the service organization implemented changes to its controls during the period covered by the service auditor's report, and the superseded controls could be relevant to meeting one or more applicable trust services criteria during a portion of the period covered by the service auditor's report, the superseded controls should be included in the population of controls to be tested. If the service organization has used the inclusive method, the service auditor considers changes to controls at both the service organization and subservice organization.

Designing and Performing Tests of Controls

3.51 When determining the nature, timing, and extent of tests of controls to be performed to obtain evidence of the operating effectiveness of controls, the service auditor considers the type of evidence that can be obtained about the performance of the control and how long that evidence will be available. The service auditor also considers whether a particular control is designed to meet one or more criteria on its own or in combination with other controls. If a combination of controls is necessary to meet a given criteria, those controls are considered together, and deviations are evaluated together. The service auditor also considers the risk that the control will not operate effectively.

3.52 The service organization's control environment or other components of internal control related to the service provided to user entities may enhance or mitigate the effectiveness of specific controls. If the service auditor determines that certain aspects of the control environment or other components of internal control are not effective, the service auditor generally would obtain more convincing evidence of the operating effectiveness of the specific controls to determine whether the related trust services criteria have been met. In some situations, the service auditor may conclude that controls are not operating effectively to meet certain related trust services criteria because of deficiencies in the control environment or other components of internal control.

3.53 For example, consider a service organization that determines bonuses based on zero processing errors. In this environment, service organization personnel may be tempted to suppress the reporting of errors in order to receive bonuses. The service auditor may decide to increase the testing of controls that prevent, or detect and correct, errors in system processing (for example, reconciliations of input to output designed to identify exceptions) or, perhaps, may even test the entire population to determine whether controls are operating effectively to meet the applicable trust services criteria.

Nature of Tests of Controls

3.54 When designing and performing tests of controls, the service auditor

a. makes inquiries and performs other procedures to obtain evidence about the following:

3.42 A service organization's controls may vary, depending on the nature of the information processed or the manner in which it is transmitted. For example, user entities may submit information to a service organization by mail, phone, fax, or Internet. Controls over the capture of that information may vary depending on the method by which the information is submitted. In order for a specified criterion to be met, the service organization's controls would need to address all the significant variations.

3.43 A service organization that has multiple controls that each independently meet a particular criterion may choose to include only one of the controls in the description. If the service auditor determines that the described control is not suitably designed to meet a particular criterion and becomes aware of one or more other controls that are suitably designed to meet the criterion, the service auditor should ask management to revise the description to include the additional control(s).

3.44 After performing the procedures and considering the guidance in paragraphs 3.34–.43, the service auditor considers whether the controls have the ability, as designed, to provide reasonable assurance that the applicable trust services criteria are met.

3.45 Paragraphs 4.29–.30 and 4.32 of this guide present illustrative explanatory paragraphs that would be added to the service auditor's report when the service auditor determines that controls are not suitably designed to meet one or more of the applicable trust services criteria.

Obtaining Evidence Regarding the Operating Effectiveness of Controls in a Type 2 Engagement

3.46 When performing a type 2 engagement, the service auditor should test the operating effectiveness of the controls stated in management's description of the service organization's system that are necessary to meet the applicable trust services criteria throughout the period covered by the service auditor's report. The service auditor is responsible for determining the nature, timing, and extent of the procedures to be performed in evaluating whether the controls are operating effectively.

3.47 From the viewpoint of the service auditor, a control is operating effectively if it functions as intended throughout the period. When the service organization uses the inclusive method, the service auditor considers the controls at both the service organization and subservice organization.

3.48 A control may be designed to address an identified risk on its own or may function in combination with another control. For example, when a supervisor reviews and approves a user's credentials prior to providing the user with access to the system, the manual control (review and approval of the user's credentials) may be complemented by a system's application control requiring that a supervisor acknowledge his or her review and approval by entering a sign-off in the system prior to providing access to the system. In this instance, both the manual and automated controls would be tested by the service auditor because the two controls are dependent on one another.

3.49 The service auditor should consider materiality when evaluating whether controls are operating with sufficient effectiveness to meet the applicable trust services criteria. Materiality with respect to the operating effectiveness of controls includes the consideration of the following:

method prevents the description from being fairly presented and causes the description to be misleading to users. The service auditor considers the extent to which

- important system functions necessary for understanding the system are performed by the subservice organization.

- controls at the subservice organization are necessary to meet the applicable trust services criteria.

- the service organization's compliance with the commitments in its statement of privacy practices is dependent on the subservice organization's compliance with those commitments.

Factors to consider in making this determination include the following:

- The number of applicable trust services criteria that would not be met if the types of controls expected to be implemented at the carved-out subservice organization that are necessary to meet the criteria, either alone or in combination with controls at the service organization, were not implemented

- The complexity of the services and the types of controls that would be expected to be implemented by the subservice organization

- The complexity of the interaction of the service organization and subservice organization.

- The ability of the service auditor to obtain sufficient appropriate evidence regarding controls at the service organization affected by controls at the carved-out subservice organization.

3.39 If the service auditor determines that the effect of the types of controls expected to be implemented at the subservice organization in meeting the applicable trust services criteria is pervasive, and the description of the service organization's system when presented using the carve-out method is misleading to users, the service auditor may

- suggest to management that the scope of the engagement be changed to the inclusive method.

- disclaim an opinion on all of the matters covered by the service auditor's report.

Paragraph 4.39 of this guide presents an explanatory paragraph that would be added to the service auditor's report when disclaiming an opinion in these circumstances, as well as the disclaimer language that replaces the opinion paragraph.

3.40 The service auditor should consider materiality with respect to the suitability of the design of controls primarily by considering qualitative factors, such as whether the controls have the ability, as designed, to provide reasonable assurance that the applicable trust services criteria would be met, and quantitative factors, such as the maximum rate of control failure that is acceptable to the service organization and whether that rate is less than the service auditor's tolerable rate of deviation.

3.41 In evaluating the suitability of the design of controls, the service auditor considers the effect of the control environment and other components of the service organization's internal control on the ability of the controls to meet the applicable trust services criteria.

assurance that the applicable trust services criteria would be met. The trust services criteria for a SOC 2^{SM} engagement are included in appendix B, "Trust Services Principles and Criteria for Security, Availability, Processing Integrity, Confidentiality, and Privacy," of this guide. In assessing whether controls are suitably designed, the service auditor considers the following:

- The events and circumstances that might prevent the applicable trust services criteria from being met

- Whether the controls, if operating effectively, would prevent, or detect and correct, those events and circumstances

3.35 The service auditor uses the information and evidence obtained in determining whether the description of the service organization's system is fairly presented to evaluate the suitability of the design of controls and obtains additional evidence by performing procedures that may include the following:

- Inquiry of service organization personnel regarding the operation of controls and the types of errors that occur

- Inspection of documents produced by the system

- Performing additional walkthroughs of control activity-related policies and procedures

- Reading system documentation

3.36 A control may meet more than one criterion or multiple controls may be needed to meet a single criterion. If a combination of controls is needed to meet one or more criteria, the service auditor considers the combination of controls jointly.

3.37 If the service organization uses the carve-out method for a subservice organization, the service auditor also evaluates whether the types of controls expected to be implemented at the carved-out subservice organization that are necessary to meet specified applicable trust services criteria, either alone or in combination with controls at the service organization, would, if operating effectively, meet the specified applicable trust services criteria. The service auditor also considers whether evidence exists that the subservice organization is aware of the service organization's requirements with regard to these types of controls and whether there is any evidence that weaknesses exist in the suitability of the design or operating effectiveness of controls at the subservice organization. Examples of procedures that may be performed to obtain such evidence include the following:

- Reading contracts with the subservice organization to determine if they identify the types of controls expected to be implemented at the subservice organization

- Obtaining an understanding of the procedures in place at the service organization to evaluate and monitor the implementation, suitability of design, and operating effectiveness of the controls at the subservice organization (for example, evaluation of a service auditor's report on the description of the subservice organization's system prepared using this guide or testing performed at the subservice organization by service organization personnel)

- Obtaining and evaluating a type 2 report on the subservice organization's system prepared using this guide

3.38 The service auditor considers whether the services provided by the subservice organization are of such a nature that the use of the carve-out

organization uses a subservice organization but refuses to disclose that fact and the functions that the subservice organization performs.

Changes in the Scope of the Engagement

3.32 Management of the service organization may request a change in the scope of the engagement prior to the completion of the engagement (for example, a change in the trust services principles to be covered, the services that the service organization provides [for example discontinuing a particular service], the boundaries of the service organization's system, the components of the system, or the use of the inclusive or carve-out method for subservice organizations). When management requests such a change in scope, the service auditor should be satisfied, before agreeing to the change, that the requirements for acceptance and continuance in paragraph 2.03 continue to be met and that a reasonable justification for the change exists. Reasonable justification may include the following:

- Changes in the needs of users of the reports
- Identification of additional system components or expansion of the boundaries of the system to be included in the description to improve the fairness of the presentation of the description
- Determination that certain system components are not relevant to the services provided
- Determination that certain services are not relevant to users
- The inability to arrange for the service auditor's access to a subservice organization

Generally, increases in the scope of the engagement are likely to have a reasonable justification. A request to decrease the scope of the engagement may not have a reasonable justification if, for example, the request is made

- to exclude portions of the system because of the likelihood that the service auditor's opinion would be modified with respect to those portions of the system.
- to prevent the disclosure of deviations identified at a subservice organization by requesting a change from the inclusive method to the carve-out method.

3.33 When a service auditor determines that a request to change the scope of an engagement derives from intent by a responsible party (for example, management of the service organization or a subservice organization) to conceal information relevant to the user, such as deficiencies in the operating effectiveness of a control, the service auditor should take appropriate action, which may include adding an explanatory paragraph to his or her report, disclaiming an opinion, or withdrawing from the engagement. If the request to change the scope of the engagement derives from refusal by management of the subservice organization to provide a written assertion or written representations, after having agreed to do so, the service auditor should disclaim an opinion due to the service auditor's inability to obtain evidence regarding the suitability of the design and operating effectiveness of controls at the subservice organization.

Evaluating the Suitability of the Design of Controls

3.34 A control is suitably designed if, individually or in combination with other controls, it would, when complied with satisfactorily, provide reasonable

following are some relevant factors to be considered when determining the timing of tests of controls:

- The nature of the controls
- The period of time during which the information will be available (for example, electronic files may be overwritten after a period of time or hard copy records may not be retained)
- Whether testing requires direct observation of a procedure that is only performed at certain times during the examination period
- Whether the control leaves evidence of its operation and, if not, whether the control must be tested through observation

3.60 Performing procedures at an interim date may assist management of the service organization in identifying deficiencies in the design or operating effectiveness of controls at an early stage in the examination and provides the service organization with an opportunity to correct the deficiencies for the remainder of the examination period. Paragraph 4.32 of this guide contains an illustrative paragraph that would be added to the service auditor's report if the service auditor concludes that controls were not suitably designed to meet an applicable trust services criterion during a portion of the period under examination.

3.61 When the service auditor performs tests of the operating effectiveness of controls at an interim period, the service auditor should determine what additional testing is necessary for the remaining period.

Extent of Tests of Controls

3.62 The service auditor should design and perform tests of controls to obtain sufficient appropriate evidence that the controls are operating effectively throughout the period to meet the applicable trust services criteria. Relevant factors in determining the extent of tests of controls include the following:

- The nature of the controls
- The frequency of the performance of the control during the period (for example, daily management review of open incidents versus monthly review of closed incidents to identify ongoing problems)
- The relevance and reliability of the evidence that can be obtained to support the conclusion that the controls are operating effectively to meet the applicable trust services criteria
- The extent to which audit evidence is obtained from tests of other controls designed to meet the same criterion
- The service organization's maximum acceptable rate of control failure
- The service auditor's tolerable rate of deviation in the operating effectiveness of the control

3.63 If the control operates frequently, the service auditor should consider using audit sampling to obtain reasonable assurance about the operating effectiveness of the control. If the control is applied on a periodic basis (for example, a monthly reconciliation of input to output), the service auditor should consider guidance appropriate for testing smaller populations. Refer further to

AU section 350, *Audit Sampling* (AICPA, *Professional Standards*), and the Audit Guide *Audit Sampling*.

3.64 The service auditor should test the operating effectiveness of the control in effect throughout the period covered by the report and determine whether the control has operated frequently enough to be assessed as operating effectively. For example, if a report covers a period of six months, and a control operates only annually, the service auditor may be unable to test the operating effectiveness of the control within the period. The shorter the test period, the greater the risk that certain controls may not have operated during the period and that the service auditor will be unable to perform sufficient testing and obtain sufficient evidence to express an opinion on the operating effectiveness of those controls.

3.65 Generally, evidence obtained in prior engagements about the satisfactory operation of controls in prior periods does not provide a basis for a reduction in testing in the current examination period, even if it is supplemented with evidence obtained during the current period. If the service auditor plans to use evidence about the operating effectiveness of controls obtained in a prior engagement, the service auditor should adapt and apply the guidance in paragraph .40 of AU section 318, *Performing Audit Procedures in Response to Assessed Risks and Evaluating the Audit Evidence Obtained* (AICPA, *Professional Standards*), which requires the service auditor to obtain evidence about whether changes in those specific controls have occurred subsequent to the prior engagement by a combination of observation, inquiry, and inspection to confirm the understanding of those specific controls. Paragraph .40 of AU section 318 refers to the guidance in paragraph .24 of AU section 326, *Audit Evidence* (AICPA, *Professional Standards*), which states that the service auditor should perform procedures to establish the continuing relevance of evidence obtained in prior periods when the service auditor plans to use such evidence in the current period. For example, in performing the prior examination, the service auditor may have determined that an automated control was functioning as intended. The service auditor should obtain evidence to determine whether changes to the automated control have been made that affect its continued effective functioning (for example, through inquiries of management and the inspection of logs to indicate whether controls have been changed). Consideration of evidence about these changes may support either increasing or decreasing the expected evidence to be obtained in the current period about the operating effectiveness of the controls.

3.66 If the service auditor intends to use evidence of the operating effectiveness of controls that was obtained in a prior period, and those controls have changed since they were last tested, the service auditor should perform additional tests of the operating effectiveness of such controls in the current period. Changes may affect the relevance of the evidence obtained in prior periods such that it may no longer be relevant. For example, changes in a system that enable the service organization to receive a new report from the system probably do not affect the relevance of prior period evidence; however, a change that causes data to be accumulated or calculated differently does affect it.

3.67 If the service auditor identified deviations in the operation of a control in a prior year, the service auditor may decide to increase the extent of testing in the current period. For example, if the opinion in the prior year's service auditor's report was qualified because of deviations in controls over the authorization of user access, the service auditor may decide to increase the number of items tested in the current examination period. This would be the case if the design or operation of the control had not been corrected in the current year, which may result in the same kinds of deviations, or if a new control had been implemented (a new control may not have been thoroughly tested and may have unexpected deficiencies in design or operating effectiveness, increasing the risk that the controls would not have operated effectively).

3.68 Generally, IT processing is inherently consistent; therefore, the service auditor may be able to limit the testing to one or a few instances of the control operation. An automated control should function consistently, unless the program, including the tables, files, or other permanent data used by the program, is changed. Once the service auditor determines that an automated control is functioning as intended, which could be determined at the time the control is initially implemented or at some other date, the service auditor should perform tests to determine that the control continues to function effectively. Such tests ordinarily would include determining that changes to the program are not made without being subject to the appropriate program change controls, that the authorized version of the program is used for processing transactions, and that other relevant IT general controls are effective.

3.69 A control may be designed to address an identified risk on its own or may function in combination with another control. Often, the effectiveness of the control will depend on both manual and automated procedures. For example, management's follow-up of system-identified security access violation events is dependent on the proper configuration and functioning of the security monitoring software.

Selecting Items to Be Tested

3.70 When determining the extent of tests of controls and whether sampling is appropriate, the service auditor should consider the characteristics of the population of the controls to be tested, including the nature of the controls, the frequency of their application, and the expected deviation rate. AU section 350 addresses planning, performing, and evaluating audit samples. If the service auditor determines that sampling is appropriate, the service auditor should apply the requirements in paragraphs .31–.43 of AU section 350 that address sampling in tests of controls. Paragraphs .01–.14 and .45–.46 of AU section 350 provide additional guidance regarding the principles underlying those paragraphs.

Controls Included in the Description That Are Not Tested

3.71 There may be situations in which the service auditor is unable to test controls related to certain applicable trust services criteria because there were no instances of the control operating during the examination period. In these situations, the service auditor's tests should identify the applicable trust services criteria for which tests of controls have not been performed and the reasons why they have not been performed.

Testing Changes to Controls

3.72 If the service organization makes changes to controls during the period that are relevant to meeting the applicable trust services criteria stated in the description, and the service auditor believes the changes would be considered significant by users, the service auditor should test the superseded controls before the change and test the new controls after the change for the period they were in effect. For example, during the period June 1, 20X0, to May 31, 20X1, Example Service Organization decided to automate a control that was previously performed manually. The service organization automated the control on December 15, 20X0. The service auditor tests the manual control for the period June 1, 20X0, to December 14, 20X0, considering the nature and frequency of the performance of the control, and then tests the automated control for the period December 15, 20X0, to May 31, 20X1, considering the guidance in paragraph 3.62 and the nature and frequency of the performance of each control. If the service auditor cannot test the superseded controls, the service auditor should disclose that fact in the description of tests and results and determine the effect on the service auditor's report.

Testing Compliance With Privacy Commitments

3.73 In a type 2 engagement that addresses the privacy principle, in addition to expressing an opinion on the design and operating effectiveness of controls, the service auditor also expresses an opinion on whether the service organization complied with the commitments in its statement of privacy practices (privacy commitments). Information obtained from the service auditor's assessment of the design and operating effectiveness of controls related to privacy contributes to his or her evaluation of the risk of material noncompliance with the service organization's privacy commitments, which includes both intentional and unintentional material noncompliance. The service auditor uses this information as part, but not all, of the reasonable basis for his or her opinion regarding the service organization's compliance with its privacy commitments.

3.74 Based on the assessment of the controls that address the trust services privacy criteria, the service auditor determines the extent to which he or she needs to perform tests to detect material noncompliance with the privacy commitments. Accordingly, the service auditor may alter the nature, timing, and extent of tests performed, based on the assessments and tests of the controls.

3.75 In an engagement in which the service auditor reports on an entity's compliance with its privacy commitments, the service auditor's consideration of materiality is affected by (a) the nature of the requirements in the statement of privacy practices; (b) the nature and frequency of identified noncompliance, with appropriate consideration of sampling risk; and (c) qualitative considerations, including the needs and expectations of the report users.

3.76 The service auditor should apply procedures to provide reasonable assurance of detecting material noncompliance. Determining these procedures and evaluating the sufficiency of the evidence obtained are matters of professional judgment. When exercising such judgment, the service auditor should consider the guidance in AU section 350 and paragraphs .51–.54 of AT section 101.

3.77 The following example illustrates how a service auditor might consider the foregoing in planning tests of compliance with privacy commitments:

> A service organization's statement of privacy practices contains a commitment not to share personal information obtained from users with other users. Based on the service auditor's evaluation and tests, the service organization's controls over access to personal information are effective in meeting the relevant criteria and in preventing one user's employees from accessing personal information provided by any other user. To test compliance with this commitment, the service auditor compares a daily log of

all accesses to personal information with a list, furnished by the user entity, of the names of user-entity employees authorized to access such information. Because the access controls related to this commitment were effective, the service auditor determined that it would only be necessary to perform this test on a limited number of daily logs throughout the period. Had the controls not been as effective or had the service auditor identified deviations while testing controls, the number of daily logs tested for compliance would need to be greater.

Using the Work of the Internal Audit Function

3.78 Paragraphs 2.16–.22 of this guide discuss the service auditor's responsibilities for the following:

- Obtaining an understanding of the responsibilities and activities of the service organization's internal audit function
- Determining whether work performed by the internal audit function is adequate for the service auditor's purposes
- Determining the planned effect of that work on the service auditor's procedures

3.79 In order for a service auditor to use specific work of the internal audit function, the service auditor should evaluate and perform procedures on that work to determine whether it is adequate for the service auditor's purposes by evaluating whether

    a. the work was performed by members of the internal audit function having adequate technical training and proficiency;

    b. the work was properly supervised, reviewed, and documented;

    c. sufficient appropriate evidence was obtained to enable the internal audit function to draw reasonable conclusions;

    d. conclusions reached are appropriate in the circumstances, and any reports prepared by the internal audit function are consistent with the results of the work performed; and

    e. exceptions relevant to the engagement or unusual matters disclosed by the internal audit function are properly resolved.

3.80 The nature, timing, and extent of the service auditor's procedures performed on specific work of the internal auditor function will depend on the service auditor's assessment of the significance of that work to the service auditor's conclusions (for example, the significance of the risks that the controls are intended to mitigate); the evaluation of the internal audit function; and the evaluation of the specific work of the internal audit function. Such procedures may include the following:

- Examination of items already examined by the internal audit function
- Examination of other similar items
- Observation of procedures performed by the internal audit function

3.81 When the internal audit function provides direct assistance to the service auditor, as described in paragraphs 2.16 and 4.10 of this guide, the service auditor should

- inform the internal auditors of their responsibilities; the objectives of the procedures they are to perform; and matters that may affect the nature, timing, and extent of the audit procedures.

- supervise, review, evaluate, and test the work performed by the internal auditors to the extent appropriate in the circumstances.

Evaluating the Results of Tests

3.82 The service auditor should evaluate the results of tests of controls and, if the ⸀port addresses the privacy principle, the results of tests of compliance ⸀h the service organization's commitments in its statement of privacy pra ⸀ces. In evaluating the results of tests, the service auditor investigates the nature and cause of any identified deviations and determines whether

- identified deviations are within the tolerable rate of deviation and are acceptable. If so, the testing that has been performed provides an appropriate basis for concluding that the control operated effectively throughout the specified period.

- additional testing of the same control or other controls designed to meet the same criterion is necessary to reach a conclusion about whether the controls related to the criterion operated effectively throughout the specified period.

- the testing that has been performed provides an appropriate basis for concluding that the control did not operate effectively throughout the specified period.

3.83 If the service auditor is unable to apply the planned testing procedures or appropriate alternative procedures to selected items, the service auditor considers the reasons for this limitation and ordinarily considers those selected items to be deviations from the prescribed policy or procedure for the purpose of evaluating the sample.

3.84 The service auditor evaluates deficiencies related to the control environment or other components of the service organization's internal control and determines the effect on the service auditor's opinion. For example, the service auditor considers how deficiencies in the control environment would alter the nature, timing, and extent of his or her procedures. In certain circumstances, identified deficiencies in the control environment may prevent controls from meeting one or more of the applicable trust services criteria, which may result in a qualified or an adverse opinion.

3.85 If the service auditor becomes aware of deviations that have resulted from intentional acts by service organization personnel, incidents of noncompliance with laws and regulations, or other adverse events not prevented or detected by a control that may affect one or more user entities, the service auditor should determine whether this information should be communicated to affected user entities and whether this communication has occurred. If the information has not been communicated, and management of the service organization is unwilling to do so, the service auditor should take appropriate action, which may include the following:

- Obtaining legal advice about the consequences of different courses of action

- Communicating with those charged with governance of the service organization

- Disclaiming an opinion, modifying the service auditor's opinion, or adding an emphasis paragraph

- Communicating with third parties (for example, a regulator) when required to do so

- Withdrawing from the engagement

3.86 If, as a result of performing the examination procedures, the service auditor becomes aware that any identified deviations have resulted from intentional acts by service organization personnel, the service auditor reassesses the risk that management's description of the service organization's system is not fairly presented; the controls are not suitably designed; the controls are not operating effectively; and if the report addresses the privacy principle, the service organization has not complied with the commitments in its statement of privacy practices. Additionally, depending on the nature of any intentional acts that are identified and the level of responsibility of the service organization personnel involved in those acts (for example, senior management versus clerical personnel), the service auditor considers the effect of the intentional act on the engagement and whether it is appropriate for the service auditor to continue with, or withdraw from, the engagement.

3.87 If the service auditor becomes aware of incidents of noncompliance with laws and regulations or other adverse events that have not been prevented or detected by a control and that may affect one or more user entities, the service auditor should determine the effect of such incidents on management's description of the service organization's system; the suitability of the design and operating effectiveness of the controls; if the report addresses the privacy principle, the service organization's compliance with the commitments in its statement of privacy practices; and the service auditor's report.

3.88 Paragraph 4.33 of this guide presents an illustrative explanatory paragraph that would be added to the service auditor's report when controls are not operating effectively.

Obtaining Written Representation

3.89 As indicated in paragraph 2.01 of this guide, one of the conditions for accepting or continuing an engagement to report on controls at a service organization is that management of the service organization agrees to the terms of the engagement by acknowledging and accepting its responsibility for providing the service auditor with written representations at the conclusion of the engagement.

3.90 The service auditor should request management to provide written representations that

  a. reaffirm its assertion that is attached to the description of the service organization's system.

  b. it has provided the service auditor with all relevant information and access agreed to.

  c. it has disclosed to the service auditor any of the following of which it is aware:

   i. Instances of noncompliance with laws and regulations or uncorrected errors attributable to the service organization that may affect one or more user entities.

ii. Knowledge of (1) any actual, suspected, or alleged intentional acts by management or the service organization's employees that could adversely affect the fairness of the presentation of management's description of the service organization's system or (2) whether the controls stated in the description were suitably designed and operating effectively to meet the applicable trust services criteria.

iii. Design deficiencies in controls.

iv. Instances when controls have not operated as described.

v. If reporting on the privacy principle, any instances of noncompliance regarding its commitments set forth in its statement of privacy practices.

vi. Any events subsequent to the period covered by management's description of the service organization's system up to the date of the service auditor's report that could have a significant effect on management's assertion or the fact that no such subsequent events have occurred.

3.91 If a service organization uses a subservice organization, and management's description of the service organization's system uses the inclusive method, the service auditor also should obtain written representations from management of the subservice organization that address the matters identified in paragraph 3.90.

3.92 The service auditor may consider it necessary to request written representations about matters in addition to those listed in paragraph 3.90, including oral representations for which no other evidential matter exists. This would be determined based on the facts and circumstances of the particular engagement (for example, if changes to the service organization's controls have occurred during the period covered by the service auditor's report, there might be a need to obtain representations that address the periods before and after the change).

3.93 The written representations required by paragraph 3.90 are separate from, and in addition to, management's written assertion.

3.94 The written representations should be in the form of a representation letter addressed to the service auditor, signed by the individuals identified by the service auditor, and dated as of the same date as the service auditor's report.

3.95 If management does not provide one or more of the requested representations, the service auditor should do the following:

- Discuss the matter with management
- Evaluate the effect of such refusal on the service auditor's assessment of the integrity of management and evaluate the effect that this may have on the reliability of management's representations and evidence in general
- Take appropriate actions, which may include disclaiming an opinion or withdrawing from the engagement

3.96 If management refuses to provide the service auditor with (*a*) representations that reaffirm its assertion or (*b*) a representation that it has provided the service auditor with all relevant information and access agreed to, the service auditor should disclaim an opinion or withdraw from the engagement. This is the case because these representations are fundamental to the engagement and affect all the other representations made by management and other service organization personnel during the course of the engagement.

3.97 If the service auditor is unable to obtain written representations regarding relevant trust services criteria and related controls at the subservice organization, management of the service organization would be unable to use the inclusive method but may be able to use the carve-out method.

3.98 Because management's written representations are an important consideration when forming the service auditor's opinion, the service auditor ordinarily would not be able to issue his or her report until he or she received the representation letter. Illustrative representation letters for a service auditor's engagement are presented in appendix C, "Illustrative Management Assertions and Related Service Auditor's Reports on Controls at a Service Organization Relevant to Security, Availability, Processing Integrity, Confidentiality, and Privacy," of this guide.

Subsequent Events

3.99 The service auditor makes inquiries about whether management is aware of any events subsequent to the period covered by management's description of the service organization's system up to the date of the service auditor's report that could have a significant effect on management's assertion and the underlying subject matter of the assertion. If the service auditor becomes aware, through inquiry or otherwise, of such an event or any other event that is of such a nature and significance that its disclosure is necessary to prevent users of the report from being misled, and information about that event is not disclosed by management in its description, the service auditor should modify his or her opinion on the fairness of the presentation of the description and disclose the event in the service auditor's report. The service auditor is responsible for determining the effect of the event on the service auditor's report, regardless of whether management appropriately discloses the event and modifies its written assertion.

3.100 The following are examples of subsequent events that could affect management's assertion or description of the service organization's system:

- After the period covered by the service auditor's report, management discovered that during the last quarter of the period covered by the service auditor's report, the IT security director provided all the programmers with access to the production data files, enabling them to modify data.
- After the period covered by the service auditor's report, management discovered that a confidentiality breach occurred at the service organization during the period covered by the service auditor's report.
- After the period covered by the service auditor's report, it was discovered that during the examination period, the signatures on a number of nonautomated transaction execution instructions that appeared to be authenticated by signature verification were not authenticated.

3.101 There may be situations in which the event discovered subsequent to the period covered by management's description of the service organization's system up to the date of the service auditor's report would likely have no effect on management's assertion because the underlying situation did not occur or exist until after the period covered by management's description of the service organization's system; however, the matter may be sufficiently important for disclosure by management in its description and, potentially, the service auditor in an emphasis paragraph of the service auditor's report. The following are examples of such subsequent events:

- The service organization was acquired by another entity.
- The service organization experienced a significant operating disruption.
- A data center-hosting service organization that provides applications and technology that enable user entities to perform essential business functions made significant changes to its information systems, including a system conversion or significant outsourcing of operations.

The service organization may want to disclose such events in a separate section of the description of the service organization's system titled, for example, "Other Information Provided by the Service Organization."

3.102 The service auditor has no responsibility to keep informed of events subsequent to the date of the service auditor's report; however, after the release of the service auditor's report, the service auditor may become aware of conditions that existed at the report date that might have affected management's assertion and the service auditor's report had the service auditor been aware of them. The evaluation of such subsequent information is similar to the evaluation of information discovered subsequent to the date of the report on an audit of financial statements, as described in AU section 561, *Subsequent Discovery of Facts Existing at the Date of the Auditor's Report* (AICPA, *Professional Standards*). The service auditor should adapt and apply the guidance in AU section 561.

Documentation

3.103 Paragraphs .100–.107 of AT section 101 describe the service auditor's responsibilities related to documentation. In addition, the service auditor considers whether users in certain industry segments (for example, government) may require additional documentation.

Consideration of Management's Assertion

3.104 Management may have provided the service auditor with an assertion at the beginning of the engagement that includes all the relevant aspects that would be expected. The service auditor may identify deficiencies in the operating effectiveness of controls that cause the service auditor to qualify the opinion. In this instance, the service auditor would evaluate the reason why management had not identified the deficiencies in the operating effectiveness of the controls and determine whether management should have known these existed and whether management is in a position to be able to provide the assertion or whether additional work needs to be done by management before they provide the final assertion that is attached to the description. In instances in which the service auditor has identified deficiencies that give rise to a qualification in the opinion, management is expected to modify their assertion to note those deficiencies.

3.105 The service auditor may determine that management's assertion does not provide sufficient detail, fails to disclose deficiencies identified by the service auditor that resulted in a qualified opinion, or contains inaccuracies. In these situations, the service auditor should request that management modify its assertion. For example, when deviations identified in the examination cause the service auditor to qualify the opinion, the service auditor should ask management to amend its assertion to reflect the identified deficiencies. If management refuses to do so, the service auditor takes appropriate action, which may include additional modifications to the service auditor's report, rendering an adverse opinion, or withdrawing from the engagement.

———————

Chapter 4

Reporting

This chapter describes the service auditor's responsibilities when reporting on a service organization's controls relevant to security, availability, processing integrity, confidentiality, or privacy. This chapter primarily focuses on the elements of a service auditor's report and modifications to the service auditor's opinion.

Responsibilities of the Service Auditor

4.01 The service auditor's responsibilities for reporting on a service organization controls (SOC) 2 engagement include the following:

- Preparing the service auditor's report, including all the report elements identified in paragraph 4.02, and modifying the report if the service auditor determines it is appropriate to do so

- For a type 2 report, preparing a written description of the tests of controls performed by the service auditor and the results of those tests

- For a type 2 report that addresses the privacy principle, preparing a written description of the service auditor's tests of the service organization's compliance with the commitments in its statement of privacy practices and the results of those tests

Contents of the Service Auditor's Report

4.02 A service auditor's type 2 report on controls relevant to security, availability, processing integrity, confidentiality, or privacy should include the following elements:

a. A title that includes the word *independent.*

b. An addressee.

c. Identification of the following:

    i. Management's description of the service organization's system and the function performed by the system or service provided by the service organization.

    ii. Any parts of management's description of the service organization's system that are not covered by the service auditor's report.

    iii. The criteria for evaluating whether management's description of the service organization's system is fairly presented.

    iv. The applicable trust services criteria for evaluating whether controls are suitably designed and operating effectively.

    v. When the report addresses the privacy principle, the service organization's statement of privacy practices.

    vi. Any services performed by a subservice organization and whether the carve-out method or inclusive method was used in relation to them. Depending on which method is used, the following should be included:

       (1) If the carve-out method was used, a statement that management's description of the service organization's system excludes controls of the subservice organization, and when the report addresses the privacy principle, that the description also excludes the subservice organization's statement of privacy practices and that the service auditor's procedures do not extend to the subservice organization.

       (2) If the inclusive method was used, a statement that management's description of the service organization's system includes applicable trust services criteria and controls for the subservice organization, and when the report addresses the privacy principle, that the description also includes the subservice organization's statement of privacy practices and that the service auditor's procedures included procedures related to the subservice organization.

  d. If management's description of the service organization's system refers to the need for complementary user-entity controls, a statement that the service auditor has not evaluated the suitability of the design or operating effectiveness of complementary user-entity controls and that the applicable trust services criteria stated in the description can be met only if complementary user-entity controls are suitably designed and operating effectively, along with the related controls at the service organization.

  e. A reference to management's assertion and a statement that management is responsible for the following:

    i. Preparing the description of the service organization's system; the assertion; and when the report covers controls over privacy, the statement of privacy practices, including the completeness, accuracy, and method of presentation of the description, assertion, and statement of privacy practices.

    ii. Providing the services covered by the description of the service organization's system.

    iii. Selecting the trust services principle(s) being reported on and stating the applicable trust services criteria and related controls in the description of the service organization's system.

    iv. Identifying any applicable trust services criteria relevant to the principle being reported on that have been omitted from the description and explaining the reason for the omission.

    v. Designing, implementing, and documenting controls that are suitably designed and operating effectively to meet the applicable trust services criteria.

    vi. When the report covers controls over privacy, complying with the commitments in its statement of privacy practices included in, or attached to, the description of the service organization's system.

f. A statement that the service auditor's responsibility is to express an opinion on the fairness of the presentation of management's description of the service organization's system; the suitability of the design and operating effectiveness of the controls to meet the applicable trust services criteria; and when the report addresses the privacy principle, the service organization's compliance with the commitments in its statement of privacy practices, based on the service auditor's examination.

g. A statement that the examination was conducted in accordance with attestation standards established by the American Institute of Certified Public Accountants and that those standards require the service auditor to plan and perform the examination to obtain reasonable assurance about whether management's description of the service organization's system is fairly presented; whether the controls are suitably designed and operating effectively throughout the specified period to meet the applicable trust services criteria; and if the report addresses the privacy principle, whether the service organization complied with the commitments in its statement of privacy practices.

h. A statement that an examination of management's description of a service organization's system and the suitability of the design and operating effectiveness of controls involves performing procedures to obtain evidence about the following:

    i. The fairness of the presentation of the description.

    ii. The suitability of the design and operating effectiveness of the controls to meet the applicable trust services criteria.

    iii. If the report addresses the privacy principle, the service organization's compliance with the commitments in its statement of privacy practices.

i. A statement that the examination included assessing the risks that management's description of the service organization's system is not fairly presented; that the controls were not suitably designed or operating effectively to meet the applicable trust services criteria; and if the report addresses the privacy principle, that the service organization did not comply with the commitments in its statement of privacy practices.

j. A statement that the examination also included testing the operating effectiveness of those controls that the service auditor considers necessary to provide reasonable assurance that the applicable trust services criteria were met, and if the report addresses the privacy principle, testing the service organization's compliance with the commitments in its statement of privacy practices.

k. A statement that the service auditor believes the examination provides a reasonable basis for his or her opinion.

l. A statement about the inherent limitations of controls, including the risk of projecting to future periods any evaluation of the fairness of the presentation of management's description of the service organization's system or conclusions about the suitability of the design or operating effectiveness of controls, and when the report addresses the privacy principle, the service organization's compliance with the commitments in its statement of privacy practices.

m. The service auditor's opinion on whether, in all material respects, based on the criteria described in management's assertion

    i. management's description of the service organization's system fairly presents the service organization's system that was designed and implemented throughout the specified period.

    ii. the controls related to the applicable trust services criteria were suitably designed to provide reasonable assurance that those criteria would be met if the controls operated effectively throughout the specified period.

    iii. the controls that the service auditor tested, which were those necessary to provide reasonable assurance that the applicable trust services criteria were met, operated effectively throughout the specified period.

    iv. if the report addresses the privacy principle, the service organization complied with the commitments in its statement of privacy practices throughout the specified period.

n. If the application of complementary user-entity controls is necessary to meet the applicable trust services criteria, a reference to this condition.

o. A reference to a part of the service auditor's report that contains a description of the service auditor's tests of controls and the results thereof and that includes the following:

    i. Identification of each of the applicable trust services criteria, the controls that were tested, whether the items tested for each control represent all or a selection of the items in the population, and the nature of the tests in sufficient detail to enable users of the report to determine the effect of such tests on their risk assessments.

    ii. If deviations have been identified in the operation of controls included in the description, the extent of testing performed by the service auditor that led to the identification of the deviations, including the number of items tested, and the number and nature of the deviations noted, even if, on the basis of tests performed, the service auditor concludes that the related criteria were met.

p. If the report addresses the privacy principle, a reference to a part of the service auditor's report that contains a description of the service auditor's tests of compliance with the service organization's commitments in its statement of privacy practices and the results thereof and that includes the following:

    i. Identification of the commitments that were tested, whether the items tested for each commitment represent all or a selection of the items in the population, and the nature of the tests in sufficient detail to enable users of the report to determine the effect of such tests on their risk assessments.

    ii. If deviations have been identified in the service organization's compliance with the commitments in its statement of privacy practices, the extent of testing performed by the service auditor that led to the identification of the deviations, including the number of items tested, and the number and nature of the deviations noted, even if, on the basis of tests performed, the service auditor concludes that the related commitment was complied with.

q. A statement indicating that the service auditor's report is intended solely for the information and use of management of the service organization and other specified parties.

r. The date of the service auditor's report.

s. The name of the service auditor and the city and state where the service auditor maintains the office that has responsibility for the engagement.

Describing Tests and the Results of Tests in a Type 2 Report[1]

4.03 A service auditor's type 2 report should contain a reference to a description of the service auditor's tests of controls and the results of those tests. If the type 2 report addresses the privacy principle, it should also contain a reference to a description of the service auditor's tests of the service organization's compliance with the commitments in its statement of privacy practices. The description should identify the controls and any privacy commitments that were tested, whether the items tested represent all or a selection of the items in the population, and the nature of the tests performed in sufficient detail to enable users to determine the effect of such tests on the user's particular objectives.

4.04 The concept of materiality is not applicable when reporting the results of tests for which deviations have been identified because the service auditor does not have the ability to determine whether a deviation will be relevant to a particular user. Consequently, the service auditor reports all deviations. If the service auditor has not identified any deviations, the service auditor may document those results with a phrase such as "No deviations noted."

4.05 The description of tests need not be a duplication of the service auditor's detailed work program, which might make the report too voluminous for users and provide more than the required level of detail. The service auditor is not required to indicate the size of the sample, unless deviations were identified during testing.

4.06 If deviations have been identified, the service auditor's description of tests and results should identify the extent of testing performed by the service auditor that led to the identification of the deviations, including the number of items tested and the number and nature of the deviations noted, even if, on the basis of tests performed, the service auditor concludes that the applicable trust services criteria were met, and the service organization complied with the commitments in its statement of privacy practices.

4.07 If deviations are identified, it may be helpful to users of the report for management to disclose, to the extent known, the causative factors for the deviation, the controls that mitigate the effect of the deviation, corrective

---

[1] For brevity, the word *tests* as used hereinafter refers to tests of the operating effectiveness of controls or tests of the service organization's compliance with the commitments in its statement of privacy practices, unless otherwise specified.

actions taken, and other qualitative factors that would assist users in understanding the effect of the deviations. Such information may be included in an attachment to the description titled "Other Information Provided by Example Service Organization That Is Not Covered by the Service Auditor's Report" or in the description and referred to in the service auditor's tests and results. If such information is included in the description, the service auditor would need to corroborate such information through inquiry, inspection of documentation, and other procedures. Information provided by management about controls that mitigate the effect of deviations or corrective actions should not include forward- looking information, such as future plans to implement controls.

4.08 The following example illustrates the documentation of tests of controls for which deviations have been identified. It is assumed that in each situation, other relevant controls and tests of controls would also be described:

- *Criteria*. Procedures exist to restrict physical access to the defined system, including, but not limited to, facilities; backup media; and other system components, such as firewalls, routers, and servers.

- *Example Service Organization's controls*. Security personnel deactivate physical security access cards of terminated employees on a daily basis using a list generated by the human resources system.

- *Service auditor's tests of controls*. Selected a sample of terminated employees from a list generated by the human resources system and compared the termination date with the access card deactivation date for each employee.

- *Results of tests of controls*. For one terminated employee in an initial sample of 25, the employee's physical access security card was not deactivated until 90 days after the employee's last day of work. In an additional sample of 15 terminated employees, no additional deviations were noted.

- *Management's response*. The terminated employee's name was not listed on the report from the human resources system until 90 days after termination. Subsequent investigation determined that the report used for removing physical access was generated based on the last payroll date of the employee, rather than the last date employed. This employee was 1 of 15 employees who were a part of a reduction in force and received the severance benefit. These employees each continued on the payroll system for 90 days after termination. The physical access cards of all employees receiving severance have been deactivated, and in addition, the report from the human resources system has been changed to generate the list based on the last date of employment.

Describing Tests and Results When Using the Internal Audit Function

4.09 If the work of the internal audit function has been used, the service auditor should not make reference to that work in the service auditor's opinion. Notwithstanding its degree of autonomy and objectivity, the internal audit function is not independent of the service organization. The service auditor has sole responsibility for the opinion expressed in the service auditor's report, and accordingly, that responsibility is not reduced by the service auditor's use of the work of the internal audit function.

4.10 If the work of the internal audit function has been used in performing tests of controls, the part of the service auditor's report that describes the service auditor's tests of controls and the results thereof should include a description of the internal auditor's work and the service auditor's procedures with respect to that work. The phrase "using the work of the internal audit function" is derived from AU section 322, *The Auditor's Consideration of the Internal Audit Function in an Audit of Financial Statements* (AICPA, *Professional Standards*), and refers to work designed and performed by the internal audit function on its own. This would include tests of controls designed and performed by the internal audit function during the period covered by the type 2 report. If the service auditor uses members of the service organization's internal audit function to provide direct assistance, including assistance in performing tests of controls that are designed by the service auditor and performed under the direction, supervision, and review of the service auditor, the description of tests of controls and results need not distinguish between the tests performed by members of the internal audit function and the tests performed by the service auditor because when the internal audit function provides direct assistance, the work performed by the internal audit function undergoes the same scrutiny as if it were performed by the service auditor's staff. When the service auditor uses members of the service organization's internal audit function to provide direct assistance, the service auditor should adapt and apply the requirements in paragraph .27 of AU section 322.

4.11 The service auditor's description of tests of controls performed by the internal audit function and the service auditor's procedures with respect to that work may be presented in a number of ways (for example, by including introductory material in the description of tests of controls indicating that certain work of the internal audit function was used in performing tests of controls or by specifically identifying the tests performed by the internal audit function and attributing those tests to the internal audit function).

4.12 The following are examples of introductory material that may be included in the description of tests of controls and results to inform readers that the service auditor has used the work of the internal audit function to perform tests of controls:

- Throughout the examination period, members of XYZ Service Organization's internal audit function performed tests of controls related to the criterion "Procedures exist to restrict logical access to the defined system, including distribution of output restricted to authorized users." Members of the internal audit function observed the controls being performed by employees, inspected documentation of the performance of the control, and reperformed a sample of control activities. The tests performed by the members of the internal audit function and the results of those tests are presented under the captions "Tests Performed" and "Results of Tests." We reperformed selected tests that had been performed by members of the internal audit function and found no exceptions.

- Members of XYZ Service Organization's internal audit function performed tests of controls for the criterion "Procedures exist to restrict logical access to the defined system, including distribution of output restricted to authorized users." The tests performed by members of the internal audit function included inquiry of employees who performed the control activities, observation of the control being performed at different times during the examination period, reperformance, and examination of the documentation for a sample of requests for system access and a sample of requests for reports. The tests performed by the members of the internal audit function and the results of those tests are presented under the captions "Tests Performed" and "Results of Tests." We tested the work of members of the internal audit function through a combination of independent testing and reperformance and noted no exceptions.

Modifications of the Service Auditor's Report

4.13 The service auditor's opinion should be modified, and the service auditor's report should contain a clear description of all the reasons for the modification if the service auditor concludes that

> *a.* management's description of the service organization's system is not fairly presented, in all material respects;
>
> *b.* the controls are not suitably designed to provide reasonable assurance that the applicable trust services criteria would be met if the controls operated as described;
>
> *c.* in the case of a type 2 report, the controls did not operate effectively throughout the specified period to meet the applicable trust services criteria stated in management's description of the service organization's system;
>
> *d.* a scope limitation exists, resulting in the service auditor's inability to obtain sufficient appropriate evidence; or
>
> *e.* in the case of a type 2 report that addresses the privacy principle, the service organization did not comply with the commitments in its statement of privacy practices.
>
> *f.* management's written assertion does not provide sufficient detail, fails to disclose deficiencies identified by the service auditor that resulted in a qualified opinion, or contains inaccuracies and management refuses to amend its assertion to reflect the identified deficiencies.
>
> *g.* other information that is not covered by the service auditor's report is attached to the description or included in a document containing the description and the service auditor's report, contains material inconsistencies, such as an apparent misstatement of fact, and management refuses to correct the information.

4.14 When determining whether to modify the service auditor's report, the service auditor considers the individual and aggregate effect of identified deviations in management's description of the service organization's system and the suitability of the design and operating effectiveness of the controls throughout the specified period. The service auditor considers quantitative and qualitative factors, such as the following:

- The nature and cause of the deviations
- The tolerable rate of deviations that the service auditor has established
- The pervasiveness of the deviations (for example, whether more than one criterion would be affected)

- The likelihood that the deviations are indicators of control deficiencies that will result in failure to meet the applicable trust services criteria

- The magnitude of such failures that could occur as a result of control deficiencies

- Whether users could be misled if the service auditor's opinion were not modified

4.15 If the service auditor decides that his or her opinion should be modified, the report should contain a clear description of all the reasons for the modification. The objective of that description is to enable report users to develop their own assessments of the effect of deficiencies and deviations on users.

4.16 If a modified opinion is appropriate, the service auditor determines whether to issue a qualified opinion, an adverse opinion, or a disclaimer of opinion.

4.17 When the service auditor has determined that a qualified opinion is appropriate, in addition to adding an explanatory paragraph to the service auditor's report before the opinion paragraph, the service auditor should also modify the opinion paragraph of the service auditor's report as follows (new language is shown in boldface italics; deleted language is shown in strikethrough):

> In our opinion, ~~in all material respects~~ *except for the matter referred to in the preceding paragraph,* based on the description criteria identified in [*name of service organization*]'s assertion and the applicable trust services criteria, *in all material respects*...

4.18 When the service auditor has determined that an adverse opinion is appropriate, in addition to adding an explanatory paragraph to the report that precedes the opinion paragraph and explains all the substantive reasons for the adverse opinion and the principal effects on the subject matter of the report, the service auditor should also modify the opinion paragraph of the service auditor's report. The following is an example of such a paragraph when the service auditor is expressing an adverse opinion on all three components of the opinion (new language is shown in boldface italics; deleted language is shown in strikethrough):

> In our opinion, ~~in all material respects~~ *because of the matter referred to in the preceding paragraph,* based on the description criteria identified in [*name of service organization*]'s assertion and the applicable trust services criteria
>
> a. the description *does not* fairly presents the [*type or name of system*] that was designed and implemented throughout the period [*date*] to [*date*].
>
> b. the controls stated in the description were *not* suitably designed to provide reasonable assurance that the applicable trust services criteria would be met if the controls operated effectively throughout the period [*date*] to [*date*].
>
> c. the controls tested, which were those necessary to provide reasonable assurance that the criteria stated in the description were met, *did not* ~~operated~~ effectively throughout the period [*date*] to [*date*].

4.19 If the service auditor is unable to obtain sufficient appropriate evidence, the service auditor should disclaim an opinion or withdraw from the engagement. If the service auditor decides to disclaim an opinion and, based on the limited procedures performed, has concluded that certain aspects of management's description of the service organization's system are not fairly presented, certain controls are not suitably designed, or certain controls did not operate effectively, the service auditor should identify these findings in the service auditor's report.

4.20 If the service auditor disclaims an opinion, the service auditor's report should not identify the procedures that were performed nor include statements describing the characteristics of a service auditor's engagement because to do so might overshadow the disclaimer. When disclaiming an opinion, in addition to adding an explanatory paragraph to the service auditor's report that describes the reason for the disclaimer and any deficiencies identified by the service auditor, the opinion paragraph would be replaced by the following disclaimer of opinion (new language is shown in boldface italics):

> *Because of the matter described in the preceding paragraph, the scope of our work was not sufficient to enable us to express, and we do not express, an opinion.*

Illustrative Explanatory Paragraphs When the Description Is Not Fairly Presented

4.21 A number of situations are presented in chapter 3, "Performing the Engagement," of this guide in which the service auditor determines that the description is not fairly presented. In practice, if the service auditor makes such a determination, the service auditor would discuss the matter with management of the service organization, describe the changes that need to be made for the description to be fairly presented, and ask management to amend the description to include the omitted information or correct the misstated information. The following paragraphs contain examples of explanatory paragraphs that would be inserted before the modified opinion paragraph of the service auditor's report if management is unwilling to amend a description that is not fairly presented. For all these paragraphs, the service auditor would modify the opinion paragraph as follows (new language is shown in boldface italics; deleted language is shown in strikethrough):

> In our opinion, ~~in all material respects~~ *except for the matter referred to in the preceding paragraph,* based on the description criteria identified in [*name of service organization*]'s assertion and the applicable trust services criteria, *in all material respects...*

4.22 The following is an example of an explanatory paragraph that would be added to the service auditor's report when the description includes controls that have not been implemented:

> The accompanying description states that Example Service Organization's system is protected against unauthorized logical access through the use of operator identification numbers and passwords. Based on inquiries of staff personnel and observation of activities, we determined that operator identification numbers and passwords are used in applications A and B but are not used in application C.

4.23 The following is an example of an explanatory paragraph that would be added to the service auditor's report when the functions and processing performed by a subservice organization are significant to the users, and the service organization has not disclosed that it uses a subservice organization and the functions that the subservice organization performs:

Example Trust Organization's description does not indicate that it uses a subservice organization for information processing, which we believe could be significant to users because controls at the subservice organization over changes to programs, as well as physical and logical access to system resources, would be relevant to users.

4.24 If management of the service organization inappropriately omits one or more applicable trust services criteria from the description of the service organization's system, the service auditor should request that management include the omitted criteria and related controls. If management refuses to do so, the service auditor should disclaim an opinion or withdraw from the engagement.

Identifying Information That Is Not Covered by the Service Auditor's Report

4.25 The service organization may want to attach to the description of the service organization's system, or include in a document containing the service auditor's report, information in addition to its description. The following are examples of such information:

- Future plans for new systems
- Other services provided by the service organization that are not included in the scope of the engagement
- Qualitative information, such as marketing claims, that may not be objectively measurable
- Responses from management to deviations identified by the service auditor when such responses have not been subject to procedures by the service auditor

4.26 Paragraph 3.16 of this guide states that such other information should be distinguished from the service organization's description of its system by excluding the information from the description. It also states that if the other information is attached to the description or included in a document that contains the description of the service organization's system and the service auditor's report, the other information should be differentiated from the information covered by the service auditor's report, for example, through the use of a title such as "Other Information Provided by Example Service Organization That Is Not Covered by the Service Auditor's Report."

4.27 Because of the nature of the other information or its presentation, the service auditor may decide to add an explanatory paragraph to the service auditor's report indicating that the other information is not covered by the service auditor's report. The following is an example of such a paragraph:

The information attached to the description titled "Other Information Provided by Example Service Organization That Is Not Covered by the Service Auditor's Report" describes the service organization's medical billing system. It is presented by the management of Example Service Organization to provide additional information and is not a part of the service organization's description of its medical records management system made available to user entities during the period from June 1, 20X0, to May 31, 20X1. Information about Example Service Organization's medical billing system has not been subjected to the procedures applied in the examination of the description of the medical records management system and the suitability of the design and operating effectiveness of controls to meet the related criteria stated in the description of the medical records management system.

4.28 The service auditor also has the option of disclaiming an opinion on information that is not covered by the service auditor's report by adding the words "and accordingly, we express no opinion on it" at the end of the explanatory paragraph illustrated in paragraph 4.27.

Illustrative Explanatory Paragraphs: Controls Are Not Suitably Designed

4.29 The following is an example of an explanatory paragraph that would be added to the service auditor's report, preceding the opinion paragraph, if the service auditor concludes that controls are not suitably designed to meet an applicable trust services criterion:

> The accompanying description of ABC Service Organization's system states on page 8 that ABC Service Organization's system supervisor makes changes to the systems only if the changes are authorized, tested, and documented. The procedures, however, do not include a requirement for approval of the change before the change is placed into operation. As a result, the controls are not suitably designed to meet the criterion "Controls provide reasonable assurance that only authorized, tested, and documented changes are made to the system."

Controls Were Not Suitably Designed to Meet a Portion of a Criterion

4.30 The service auditor may conclude that the controls are not suitably designed to meet part of a criterion. The following is an example of an explanatory paragraph that would be added to the service auditor's report, preceding the opinion paragraph, if the service auditor determines that controls are not suitably designed to meet part of a criterion:

> The criteria for the privacy principle include the criterion "Personal information is provided to the individual in an understandable form; in a reasonable time frame; and at a reasonable cost, if any." Management reviews requests by individuals for copies of their personal information on a quarterly basis and approves or denies access in accordance with HIPAA Administrative Simplification regulations. Individuals who request copies of such information may have to wait up to 12 weeks for a decision regarding such access, resulting in an unreasonable time frame for its provision. As a result, controls are not suitably designed to meet the portion of the criterion "Personal information is provided to the individual in a reasonable time frame."

4.31 The service auditor focuses on the suitability of the design of controls to meet the related applicable trust services criteria during the period covered by the service auditor's report, not the suitability of the design of controls to meet criteria in future periods when conditions may change. For example, if computer programs are correctly processing data during the period covered by the service auditor's report, and the design of the controls will need to be changed in future periods to accommodate conditions that will exist in the future, the service auditor would not be required to report this information as a design deficiency in his or her report.[2] However, if a service auditor becomes aware of the need for change to the design of controls at the service organization to address future conditions, the service auditor, in his or her judgment, may choose to communicate this information to the service organization's management and may consider advising management to disclose this information and its plans for changing the design of its controls to address the expected future conditions in a section of the service auditor's document titled "Other Information Provided by the Service Organization That Is Not Covered by the Service Auditor's Report."

Controls Were Not Suitably Designed During a Portion of the Period

4.32 The following is an example of an explanatory paragraph that would be added to the service auditor's report, preceding the opinion paragraph, if the service auditor concludes that controls are not suitably designed to meet an applicable trust services criterion for a portion of the period under examination:

> The accompanying description of ABC Service Organization's system states on page 8 that ABC Service Organization's system supervisor makes changes to the system only if the changes are authorized, tested, and documented. During the period January 1, 20XX, to March 31, 20XX, the procedures, however, did not include a requirement for changes to be authorized, tested, and documented before being placed into operation. On April 1, 20XX, ABC Service Organization implemented a procedure requiring that all changes be authorized, tested, and documented by the director of application development before being placed into operation. As a result, during the period January 1, 20XX, to March 31, 20XX, the controls were not suitably designed to meet the criterion "Controls provide reasonable assurance that only authorized, tested, and documented changes are made to the system."

Illustrative Explanatory Paragraph: Controls Are Not Operating Effectively

4.33 The service auditor may conclude that controls are suitably designed but are not operating effectively to meet one or more of the applicable trust services criteria. The following is an example of an explanatory paragraph that may be added to the service auditor's report, preceding the opinion paragraph, if the service auditor determines that controls are not operating effectively:

> ABC Service Organization states in the description of its system that the director of IT may approve emergency changes to the system without receiving a written request for such changes, as long as the changes are documented within 48 hours after implementation into production. However, as noted on page 155 of the description of tests of controls and the results thereof, controls related to the authorization of emergency changes were not performed and, therefore, were not operating effectively throughout the period [date] to [date]. This control deficiency resulted in not meeting the criterion "Procedures exist to provide that emergency changes are documented and authorized in a timely manner."

---

[2] See paragraph A39 of Statement on Standards for Attestation Engagements No. 16, *Reporting on Controls at a Service Organization* (AICPA, *Professional Standards*, AT sec. 801), for similar guidance related to internal control over financial reporting.

In addition, the service auditor modifies the opinion paragraph of the service auditor's report on operating effectiveness as follows (new language is shown in boldface italics; deleted language is shown in strikethrough):

> In our opinion, ~~in all material respects,~~ ***except for the matter described in the preceding paragraph,*** based on the description criteria identified in [*name of service organization*]'s assertion and the applicable trust services criteria, ***in all material respects***...

Scope Limitation: Service Auditor Is Unable to Obtain Sufficient Appropriate Evidence

4.34 The following is an example of an explanatory paragraph that would be added to the service auditor's report if the service auditor is unable to obtain sufficient appropriate evidence regarding the operating effectiveness of controls to meet a criterion:

> The accompanying description of ABC Service Organization's system states on page 45 that ABC Service Organization makes system changes only if they are authorized, tested, and documented. Documentation of the authorization and testing of proposed system changes was destroyed on July 15, 20X0, and we were unable to obtain sufficient evidence that system changes were authorized and tested prior to July 15, 20X0. As a result, we were unable to determine whether controls were operating effectively during the period January 1, 20X0, to July 14, 20X0, to meet the criterion "Procedures exist to provide that only authorized, tested, and documented changes are made to the system."

Reporting on Compliance With the Commitments in the Statement of Privacy Practices When the Type 2 Report Addresses the Privacy Principle

4.35 A service auditor's type 2 report that covers controls over privacy includes the service auditor's opinion on whether the service organization complied with the commitments in its statement of privacy practices throughout the period covered by the service auditor's report. The following are situations that may result in a modification of the service auditor's report:

- The statement of privacy practices is not included with management's description of the service organization's system or is incomplete.
- Privacy commitments are not clearly described in management's privacy statement.
- The results of tests performed do not provide sufficient appropriate evidence to conclude that the service organization complied with the commitments in its statement of privacy practices throughout the examination period.

4.36 The following are examples of explanatory paragraphs that may be added to the service auditor's report, preceding the opinion paragraph, if the service auditor determines that the service organization did not comply with the commitments in its statement of privacy practices (new language is shown in boldface italics; deleted language is shown in strikethrough):

- The accompanying statement of privacy practices states on page 40 that Example Service Organization requires all vendors with whom it shares personal information to sign a data-sharing agreement requiring these vendors to adhere to privacy practices similar to those established by Example Service Organization. The results of our tests indicated that two vendors with whom personal information was shared had not signed a data-sharing agreement. As a result, the commitment "All vendors with whom the service organization shares personal information are required to sign a data-sharing agreement that requires these vendors to follow privacy practices similar to ours" was not met.

In our opinion, ~~in all material respects,~~ *except for the matter described in the preceding paragraph,* based on the description criteria identified in [*name of service organization*]'s assertion and the applicable trust services criteria, *in all material respects...*

- Example Service Organization states in its statement of privacy practices on page [*aa*] that Example Service Organization securely disposes of all copies, including archived and backup copies, of personal information records. However, as noted on page 45 of the description of tests of controls and the results thereof, backup copies of records were not disposed of securely. This results in a failure to meet the service organization's commitment "Archived and backup copies of personal information are disposed of securely."

In our opinion, ~~in all material respects,~~ *except for the matter described in the preceding paragraph,* based on the description criteria identified in [*name of service organization*]'s assertion and the applicable trust services criteria, *in all material respects...*

Reporting When the Service Organization Uses the Carve-Out Method to Present a Subservice Organization

4.37 The following are modifications to the scope paragraph of a type 2 report for use in engagements in which the service organization uses a subservice organization and presents its description using the carve-out method (new language is shown in boldface italics):

Scope

We have examined the attached description titled "XYZ Service Organization's Description of the Adaptable Cloud Computing System Throughout the Period January 1, 200X, to December 31, 200X"[3] (the description) and the suitability of the design and operating effectiveness of controls to meet the criteria for the privacy principle set forth in TSP section 100, *Trust Services Principles, Criteria, and Illustrations for Security, Availability, Processing Integrity, Confidentiality, and Privacy* (AICPA, *Technical Practice Aids*) (applicable trust services criteria), throughout the period January 1, 20X1, to December 31, 20X1.

XYZ Service Organization uses a service organization (subservice organization) to perform certain processing of customers' personal information. The description indicates that certain applicable trust services criteria can only be met if controls at the subservice organization are suitably designed and operating effectively. The description presents XYZ Service Organization's system; its controls relevant to the applicable trust services criteria; and the types of

---

[3] The title of the description of the service organization's system in the service auditor's report should match the title used by management of the service organization in its description.

controls that the service organization expects to be implemented, suitably designed, and operating effectively at the subservice organization to meet certain applicable trust services criteria. The description does not include any of the controls implemented at the subservice organization. Our examination did not extend to the services provided by the subservice organization or the subservice organization's compliance with the commitments in its statement of privacy practices.

4.38 Following are modifications to the applicable subparagraphs of the opinion paragraph of a type 2 report for use in engagements in which the service organization uses a subservice organization and presents its description using the carve-out method (new language is shown in boldface italics):

In our opinion, in all material respects, based on the description criteria identified in XYZ Service Organization's assertion and the applicable trust services criteria

> *a.* the description fairly presents XYZ Service Organization's [*type or name of*] system and the related privacy practices that were designed and implemented throughout the period [*date*] to [*date*].
>
> *b.* the controls stated in the description were suitably designed to provide reasonable assurance that the applicable trust services criteria would be met if the controls operated effectively throughout the period [*date*] to [*date*], **and the subservice organization applied, throughout the period [date] to [date], the types of controls expected to be implemented at the subservice organization and incorporated in the design of the system**.
>
> *c.* the controls we tested, which **together with the types of controls expected to be implemented at the subservice organization and incorporated in the design of the system, if operating effectively,** were those necessary to provide reasonable assurance that the applicable trust services criteria were met, operated effectively throughout the period [*date*] to [*date*].
>
> *d.* XYZ Service Organization complied with the commitments in its statement of privacy practices throughout the period [*date*] to [*date*] **if the subservice organization complied with those aspects of such privacy practices that it performed**.

All other report paragraphs are unchanged.

Disclaiming an Opinion When the Service Organization Uses the Carve-Out Method to Present a Subservice Organization

4.39 If the service auditor disclaims an opinion because of matters related to the carved-out subservice organization, such as those described in paragraph 3.38 of this guide (for example, because the subservice organization performs control procedures that are necessary for the service organization to meet the applicable trust services criteria), the service auditor's report should not identify the procedures that were performed or include statements describing the characteristics of a service auditor's engagement because to do so might overshadow the disclaimer. The service auditor would describe the carve-out using an additional paragraph following the scope paragraph (see the illustration in paragraph 4.37). When disclaiming an opinion in such circumstances, the service auditor would add an explanatory paragraph to the service auditor's report that describes the reason for the disclaimer and any deficiencies identified by the service auditor. The following is an example of such a paragraph (new language is shown in boldface italics):

> *The accompanying description of XYZ Service Organization's system indicates that responsibility for important aspects of the personal information life cycle, the controls required for the service organization to meet the trust services criteria applicable to the privacy principle, and performing activities to determine compliance with the commitments in the service organization's statement of privacy practices has been delegated to the subservice organization. Such matters were not included in the scope of our examination.*

When disclaiming an opinion, in addition to adding such an explanatory paragraph to the service auditor's report, the opinion paragraph would be replaced by the following disclaimer of opinion: (new language is shown in boldface italics):

> *Because of the matter described in the preceding paragraph, the scope of our work was not sufficient to enable us to express, and we do not express, an opinion.*

Reporting When the Service Organization Uses the Inclusive Method to Present a Subservice Organization

4.40 Following are modifications to a service auditor's type 2 report for use in engagements in which the service organization uses a subservice organization and presents its description using the inclusive method (new language is shown in boldface italics; deleted language is shown in strikethrough):

Scope

We have examined the attached description titled "XYZ Service Organization's **and ABC Subservice Organization's** Description of the Adaptable Cloud Computing System Throughout the Period January 1, 20X1, to December 31, 20X1" (the description) and the suitability of the design and operating effectiveness of controls to meet the criteria for the security, availability, processing integrity, and confidentiality principles set forth in TSP section 100, *Trust Services Principles, Criteria, and Illustrations for Security, Availability, Processing Integrity, Confidentiality, and Privacy* (AICPA, *Technical Practice Aids*) (applicable trust services criteria), throughout the period January 1, 20X1, to December 31, 20X1. **ABC Subservice Organization is an independent service organization that provides certain computer processing services to XYZ Service Organization. XYZ Service Organization's description includes a description of those elements of its system provided by ABC Subservice Organization, the controls of which help meet certain applicable trust services criteria.**

*Service organization's **and subservice organization's** responsibilities*

XYZ Service Organization **and ABC Subservice Organization** ha~~ve~~s provided their attached assertion~~s~~ titled [*title of service organization's assertion*] and [*title of subservice organization assertion*], which ~~is~~ **are** based on the criteria identified in *those* ~~management's~~ assertion*s*. XYZ Service Organization *and ABC Subservice Organization*~~is~~*are* responsible for (1) preparing the description and the assertion*s*; (2) the completeness, accuracy, and method of presentation of both the description and assertion*s*; (3) providing the services covered by the description; (4) specifying the controls that meet the applicable trust services criteria and stating them in the description; and (5) designing, implementing, and documenting the controls to meet the applicable trust services criteria.

Service auditor's responsibilities

Our responsibility is to express an opinion on the fairness of the presentation of the description based on the description criteria set forth in XYZ Service Organization's *and ABC Subservice Organization's* assertion*s* and on the suitability of the design and operating effectiveness of the controls to meet the applicable trust services criteria, based on our examination. We conducted our examination in accordance with attestation standards established by the American Institute of Certified Public Accountants. Those standards require that we plan and perform our examination to obtain reasonable assurance about whether, in all material respects, (1) the description is fairly presented based on the description criteria, and (2) the controls were suitably designed and operating effectively to meet the applicable trust services criteria throughout the period [*date*] to [*date*].

Inherent limitations

Because of their nature and inherent limitations, controls at a service organization *or subservice organization* may not always operate effectively to meet the applicable trust services criteria. Also, the projection to the future of any evaluation of the fairness of the presentation of the description or conclusions about the suitability of the design or operating effectiveness of the controls to meet the applicable trust services criteria is subject to the risks that the system may change or that controls at a service organization *or subservice organization* may become inadequate or fail.

Opinion

In our opinion, in all material respects, based on the criteria identified in XYZ Service Organization's *and ABC Subservice Organization's* assertion*s*

    a. the description fairly presents XYZ Service Organization's [*type or name of*] system *and the elements of the system provided by ABC Subservice Organization* that ~~was~~ *were* designed and implemented throughout the period [*date*] to [*date*].

    b. the controls *of XYZ Service Organization and ABC Subservice Organization* stated in the description were suitably designed to provide reasonable assurance that the applicable trust services criteria would be met if the controls operated effectively throughout the period [*date*] to [*date*].

    c. the controls *of XYZ Service Organization and ABC Subservice Organization* that were tested, which were those necessary to provide reasonable assurance that the applicable trust services criteria were met, operated effectively throughout the period from [*date*] to [*date*].

Restricted use

This report and the description of tests of controls and the results thereof are intended solely for the information and use of XYZ Service Organization *and ABC Subservice Organization*; user entities of XYZ Service Organization's [*type or name of*] system; and those prospective user entities, independent auditors, and practitioners providing services to such user entities and regulators who have sufficient knowledge and understanding of

- the nature of the service provided by the service organization.
- how the service organization's system interacts with user entities, subservice organizations, and other parties.
- internal control and its limitations.
- complementary user-entity controls and how they interact with related controls at the service organization *and subservice organization* to meet the applicable trust services criteria.
- the applicable trust services criteria.
- the risks that may threaten the achievement of the applicable trust services criteria and how controls address those risks.

This report is not intended to be and should not be used by anyone other than these specified parties.

Intended Users of the Report

4.41 Paragraph .79 of AT section 101, *Attest Engagements* (AICPA, *Professional Standards*), in part, includes the following discussion of the circumstances in which a report is intended solely for the information and use of specified parties:

> The need for restriction on the use of a report may result from a number of circumstances, including the purpose of the report, the criteria used in preparation of the subject matter, the extent to which the procedures performed are known or understood, and the potential for the report to be misunderstood when taken out of the context in which it was intended to be used.

4.42 SOC 2^{SM} reports have the potential to be misunderstood when taken out of the context in which they were intended to be used. Accordingly, the service auditor's report should include a statement indicating that the report is intended solely for the information and use of management of the service organization and other specified parties who have sufficient knowledge and understanding of the following:

- The nature of the service provided by the service organization
- How the service organization's system interacts with user entities, subservice organizations, or other parties
- Internal control and its limitations
- Complementary user-entity controls and how they interact with related controls at the service organization to meet the applicable trust services criteria
- The applicable trust services criteria
- The risks that may threaten the achievement of the applicable trust services criteria and how controls address those risks

User entities commonly are specified parties. However, in some instances (for example, when the report is intended for use by a regulator), user entities may not be a specified party. Distribution of the report for general marketing purposes creates a greater likelihood that some users of the report will not have the required knowledge and may misunderstand the report.

4.43 Report users who are most likely to have such knowledge include management of the service organization; management of the user entities; practitioners evaluating or reporting on controls at a user entity; regulators; and others performing services related to controls at the service organization, such as a service auditor reporting on controls at a user entity that is also a service provider to other user entities.

4.44 Management of a prospective user entity may need to obtain an understanding of a service organization's system related to security, availability, processing integrity, confidentiality, or privacy and the historic operating effectiveness of controls at the service organization, either as part of its vendor selection process or to comply with regulatory requirements for vendor acceptance. To understand and make appropriate use of a SOC 2 report, management of a prospective user entity will need the knowledge and understanding identified in paragraph 4.42. When management of a prospective user entity has such knowledge, a SOC 2 report is likely to be helpful to management in evaluating the service organization's system and controls. Accordingly, management of a prospective user entity that has such knowledge would be an appropriate user of a SOC 2 report. Conversely, management of a prospective user entity that does not have such knowledge is unlikely to be an appropriate user of such a report. When certain prospective user entities are intended users of the report, the service auditor's identification of the intended users of the report should include the knowledge and understanding identified in paragraph 4.42.

Illustrative Type 2 Reports

4.45 Although this guide specifies the information to be included in a description of a service organization's system, it is not specific about the format for these reports. Service organizations and service auditors may organize and present the required information in a variety of formats.

4.46 Appendix C, "Illustrative Management Assertions and Related Service Auditor's Reports on Controls at a Service Organization Relevant to Security, Availability, Processing Integrity, Confidentiality, and Privacy," of this guide contains two examples of type 2 reports. These reports illustrate the following:

- A type 2 report on controls at a service organization relevant to security, availability, processing integrity, and confidentiality

- A type 2 report on controls at a service organization relevant to privacy

4.47 Appendix D, "Illustrative Type 2 Service Organization Controls Report," of this guide contains an example of a type 2 SOC 2 report. This illustrative type 2 SOC 2 report, "Report on Example Service Organization's Description of Its Transportation Management System and on the Suitability of the Design and Operating Effectiveness of Its Controls Relevant to Security Throughout the Period January 1, 20X1, to December 31, 20X1," contains all of the components of a type 2 SOC 2 report.

Appendix A

Information for Management of a Service Organization

Introduction and Background

Many entities function more efficiently and profitably by outsourcing tasks or entire functions to other organizations (service organizations) that have the personnel, expertise, equipment, or technology to accomplish these tasks or functions. Many of these service organizations collect, process, transmit, store, organize, maintain, and dispose of information for other entities. Entities that use service organizations are known as *user entities*. Examples of the services provided by service organizations include the following:

- *Cloud computing*. Providing on-demand access to a shared pool of configurable computing resources (for example, networks, servers, storage, and applications). Additional information about cloud computing is presented in appendix E, "Service Auditor Considerations in Performing SOC 2^{SM} or SOC 3^{SM} Engagements for Cloud Computing Service Organizations."

- *Managed security*. Managing access to networks and computing systems for user entities (for example, granting access to a system and preventing, or detecting and mitigating, system intrusion).

- *Customer support*. Providing customers of user entities with online or telephonic postsales support and service management. Examples of these services are warranty inquiries and investigating and responding to customer complaints.

- *Sales force automation*. Providing and maintaining software to automate business tasks for user entities that have a sales force. Examples of such tasks are order processing, information sharing, order tracking, contact management, customer management, sales forecast analysis, and employee performance evaluation.

- *Health care claims management and processing*. Providing medical providers, employers, and insured parties of employers with systems that enable medical records and related health insurance claims to be processed securely and confidentially.

- *Enterprise IT outsourcing services*. Managing, operating, and maintaining user entities' IT data centers, infrastructure, and application systems and related functions that support IT activities, such as network, production, security, change management, hardware, and environmental control activities.

One of the critical roles of management and those charged with governance in any entity is to identify and assess risks to the entity and address those risks through effective internal control. When an entity outsources tasks or functions to a service organization and becomes a user entity, it replaces many of the risks associated with performing those tasks or functions with risks associated with outsourcing, particularly risks related to how the service organization performs the tasks or functions and how that may affect the user entity's compliance with requirements. Although a task or function is outsourced, management of the user entity retains responsibility for managing these risks and needs to monitor the services provided by the service organization.

To carry out its responsibilities related to the outsourced tasks or functions, management of a user entity needs information about the system by which the service organization provides services, including the service organization's controls[1] over that system. User-entity management may also need assurance that the system information provided by the service organization is accurate and that the service organization actually operates in accordance with that information.

To obtain assurance, user entities often ask the service organization for a CPA's report on the service organization's system. Historically, such requests have focused on controls at the service organization that affect user entities' financial reporting. However, user entities are now requesting reports that address the security, availability, or processing integrity of the system or the confidentiality or privacy of the information processed by the system. In this document, these attributes of a system are referred to as *principles*.

The AICPA is alerting CPAs to the various types of engagements that a CPA may perform when reporting on controls at a service organization and has identified these reports as service organization controls (SOC) reports. The objective of this effort is to help CPAs select the appropriate reporting option depending on the subject matter addressed by the controls. The following three types of SOC reports are designed to help CPAs meet specific service organization and user entity needs:

- *SOC 1^SM report.* These reports are intended to meet the needs of entities that use service organizations (user entities) and the CPAs who audit the user entities' financial statements (user auditors) when evaluating the effect of controls at the service organization on the user entities' financial statements. User auditors use these reports to plan and perform audits of the user entities' financial statements. SOC 1 engagements are performed in accordance with Statement on Standards for Attestation Engagements (SSAE) No. 16, *Reporting on Controls at a Service Organization* (AICPA, *Professional Standards*, AT sec. 801), and the AICPA Guide *Service Organizations: Applying SSAE No. 16*, Reporting on Controls at a Service Organization *(SOC 1^SM)* provides implementation guidance for these engagements.

- *SOC 2^SM report.* These reports are intended to meet the needs of a broad range of users who need information and assurance about controls at a service organization that affect the security, availability, or processing integrity of the systems that the service organization uses to process users' data or the confidentiality or privacy of the information processed by these systems. Examples of stakeholders who may need these reports are management or those charged with governance of the user entities and service organization, customers of the service organization, regulators, business partners, suppliers, and others who have an understanding of the service organization and its controls. These reports include a detailed description of the service organization's system; the criteria in TSP section 100, *Trust*

---

[1] From a governance and internal control perspective, *controls* are policies and procedures that address risks associated with financial reporting, operations, or compliance and, when operating effectively, enable an entity to meet specified criteria.

Services Principles, Criteria, and Illustrations for Security, Availability, Processing Integrity, Confidentiality, and Privacy (AICPA, *Technical Practice Aids*), applicable to the principle being reported on; the controls designed to meet these criteria; a written assertion by management regarding the description and the design and operation of the controls; and a service auditor's report (the letter) in which the service auditor expresses an opinion on whether the description is fairly presented and the controls are suitability designed and operating effectively. The report also includes the service auditor's description of tests performed and results of the tests. These reports can play an important role in the following:

— Vendor management programs[2]

— Internal corporate governance and risk management processes

— Regulatory compliance

These engagements are performed in accordance with AT section 101, *Attest Engagements* (AICPA, *Professional Standards*). The AICPA Guide *Reporting on Controls at a Service Organization Relevant to Security, Availability, Processing Integrity, Confidentiality, or Privacy (SOC 2^{SM})*, contains performance and reporting guidance for these engagements.

- *SOC 3 report.* These reports are designed to meet the needs of a wider range of users who need assurance about controls at a service organization that affect the security, availability, or processing integrity of the systems used by a service organization to process users' information, or the confidentiality or privacy of that information, but do not have the need for, or knowledge necessary to effectively use, a SOC 2 report. These reports comprise a written assertion by management regarding the suitability of the design and operating effectiveness of the controls implemented, a CPA's report on the suitability of the design and operating effectiveness of the controls, and a description of the system and its boundaries. This description generally is brief and does not include the detail provided in a SOC 2 system description. The criteria for evaluating the controls are the criteria in TSP section 100 that are relevant to the principle being reported on (the same criteria as in a SOC 2 report). Because they are general-use reports, SOC 3 reports can be freely distributed or posted on a website. If the report is unqualified, the service organization is eligible to display on its website the SysTrust for Service Organizations seal. For more information about the SysTrust for Service Organization seal program, go to www.webtrust.org. SOC 3 engagements are performed in accordance with AT section 101. Appendix C, "Practitioner Guidance on Scoping and Reporting Issues," of TSP section 100 contains illustrative reports and other implementation guidance for these engagements.

---

[2] *Vendor management*, in this context, is a user entity's management of the services provided by a service organization.

The Trust Service Principles

The following are the five attributes of a reliable system,[3] which are also referred as the *trust services principles*:

    a. Security. The system is protected against unauthorized access (both physical and logical).

    b. Availability. The system is available for operation and use as committed or agreed.

    c. Processing integrity. System processing is complete, accurate, timely, and authorized.

    d. Confidentiality. Information designated as confidential is protected as committed or agreed.

    e. Privacy. Personal information[4] is collected, used, retained, disclosed, and disposed of in conformity with the commitments in the entity's privacy notice and criteria set forth in *Generally Accepted Privacy Principles* issued jointly by the AICPA and the Canadian Institute of Chartered Accountants.

In a SOC 2 engagement, management of the service organization selects the trust services principle(s) that will be covered by the SOC 2 report. The trust services criteria for the principle(s) covered by the report are referred to as the *applicable trust services criteria*.

Service organization management implements controls over its systems to prevent adverse events from occurring or detect such events as errors, privacy breaches, and theft or loss of information. For example, a control that terminates access to a system after three unsuccessful login attempts is designed to prevent unauthorized access to the system. Management of the service organization may engage a CPA to report on the design and operating effectiveness of controls over its systems. Controls that are suitably designed are able to meet the criteria they were designed to meet if they operate effectively. Controls that operate effectively actually do meet the criteria they were designed to meet over a period of time.

The SOC 2 guide provides guidance to a service auditor examining and reporting on the fairness of the presentation of a description of a service organization's system; the suitability of the design of the service organization's controls over the system as they relate to one or more of the trust services principles; and in certain reports, the operating effectiveness of those controls. This appendix is intended to

- assist management of a service organization in preparing its description of the service organization's system, which serves as the basis for a SOC 2 examination engagement.

- familiarize management with its responsibilities when it engages a service auditor to perform a SOC 2 engagement.

---

[3] A *reliable system* is defined in TSP section 100, *Trust Services Principles, Criteria, and Illustrations for Security, Availability, Processing Integrity, Confidentiality, and Privacy* (AICPA, *Technical Practice Aids*), as a system that is capable of operating without material error, fault, or failure during a specified period in a specified environment.

[4] *Personal information* (sometimes referred to as *personally identifiable information*) is information that is about, or can be related to, an identifiable individual.

This appendix is not intended to provide guidance to

- management of a service organization in preparing the description of a service organization's system for a SOC 1 or SOC 3 report.
- management of a user entity in assessing a service organization's controls that are likely to be relevant to user entities' internal control over financial reporting.
- auditors of user entities (user auditors) in planning and performing an audit of a user entity's financial statements.

In the remainder of this appendix, references to controls over a system mean controls over a system related to one or more of the trust services principles.

Responsibilities of Management of a Service Organization

In a SOC 2 engagement, management of a service organization is responsible for the following:

- Determining the type of engagement to be performed; which principle(s) will be addressed in the engagement; the scope of the engagement, as discussed in the first paragraph of the section of this appendix titled "Defining the Scope of the Engagement"; and whether any subservice organizations will be included in, or carved out of, the description and the service auditor's report. (*Subservice organizations* are organizations to which the service organization outsources aspects of the services that it provides.)
- Preparing a description of the service organization's system.
- Providing a written assertion.
- Providing written representations.
- Having a reasonable basis for its assertion.

Determining the Type of Engagement to Be Performed

This guide provides for the following two types of SOC 2 engagements and related reports:

- Report on management's description of a service organization's system and the suitability of the design of controls (referred to as a *type 1 report*)
- Report on management's description of a service organization's system and the suitability of the design and operating effectiveness of controls (referred to as a *type 2 report*)

Both type 1 and type 2 reports include the following:

- Management's description of the service organization's system
- A written assertion by management of the service organization about the matters in the first paragraph of the section of this appendix titled "Providing a Written Assertion"
- A service auditor's report that expresses an opinion on the matters in the first paragraph of the section of this appendix titled "Providing a Written Assertion"

A type 2 report also contains a description of the service auditor's tests of the controls and the results of the tests, and when the report addresses the privacy principle, a description of the service auditor's tests of the service organization's compliance with the commitments in its statement of privacy practices and the results of those tests.

Management's written assertion is attached to the description of the service organization's system.

A type 1 report, which does not include tests of the operating effectiveness of controls, provides user entities with information that will enable them to understand and assess the design of the controls. However, a type 1 report does not provide sufficient information for user entities to assess the operating effectiveness of the controls. A type 1 report may be useful if the service organization[5]

- has not been in operation for a sufficient length of time to enable the service auditor to gather sufficient appropriate evidence regarding the operating effectiveness of controls.

- has recently made significant changes to the system and related controls and does not have a sufficient history with a stable system to enable a type 2 engagement to be performed.

Defining the Scope of the Engagement

In determining the scope of a SOC 2 engagement, management of a service organization considers the following:

- The services, business units, functional areas, business processes, and activities or applications that will be of interest to users because of concerns regarding compliance with laws or regulations or governance or because the service organization has made commitments to user entities to provide a type 1 or type 2 report.

- The trust services principles that will be covered by the report. Management makes this determination by understanding the needs of report users and the service organization's goals in engaging a service auditor to perform the examination. The engagement may cover one, multiple, or all of the principles.

- The period to be covered by the description and report (for a type 1 report, this would be the as of date of the description and report).

- Whether controls at subservice organizations are relevant to meeting one or more of the applicable trust services criteria. (Subservice organizations may be separate entities from the service organization or entities related to the service organization.)

To increase the likelihood that the description and service auditor's report will be useful to report users, management of the service organization may decide to discuss with user entities matters such as the services, trust services principles, and period or as of date to be covered by the description and service auditor's report.

---

[5] A user of a type 1 report may misunderstand the nature of the engagement and incorrectly assume that controls are operating effectively or that the entity has complied with the practices in its privacy notice, even though the service auditor has not provided such an opinion or performed sufficient procedures to express such an opinion. When the report user is a regulatory agency or body, this misunderstanding may result in regulatory compliance risk, particularly in a report that addresses the privacy principle.

If a service organization uses a subservice organization, the description of the service organization's system may either (*a*) include the subservice organization's services by using the inclusive method or (*b*) exclude the subservice organization's services by using the carve-out method.

When the carve-out method is used, management's description of the service organization's system identifies the nature of the services and functions performed by the subservice organization and the types of controls that management expects to be implemented at the subservice organization but excludes details of the subservice organization's system and controls.

A service organization's description prepared using the carve-out method generally is most useful if the services provided by the subservice organization are not extensive or if a type 1 or type 2 report that meets the needs of user entities is available from the subservice organization.

When the inclusive method is used, management's description of the service organization's system includes a description of the nature of the services and functions performed by the subservice organization, as well the applicable trust services criteria and controls implemented by the subservice organization. Controls of the service organization are presented separately from those of the subservice organization.

Although the inclusive method provides more information for user entities, it may not be appropriate or feasible in all circumstances. In determining which approach to use, the service organization considers (*a*) the nature and extent of the information about the subservice organization that user entities may need and (*b*) the practical difficulties entailed in implementing the inclusive method.

The inclusive method is difficult to implement in certain circumstances. The approach entails extensive planning and communication among the service auditor, the service organization, and the subservice organization. If a service organization uses the inclusive method of presentation, matters such as the following generally will need to be coordinated by all the parties involved, preferably in advance:

- The scope of the description and the timing of the examination and tests of controls
- Responsibility for preparing the section of the description that relates to the services provided by the subservice organization
- The content of the subservice organization's written representations and the members of the subservice organization's management who will be responsible for the written representations
- An agreement regarding access to the subservice organization's premises, personnel, and systems
- Fees
- Identification of the parties for whom use of the report is intended

These issues become more complex if multiple subservice organizations are involved, and the inclusive method is used. The inclusive approach is facilitated if the service organization and subservice organization are related parties or have a contractual relationship that provides for inclusive reports and visits by service auditors.

If more than one subservice organization is relevant to user entities, management of the service organization may use the inclusive method for one or more subservice organizations and the carve-out method for one or more of the other subservice organizations.

If the service organization uses the inclusive method, the service organization would obtain a written assertion from management of the subservice organization covering the subservice organization's services. That assertion would also be attached to the description of the service organization's system. If management of the subservice organization will not provide a written assertion, the service organization cannot use the inclusive method but may instead be able to use the carve-out method.

If the service organization's controls and monitoring of the activities of a subservice organization are sufficient to meet the applicable trust services criteria, the controls at the subservice organization are not necessary to meet those criteria. In such instances, the service organization's assertion is based solely on controls at the service organization, and consequently, neither the inclusive nor carve-out method is applicable. In these situations, the description need not describe the subservice organization's activities, unless such information is needed to help users understand the service organization's system.

Preparing the Description of the Service Organization's System

Management of a service organization is responsible for preparing the description, including the completeness, accuracy, and method of presentation of the description. No one particular format for the description is prescribed, and the extent of the description may vary, depending on the size and complexity of the service organization and its activities. The description may be presented using various formats, such as narratives, flowcharts, tables, and graphics, but should meet the criteria set forth in the section of this appendix titled "Criteria for Management's Description of the Service Organization's System."

Appendix B, "Trust Services Principles and Criteria for Security, Availability, Processing Integrity, Confidentiality, and Privacy," of this guide contains the control criteria for each of the trust services principles. All the criteria related to the trust services principle(s) being reported on (applicable trust services criteria) should be included in management's description. For example, if a service auditor is reporting on the design and operating effectiveness of controls at a service organization relevant to the security of user entities' information, all the control criteria related to security should be addressed by the description. If the description does not describe controls for one or more control criteria, the description should include an explanation of why such criteria are not addressed by a control. Omission of controls related to one or more of the applicable trust services criteria would be appropriate if the omitted criteria are not applicable to the services provided by the service organization.

For example, in an engagement to report on the privacy principle in which personal information is collected from individuals by user entities, not the service organization, it would be appropriate to omit controls for the criteria related to collection and describe the reason for such omission. However, for certain criteria, a policy prohibiting certain activities is not sufficient to render a criterion not applicable. For example, in a SOC 2 report that addresses the privacy principle, it would not be appropriate for a service organization to omit controls for the criteria related to disclosure of personal information to third parties based only on the fact that the service organization's policies forbid such disclosure. Such policies would need to be suitably designed, implemented, and operating effectively to conclude that they prevent such disclosure.

The description need not address every aspect of the service organization's system or the services provided to user entities. Certain aspects of the services provided may not be relevant to user entities or may be beyond the scope of the engagement. For example, a service organization's processes related to availability are not likely to be relevant in an engagement that addresses only the security principle. Similarly, although the description should include procedures within both manual and automated systems by which services are provided, it need not necessarily include every step in the process.

The description needs to meet certain criteria in order to be fairly presented. These criteria are set forth in the section of this appendix titled "Criteria for Management's Description of the Service Organization's System." As a part of the SOC 2 engagement, the service auditor evaluates the fairness of the presentation of the description using these criteria.

Providing a Written Assertion

Management of the service organization prepares a written assertion that is to be attached to the description of the service organization's system. In its assertion, management confirms, to the best of its knowledge and belief, that

> *a.* management's description of the service organization's system fairly presents the service organization's system that was designed and implemented throughout the specified period, based on the criteria in the section of this appendix titled "Criteria for Management's Description of the Service Organization's System."
>
> *b.* the controls stated in management's description of the service organization's system were suitably designed throughout the specified period to meet the applicable trust services criteria.
>
> *c.* the controls stated in management's description of the service organization's system operated effectively throughout the specified period to meet the applicable trust services criteria (type 2 report only).
>
> *d.* when management's description of the service organization's system includes controls over privacy, the service organization complied with the commitments in its statement of privacy practices throughout the specified period (type 2 report only).

Paragraph .23 of AT section 101 requires that criteria be available to users. Because the criteria in paragraphs 1.34–.35 of this guide may not be readily available to report users, management of the service organization should include in its assertion all of the description criteria in paragraphs 1.34–.35 of this guide. Although all of the criteria should be included in management's assertion, certain description criteria may not be pertinent to a particular service organization or system; for example, the criterion in paragraph 1.34*a*(v) would not be pertinent to a service organization that does not prepare and deliver reports or other information to user entities or other parties, and the criterion in paragraph 1.34*a*(vii)(2) would not be pertinent to a service organization that does not use a subservice organization. If certain description criteria are not pertinent to a service organization, report users generally find it useful if management presents all of the description criteria and indicates which criteria are not pertinent to the service organization and the reasons therefore. Management may do so either in its system description or in a note to the specific description criteria.

Management of the service organization needs to have a reasonable basis for its written assertion, which typically is based on management's monitoring activities and other procedures.

Management's monitoring activities may provide a portion of the basis for making its assertion regarding the design and operating effectiveness of controls or may be a sufficient basis on its own. Monitoring of controls is a process to assess the effectiveness of internal control performance over time. It involves assessing the effectiveness of controls on a timely basis, identifying and reporting deficiencies to appropriate individuals within the service organization, and taking necessary corrective actions. Management accomplishes monitoring of controls through ongoing activities, separate evaluations, or a combination of the two. Ongoing monitoring activities are often built into the normal recurring activities of an entity and include regular management and supervisory activities. Internal auditors or personnel performing similar functions may contribute to the monitoring of a service organization's activities. Monitoring activities may also include using information communicated by external parties, such as customer complaints and regulator comments, which may indicate problems or highlight areas in need of improvement. The greater the degree and effectiveness of ongoing monitoring, the less need for separate evaluations. Usually, some combination of ongoing monitoring and separate evaluations will help ensure that internal control maintains its effectiveness over time. The service auditor's report on controls is not a substitute for the service organization's own processes that provide a reasonable basis for its assertion.

When monitoring does not provide a basis for management's assertion regarding the design and operating effectiveness of controls, service organization management may need to perform its own tests of the service organization's controls.

Additional Management Responsibilities

The following are some of the additional responsibilities that management of the service organization will have throughout the engagement:

- Providing access to all information, such as information in records, documentation, service level agreements, internal audit reports and other reports that management is aware of, that is relevant to the description of the service organization's system or the design and operating effectiveness of controls and management's assertion.

- Providing additional information that the service auditor may request from management for the purpose of the examination engagement.

- Providing unrestricted access to personnel within the service organization from whom the service auditor determines it is necessary to obtain evidence relevant to the service auditor's engagement.

- Disclosing to the service auditor any deficiencies in the design of controls of which management is aware.

- Disclosing to the service auditor all instances of which management is aware when controls have not operated with sufficient effectiveness to meet the applicable trust services criteria.

- Disclosing to the service auditor incidents of noncompliance with laws and regulations, fraud, or uncorrected errors attributable to management or other service organization personnel that are clearly not trivial and may affect one or more user entities and whether such incidents have been communicated appropriately to affected user entities.

- Providing written representations at the conclusion of the engagement. When the inclusive method is used, management of the service organization and subservice organization are responsible for providing separate representations. In its representations, management includes statements that

  — reaffirm its written assertion attached to the description.

  — the service organization has provided the service auditor with all relevant information and the access agreed to.

  — the service organization has disclosed to the service auditor any of the following of which it is aware:

    - Instances of noncompliance with laws or regulations or uncorrected errors attributable to the service organization that may affect one or more user entities.

    - Knowledge of any actual, suspected, or alleged intentional acts by management of the service organization or its employees that could adversely affect the fairness of the presentation of management's description of the service organization's system or whether the controls stated in the description were suitably designed and operating effectively to meet the applicable trust services criteria.

    - Deficiencies in the design of controls.

    - Instances when controls have not operated as described.

    - Any events subsequent to the period covered by management's description of the service organization's system up to the date of the service auditor's report that could have a significant effect on management's assertion or the fact that no such subsequent events have occurred.

Criteria for Management's Description of the Service Organization's System

The criteria for determining whether the description of the service organization's system is fairly presented are as follows:

   a. The description contains the following information:

   i. The types of services provided.

   ii. The components of the system used to provide the services, which are the following:

      (1) *Infrastructure.* The physical and hardware components of a system (facilities, equipment, and networks).

      (2) *Software.* The programs and operating software of a system (systems, applications, and utilities).

      (3) *People.* The personnel involved in the operation and use of a system (developers, operators, users, and managers).

(4) *Procedures.* The programmed and manual procedures involved in the operation of a system.

(5) *Data.* The information used and supported by a system (transaction streams, files, databases, and tables).

iii. The boundaries of the system covered by the description.

iv. How the service organization's system captures and addresses significant events and conditions[6]

v. The process used to prepare and deliver reports and other information to user entities or other parties.

vi. For information provided to, or received from, subservice organizations and other parties,

(1) how the information is provided or received and the role of the subservice organizations or other parties.

(2) the procedures that the service organization performs to determine that such information and its processing, maintenance, and storage are subject to appropriate controls.

vii. For each principle being reported on, the related criteria in TSP section 100 (applicable trust services criteria) and the related controls designed to meet those criteria, including, as applicable, the following:

(1) Complementary user-entity controls contemplated in the design of the service organization's system.

(2) When the inclusive method is used to present a subservice organization, controls at the subservice organization.

viii. If the service organization presents the subservice organization using the carve-out method,

(1) the nature of the services provided by the subservice organization.

(2) any aspects of the personal information life cycle for which responsibility has been delegated to the subservice organization.

(3) each of the applicable trust services criteria that are intended to be met by controls at the subservice organization, alone or in combination with controls at the service organization, and the types of controls expected to be implemented at carved-out subservice organizations to meet those criteria.

(4) when the report addresses the privacy principle, the types of activities that the subservice organization would need to perform to comply with the service organization's privacy commitments.

ix. Identifying any applicable trust services criteria that are not addressed by a control at the service organization or subservice organization and the reasons therefore.

---

[6] For example, the setup of access rights for new users of the system.

    x. Other aspects of the service organization's control environment, risk assessment process, information and communication systems, and monitoring of controls that are relevant to the services provided and the applicable trust services criteria.

    xi. In the case of a type 2 report, relevant details of changes to the service organization's system during the period covered by the description.

b. The description does not omit or distort information relevant to the service organization's system while acknowledging that the description is prepared to meet the common needs of a broad range of users and may not, therefore, include every aspect of the system that each individual user may consider important to his or her own particular needs.

c. For engagements to report on the privacy principle

    i. the types of personal information collected from individuals or obtained from user entities or other parties[7] and how such information is collected and, if collected by user entities, how it is obtained by the service organization.

    ii. the process for (1) identifying specific requirements in agreements with user entities and laws and regulations applicable to the personal information and (2) implementing controls and practices to meet those requirements.

    iii. if the service organization provides the privacy notice to individuals about whom personal information is collected, used, retained, disclosed, and disposed of or anonymized, the privacy notice prepared in conformity with the relevant criteria for a privacy notice set forth in TSP section 100.

    iv. if the service organization presents the subservice organization using the carve-out method

        (1) any aspects of the personal information life cycle for which responsibility has been delegated to the subservice organization and

        (2) the types of activities that the subservice organization would need to perform to comply with the service organization's privacy commitments.

    v. if the user entities, rather than the service organization, are responsible for providing the privacy notice to individuals, a statement regarding how the privacy notice is communicated to individuals, that the user entities are responsible for communicating such notice to individuals, and that the service organization is responsible for communicating its privacy practices to the user entities in its statement of privacy practices, which includes the following information:

        (1) A summary of the significant privacy and related security requirements common to most agreements between the

---

[7] An example of an entity that collects personal information from user entities is a credit-reporting bureau that maintains information about the creditworthiness of individuals.

service organization and its user entities and any requirements in a particular user-entity's agreement that the service organization meets for all or most user entities.

(2) A summary of the significant privacy and related security requirements mandated by law, regulation, industry, or market requirements that are not included in user-entity agreements but that the service organization meets for all or most user entities.

(3) The purposes, uses, and disclosures of personal information as permitted by user-entity agreements and beyond those permitted by such agreements but not prohibited by such agreements and the service organization's commitments regarding the purpose, use, and disclosure of personal information that are prohibited by such agreements.

(4) A statement that the information will be retained for a period no longer than necessary to fulfill the stated purposes or contractual requirements or for the period required by law or regulation, as applicable, or a statement describing other retention practices.

(5) A statement that the information will be disposed of in a manner that prevents loss, theft, misuse, or unauthorized access to the information.

(6) If applicable, how the service organization supports any process permitted by user entities for individuals to obtain access to their information to review, update, or correct it.

(7) If applicable, a description of the process to determine that personal information is accurate and complete and how the service organization implements correction processes permitted by user entities.

(8) If applicable, how inquiries, complaints, and disputes from individuals (whether directly from the individual or indirectly through user entities) regarding their personal information are handled by the service organization.

(9) A statement regarding the existence of a written security program and what industry or other standards it is based on.

(10) Other relevant information related to privacy practices deemed appropriate for user entities by the service organization.

vi. if the user entities, rather than the service organization, are responsible for providing the privacy notice to individuals, the service organization's statement of privacy practices.

———————

Appendix B

Trust Services Principles and Criteria for Security, Availability, Processing Integrity, Confidentiality, and Privacy

TSP Section 100 Principles and Criteria

Security Principle and Criteria Table

The system is protected against unauthorized access (both physical and logical)

	Criteria
1.0	**Policies: The entity defines and documents its policies for the security of its system.**
1.1	The entity's security policies are established and periodically reviewed and approved by a designated individual or group.
1.2	The entity's security policies include, but may not be limited to, the following matters:

    a. Identifying and documenting the security requirements of authorized users

    b. Classifying data based on its criticality and sensitivity and that classification is used to define protection requirements, access rights and access restrictions, and retention and destruction requirements

    c. Assessing risks on a periodic basis

    d. Preventing unauthorized access

    e. Adding new users, modifying the access levels of existing users, and removing users who no longer need access

    f. Assigning responsibility and accountability for system security

    g. Assigning responsibility and accountability for system changes and maintenance

    h. Testing, evaluating, and authorizing system components before implementation

    i. Addressing how complaints and requests relating to security issues are resolved

    j. Identifying and mitigating security breaches and other incidents

    k. Providing for training and other resources to support its system security policies

    l. Providing for the handling of exceptions and situations not specifically addressed in its system security policies

(continued)

Criteria

	m. Providing for the identification of and consistency with applicable laws and regulations, defined commitments, service-level agreements, and other contractual requirements
	n. Providing for sharing information with third parties
1.3	Responsibility and accountability for developing and maintaining the entity's system security policies, and changes and updates to those policies, are assigned.
2.0	**Communications: The entity communicates its defined system security policies to responsible parties and authorized users.**
2.1	The entity has prepared an objective description of the system and its boundaries and communicated such description to authorized users.
2.2	The security obligations of users and the entity's security commitments to users are communicated to authorized users.
2.3	Responsibility and accountability for the entity's system security policies and changes and updates to those policies are communicated to entity personnel responsible for implementing them.
2.4	The process for informing the entity about breaches of the system security and for submitting complaints is communicated to authorized users.
2.5	Changes that may affect system security are communicated to management and users who will be affected.
3.0	**Procedures: The entity placed in operation procedures to achieve its documented system security objectives in accordance with its defined policies.**
3.1	Procedures exist to (1) identify potential threats of disruption to systems operation that would impair system security commitments and (2) assess the risks associated with the identified threats.
3.2	Procedures exist to restrict logical access to the defined system including, but not limited to, the following matters:
	a. Logical access security measures to restrict access to information resources not deemed to be public.
	b. Identification and authentication of users.
	c. Registration and authorization of new users.
	d. The process to make changes and updates to user profiles.
	e. Distribution of output restricted to authorized users.
	f. Restriction of access to offline storage, backup data, systems, and media.
	g. Restriction of access to system configurations, superuser functionality, master passwords, powerful utilities, and security devices (for example, firewalls).

Criteria

3.3	Procedures exist to restrict physical access to the defined system including, but not limited to, facilities, backup media, and other system components such as firewalls, routers, and servers.
3.4	Procedures exist to protect against unauthorized access to system resources.
3.5	Procedures exist to protect against infection by computer viruses, malicious code, and unauthorized software.
3.6	Encryption or other equivalent security techniques are used to protect user authentication information and the corresponding session transmitted over the Internet or other public networks.

Criteria related to execution and incident management used to achieve objectives

3.7	Procedures exist to identify, report, and act upon system security breaches and other incidents.

Criteria related to the system components used to achieve the objectives

3.8	Procedures exist to classify data in accordance with classification policies and periodically monitor and update such classifications as necessary
3.9	Procedures exist to provide that issues of noncompliance with security policies are promptly addressed and that corrective measures are taken on a timely basis.
3.10	Design, acquisition, implementation, configuration, modification, and management of infrastructure and software are consistent with defined system security policies to enable authorized access and to prevent unauthorized access.
3.11	Procedures exist to provide that personnel responsible for the design, development, implementation, and operation of systems affecting security have the qualifications and resources to fulfill their responsibilities.

Change management-related criteria applicable to the system's security

3.12	Procedures exist to maintain system components, including configurations consistent with the defined system security policies.
3.13	Procedures exist to provide that only authorized, tested, and documented changes are made to the system.
3.14	Procedures exist to provide that emergency changes are documented and authorized timely.
4.0	**Monitoring: The entity monitors the system and takes action to maintain compliance with its defined system security policies.**
4.1	The entity's system security is periodically reviewed and compared with the defined system security policies.

(continued)

	Criteria
4.2	There is a process to identify and address potential impairments to the entity's ongoing ability to achieve its objectives in accordance with its defined system security policies.
4.3	Environmental, regulatory, and technological changes are monitored and their effect on system security is assessed on a timely basis and policies are updated for that assessment.

Availability Principle and Criteria Table

The system is available for operation and use as committed or agreed.

	Criteria
1.0	**Policies: The entity defines and documents its policies for the availability of its system.**
1.1	The entity's system availability and related security policies are established and periodically reviewed and approved by a designated individual or group.
1.2	The entity's system availability and related security policies include, but may not be limited to, the following matters:
	a. Identifying and documenting the system availability and related security requirements of authorized users.
	b. Classifying data based on its criticality and sensitivity and that classification is used to define protection requirements, access rights and access restrictions, and retention and destruction requirements
	c. Assessing risks on a periodic basis
	d. Preventing unauthorized access.
	e. Adding new users, modifying the access levels of existing users, and removing users who no longer need access.
	f. Assigning responsibility and accountability for system availability and related security.
	g. Assigning responsibility and accountability for system changes and maintenance.
	h. Testing, evaluating, and authorizing system components before implementation.
	i. Addressing how complaints and requests relating to system availability and related security issues are resolved.
	j. Identifying and mitigating system availability and related security breaches and other incidents.
	k. Providing for training and other resources to support its system availability and related security policies.
	l. Providing for the handling of exceptions and situations not specifically addressed in its system availability and related security policies.

Criteria

m.	Providing for the identification of and consistency with, applicable laws and regulations, defined commitments, service-level agreements, and other contractual requirements.
n.	Recovering and continuing service in accordance with documented customer commitments or other agreements.
o.	Monitoring system capacity to achieve customer commitments or other agreements regarding availability
1.3	Responsibility and accountability for developing and maintaining the entity's system availability and related security policies, and changes and updates to those policies, are assigned.

2.0	**Communications: The entity communicates the defined system availability policies to responsible parties and authorized users.**
2.1	The entity has prepared an objective description of the system and its boundaries and communicated such description to authorized users.
2.2	The availability and related security obligations of users and the entity's availability and related security commitments to users are communicated to authorized users.
2.3	Responsibility and accountability for the entity's system availability and related security policies and changes and updates to those policies are communicated to entity personnel responsible for implementing them.
2.4	The process for informing the entity about system availability issues and breaches of system security and for submitting complaints is communicated to authorized users.
2.5	Changes that may affect system availability and system security are communicated to management and users who will be affected.

3.0	**Procedures: The entity placed in operation procedures to achieve its documented system availability objectives in accordance with its defined policies.**
3.1	Procedures exist to (1) identify potential threats of disruptions to systems operation that would impair system availability commitments and (2) assess the risks associated with the identified threats.
3.2	Measures to prevent or mitigate threats have been implemented consistent with the risk assessment when commercially practicable.
3.3	Procedures exist to provide for backup, offsite storage, restoration, and disaster recovery consistent with the entity's defined system availability and related security policies.
3.4	Procedures exist to provide for the integrity of backup data and systems maintained to support the entity's defined system availability and related security policies.

(continued)

	Criteria
	Security-related criteria relevant to the system's availability
3.5	Procedures exist to restrict logical access to the defined system including, but not limited to, the following matters:
	a. Logical access security measures to restrict access to information resources not deemed to be public.
	b. Identification and authentication of users.
	c. Registration and authorization of new users.
	d. The process to make changes and updates to user profiles.
	e. Restriction of access to offline storage, backup data, systems and media.
	f. Restriction of access to system configurations, superuser functionality, master passwords, powerful utilities, and security devices (for example, firewalls).
3.6	Procedures exist to restrict physical access to the defined system including, but not limited to, facilities, backup media, and other system components such as firewalls, routers, and servers.
3.7	Procedures exist to protect against unauthorized access to system resources.
3.8	Procedures exist to protect against infection by computer viruses, malicious codes, and unauthorized software.
3.9	Encryption or other equivalent security techniques are used to protect user authentication information and the corresponding session transmitted over the Internet or other public networks.
	Criteria related to execution and incident management used to achieve objectives
3.10	Procedures exist to identify, report, and act upon system availability issues and related security breaches and other incidents.
	Criteria related to the system components used to achieve the objectives
3.11	Procedures exist to classify data in accordance with classification policies and periodically monitor and update such classifications as necessary.
3.12	Procedures exist to provide that issues of noncompliance with system availability and related security policies are promptly addressed and that corrective measures are taken on a timely basis.
3.13	Design, acquisition, implementation, configuration, modification, and management of infrastructure and software are consistent with defined system availability and related security policies.
3.14	Procedures exist to provide that personnel responsible for the design, development, implementation, and operation of systems affecting availability and security have the qualifications and resources to fulfill their responsibilities.

Criteria

	Change management-related criteria applicable to the system's availability
3.15	Procedures exist to maintain system components, including configurations consistent with the defined system availability and related security policies.
3.16	Procedures exist to provide that only authorized, tested, and documented changes are made to the system.
3.17	Procedures exist to provide that emergency changes are documented and authorized (including after-the-fact approval).
4.0	**Monitoring: The entity monitors the system and takes action to maintain compliance with its defined system availability policies.**
4.1	The entity's system availability and security performance is periodically reviewed and compared with the defined system availability and related security policies.
4.2	There is a process to identify and address potential impairments to the entity's ongoing ability to achieve its objectives in accordance with its defined system availability and related security policies.
4.3	Environmental, regulatory, and technological changes are monitored, and their effect on system availability and security is assessed on a timely basis; policies are updated for that assessment.

Processing Integrity Principle and Criteria Table

System processing is complete, accurate, timely, and authorized.

Criteria

1.0	**Policies: The entity defines and documents its policies for the processing integrity of its system.**
1.1	The entity's processing integrity and related security policies are established and periodically reviewed and approved by a designated individual or group.
1.2	The entity's system processing integrity and related security policies include, but may not be limited to, the following matters:
	a. Identifying and documenting the system processing integrity and related security requirements of authorized users
	b. Classifying data based on their criticality and sensitivity; that classification is used to define protection requirements, access rights and access restrictions, and retention and destruction requirements
	c. Assessing risks on a periodic basis
	d. Preventing unauthorized access

(continued)

Criteria

   e. Adding new users, modifying the access levels of existing users, and removing users who no longer need access

   f. Assigning responsibility and accountability for system processing integrity and related security

   g. Assigning responsibility and accountability for system changes and maintenance

   h. Testing, evaluating, and authorizing system components before implementation

   ι. Addressing how complaints and requests relating to system processing integrity and related security issues are resolved

   j. Identifying and mitigating errors and omissions and other system processing integrity and related security breaches and other incidents

   k. Providing for training and other resources to support its system processing integrity and related system security policies

   l. Providing for the handling of exceptions and situations not specifically addressed in its system processing integrity and related system security policies

   m. Providing for the identification of and consistency with applicable laws and regulations, defined commitments, service-level agreements, and other contractual requirements

1.3   Responsibility and accountability for developing and maintaining entity's system processing integrity and related system security policies; changes, updates, and exceptions to those policies are assigned.

2.0   Communications: The entity communicates its documented system processing integrity policies to responsible parties and authorized users.

2.1   The entity has prepared an objective description of the system and its boundaries and communicated such description to authorized users.

   If the system is an e-commerce system, additional information provided on its website includes, but may not be limited to, the following matters:

   a. Descriptive information about the nature of the goods or services that will be provided, including, where appropriate,

   — condition of goods (whether they are new, used, or reconditioned).

   — description of services (or service contract).

   — sources of information (where it was obtained and how it was compiled).

   b. The terms and conditions by which it conducts its e-commerce transactions including, but not limited to, the following matters:

Criteria

- Time frame for completion of transactions (*transaction* means fulfillment of orders where goods are being sold and delivery of service where a service is being provided)
- Time frame and process for informing customers of exceptions to normal processing of orders or service requests
- Normal method of delivery of goods or services, including customer options, where applicable
- Payment terms, including customer options, if any
- Electronic settlement practices and related charges to customers
- How customers may cancel recurring charges, if any
- Product return policies and limited liability, where applicable

c. Where customers can obtain warranty, repair service, and support related to the goods and services purchased on its website.

d. Procedures for resolution of issues regarding processing integrity. These may relate to any part of a customer's e-commerce transaction, including complaints related to the quality of services and products, accuracy, completeness, and the consequences for failure to resolve such complaints.

2.2 The processing integrity and related security obligations of users and the entity's processing integrity and related security commitments to users are communicated to authorized users.

2.3 Responsibility and accountability for the entity's system processing integrity and related security policies, and changes and updates to those policies, are communicated to entity personnel responsible for implementing them.

2.4 The process for obtaining support and informing the entity about system processing integrity issues, errors and omissions, and breaches of systems security and for submitting complaints is communicated to authorized users.

2.5 Changes that may affect system processing integrity and system security are communicated to management and users who will be affected.

3.0 **Procedures: The entity placed in operation procedures to achieve its documented system processing integrity objectives in accordance with its defined policies.**

3.1 Procedures exist to (1) identify potential threats of disruptions to systems operations that would impair processing integrity commitments and (2) assess the risks associated with the identified threats.

3.2 The procedures related to completeness, accuracy, timeliness, and authorization of inputs are consistent with the documented system processing integrity policies.

(continued)

Criteria

	If the system is an e-commerce system, the entity's procedures include, but may not be limited to, the following matters:
	a. The entity checks each request or transaction for accuracy and completeness.
	b. Positive acknowledgment is received from the customer before the transaction is processed.
3.3	The procedures related to completeness, accuracy, timeliness, and authorization of system processing, including error correction and database management, are consistent with documented system processing integrity policies.
	If the system is an e-commerce system, the entity's procedures include, but are not necessarily limited to, the following matters:
	a. The correct goods are shipped in the correct quantities in the time frame agreed upon, or services and information are provided to the customer as requested.
	b. Transaction exceptions are promptly communicated to the customer.
	c. Incoming messages are processed and delivered accurately and completely to the correct IP address.
	d. Outgoing messages are processed and delivered accurately and completely to the service provider's (SP's) Internet access point.
	e. Messages remain intact while in transit within the confines of the SP's network.
3.4	The procedures related to completeness, accuracy, timeliness, and authorization of outputs are consistent with the documented system processing integrity policies.
	If the system is an e-commerce system, the entity's procedures include, but are not necessarily limited to, the following matters: • The entity displays sales prices and all other costs and fees to the customer before processing the transaction. • Transactions are billed and electronically settled as agreed. • Billing or settlement errors are promptly corrected.
3.5	There are procedures to enable tracing of information inputs from their source to their final disposition and vice versa.
	Security-related criteria relevant to the system's processing integrity
3.6	Procedures exist to restrict logical access to the defined system including, but not limited to, the following matters:
	a. Logical access security measures to access information not deemed to be public
	b. Identification and authentication of authorized users
	c. Registration and authorization of new users
	d. The process to make changes and updates to user profiles

Criteria

e.   Distribution of output restricted to authorized users

f.   Restriction of access to offline storage, backup data, systems, and media

g.   Restriction of access to system configurations, superuser functionality, master passwords, powerful utilities, and security devices (for example, firewalls)

3.7   Procedures exist to restrict physical access to the defined system including, but not limited to, facilities, offline storage media, backup media and systems, and other system components such as firewalls, routers, and servers.

3.8   Procedures exist to protect against unauthorized access to system resources.

3.9   Procedures exist to protect against infection by computer viruses, malicious code, and unauthorized software.

3.10   Encryption or other equivalent security techniques are used to protect user authentication information and the corresponding session transmitted over the Internet or other public networks.

Criteria related to execution and incident management used to achieve objectives

3.11   Procedures exist to identify, report, and act upon system processing integrity issues and related security breaches and other incidents.

Criteria related to the system components used to achieve the objectives

3.12   Procedures exist to classify data in accordance with classification policies and periodically monitor and update such classifications as necessary

3.13   Procedures exist to provide that issues of noncompliance with system processing integrity and related security policies are promptly addressed and that corrective measures are taken on a timely basis.

3.14   Design, acquisition, implementation, configuration, modification, and management of infrastructure and software are consistent with defined processing integrity and related security policies.

3.15   Procedures exist to provide that personnel responsible for the design, development, implementation, and operation of systems affecting processing integrity and security have qualifications and resources to fulfill their responsibilities.

Change management-related criteria applicable to the system's processing integrity

3.16   Procedures exist to maintain system components, including configurations consistent with the defined system processing integrity and related security policies.

3.17   Procedures exist to provide that only authorized, tested, and documented changes are made to the system.

(continued)

	Criteria
3.18	Procedures exist to provide that emergency changes are documented and authorized (including after-the-fact approval).
	Availability-related criteria applicable to the system's processing integrity
3.19	Procedures exist to protect the system against potential risks (for example, environmental risks, natural disasters, and routine operational errors and omissions) that might impair system processing integrity.
3.20	Procedures exist to provide for restoration and disaster recovery consistent with the entity's defined processing integrity policies.
3.21	Procedures exist to provide for the completeness, accuracy, and timeliness of backup data and systems.
4.0	**Monitoring: The entity monitors the system and takes action to maintain compliance with the defined system processing integrity policies.**
4.1	System processing integrity and security performance are periodically reviewed and compared with the defined system processing integrity and related security policies.
4.2	There is a process to identify and address potential impairments to the entity's ongoing ability to achieve its objectives in accordance with its defined system processing integrity and related security policies.
4.3	Environmental, regulatory, and technological changes are monitored, their impact on system processing integrity and security is assessed on a timely basis, and policies are updated for that assessment.

Confidentiality Principle and Criteria Table

Information designated as confidential is protected by the system as committed or agreed.

	Criteria
1.0	**Policies: The entity defines and documents its policies related to the system protecting confidential information, as committed or agreed.**
1.1	The entity's system confidentiality and related security policies are established and periodically reviewed and approved by a designated individual or group.

Criteria

1.2	The entity's policies related to the system's protection of confidential information and security include, but are not limited to, the following matters:

    a. Identifying and documenting the confidentiality and related security requirements of authorized users

    b. Classifying data based on its criticality and sensitivity that is used to define protection requirements, access rights and access restrictions, and retention and destruction requirements

    c. Assessing risk on a periodic basis

    d. Preventing unauthorized access

    e. Adding new users, modifying the access levels of existing users, and removing users who no longer need access

    f. Assigning responsibility and accountability for confidentiality and related security

    g. Assigning responsibility and accountability for system changes and maintenance

    h. Testing, evaluating, and authorizing system components before implementation

    i. Addressing how complaints and requests relating to confidentiality and related security issues are resolved

    j. Handling confidentiality and related security breaches and other incidents

    k. Providing for training and other resources to support its system confidentiality and related security policies

    l. Providing for the handling of exceptions and situations not specifically addressed in its system confidentiality and related security policies

    m. Providing for the identification of and consistency with, applicable laws and regulations, defined commitments, service-level agreements, and other contractual requirements

    n. Sharing information with third parties

1.3	Responsibility and accountability for developing and maintaining the entity's system confidentiality and related security policies, and changes and updates to those polices, are assigned.
2.0	**Communications: The entity communicates its defined policies related to the system's protection of confidential information to responsible parties and authorized users.**
2.1	The entity has prepared an objective description of the system and its boundaries and communicated such description to authorized users.
2.2	The system confidentiality and related security obligations of users and the entity's confidentiality and related security commitments to users are communicated to authorized users before the confidential information is provided. This

(continued)

AAG-SOP APP B

communication includes, but is not limited to, the following matters:

a. How information is designated as confidential and ceases to be confidential. The handling, destruction, maintenance, storage, back-up, and distribution or transmission of confidential information.

b. How access to confidential information is authorized and how such authorization is rescinded.

c. How confidential information is used.

d. How confidential information is shared.

e. If information is provided to third parties, disclosures include any limitations on reliance on the third party's confidentiality practices and controls. Lack of such disclosure indicates that the entity is relying on the third party's confidentiality practices and controls that meet or exceed those of the entity.

f. Practices to comply with applicable laws and regulations addressing confidentiality.

2.3 Responsibility and accountability for the entity's system confidentiality and related security policies and changes and updates to those policies are communicated to entity personnel responsible for implementing them.

2.4 The process for informing the entity about breaches of confidentiality and system security and for submitting complaints is communicated to authorized users.

2.5 Changes that may affect confidentiality and system security are communicated to management and users who will be affected.

3.0 Procedures: The entity placed in operation procedures to achieve its documented system confidentiality objectives in accordance with its defined policies.

3.1 Procedures exist to (1) identify potential threats of disruptions to systems operations that would impair system confidentiality commitments and (2) assess the risks associated with the identified threats.

3.2 The system procedures related to confidentiality of inputs are consistent with the documented confidentiality policies.

3.3 The system procedures related to confidentiality of data processing are consistent with the documented confidentiality policies.

3.4 The system procedures related to confidentiality of outputs are consistent with the documented confidentiality policies.

3.5 The system procedures provide that confidential information is disclosed to parties only in accordance with the entity's defined confidentiality and related security policies.

3.6 The entity has procedures to obtain assurance or representation that the confidentiality policies of third parties to whom information is transferred and upon which the entity relies are

Criteria

in conformity with the entity's defined system confidentiality and related security policies and that the third party is in compliance with its policies.

3.7 In the event that a disclosed confidentiality practice is discontinued or changed to be less restrictive, the entity has procedures to protect confidential information in accordance with the system confidentiality practices in place when such information was received, or obtains customer consent to follow the new confidentiality practice with respect to the customer's confidential information.

System security-related criteria relevant to confidentiality

3.8 Procedures exist to restrict logical access to the system and the confidential information resources maintained in the system including, but not limited to, the following matters:

a. Logical access security measures to restrict access to information resources not deemed to be public

b. Identification and authentication of all users.

c. Registration and authorization of new users.

d. The process to make changes and updates to user profiles.

e. Procedures to prevent customers, groups of individuals, or other entities from accessing confidential information other than their own.

f. Procedures to limit access to confidential information to only authorized employees based upon their assigned roles and responsibilities.

g. Distribution of output containing confidential information restricted to authorized users.

h. Restriction of access to offline storage, backup data, systems, and media.

i. Restriction of access to system configurations, superuser functionality, master passwords, powerful utilities, and security devices (for example, firewalls).

3.9 Procedures exist to restrict physical access to the defined system including, but not limited to, facilities, backup media, and other system components such as firewalls, routers, and servers.

3.10 Procedures exist to protect against unauthorized access to system resources.

3.11 Procedures exist to protect against infection by computer viruses, malicious code, and unauthorized software.

3.12 Encryption or other equivalent security techniques are used to protect transmissions of user authentication and other confidential information passed over the Internet or other public networks.

(continued)

	Criteria
	Criteria related to execution and incident management used to achieve the objectives
3.13	Procedures exist to identify, report, and act upon system confidentiality and security breaches and other incidents.
	Criteria related to the system components used to achieve the objectives
3.14	Procedures exist to provide that system data are classified in accordance with the defined confidentiality and related security policies.
3.15	Procedures exist to provide that issues of noncompliance with defined confidentiality and related security policies are promptly addressed and that corrective measures are taken on a timely basis.
3.16	Design, acquisition, implementation, configuration, modification, and management of infrastructure and software are consistent with defined confidentiality and related security policies.
3.17	Procedures exist to help ensure that personnel responsible for the design, development, implementation, and operation of systems affecting confidentiality and security have the qualifications and resources to fulfill their responsibilities.
	Change management-related criteria relevant to confidentiality
3.18	Procedures exist to maintain system components, including configurations consistent with the defined system confidentiality and related security policies.
3.19	Procedures exist to provide that only authorized, tested, and documented changes are made to the system.
3.20	Procedures exist to provide that emergency changes are documented and authorized (including after-the-fact approval).
3.21	Procedures exist to provide that confidential information is protected during the system development, testing, and change processes in accordance with defined system confidentiality and related security policies.
4.0	**Monitoring: The entity monitors the system and takes action to maintain compliance with its defined confidentiality policies.**
4.1	The entity's system confidentiality and security performance is periodically reviewed and compared with the defined system confidentiality and related security policies.
4.2	There is a process to identify and address potential impairments to the entity's ongoing ability to achieve its objectives in accordance with its system confidentiality and related security policies.
4.3	Environmental, regulatory, and technological changes are monitored, and their impact on system confidentiality and security is assessed on a timely basis. System confidentiality policies and procedures are updated for such changes as required.

Generally Accepted Privacy Principles and Criteria

Ref.	Management Principle and Criteria
1.0	**The entity defines, documents, communicates, and assigns accountability for its privacy policies and procedures.**

1.1	**Policies and Communications**

1.1.0 **Privacy Policies**
The entity defines and documents its privacy policies with respect to the following:

a. Notice (See 2.1.0)

b. Choice and consent (See 3.1.0)

c. Collection (See 4.1.0)

d. Use, retention, and disposal (See 5.1.0)

e. Access (See 6.1.0)

f. Disclosure to third parties (See 7.1.0)

g. Security for privacy (See 8.1.0)

h. Quality (See 9.1.0)

i. Monitoring and enforcement (See 10.1.0)

1.1.1 **Communication to Internal Personnel**

Privacy policies and the consequences of noncompliance with such policies are communicated, at least annually, to the entity's internal personnel responsible for collecting, using, retaining, and disclosing personal information. Changes in privacy policies are communicated to such personnel shortly after the changes are approved.

1.1.2 **Responsibility and Accountability for Policies**

Responsibility and accountability are assigned to a person or group for developing, documenting, implementing, enforcing, monitoring, and updating the entity's privacy policies. The names of such person or group and their responsibilities are communicated to internal personnel.

1.2 **Procedures and Controls**

1.2.1 **Review and Approval**

Privacy policies and procedures, and changes thereto, are reviewed and approved by management.

1.2.2 **Consistency of Privacy Policies and Procedures With Laws and Regulations**

Policies and procedures are reviewed and compared to the requirements of applicable laws and regulations at least annually and whenever changes to such laws and regulations are made. Privacy policies and procedures are revised to conform with the requirements of applicable laws and regulations.

(continued)

Ref.	Management Principle and Criteria

1.2.3   **Personal Information Identification and Classification**

The types of personal information and sensitive personal information and the related processes, systems, and third parties involved in the handling of such information are identified. Such information is covered by the entity's privacy and related security policies and procedures.

1.2.4   **Risk Assessment**

A risk assessment process is used to establish a risk baseline and to, at least annually, identify new or changed risks to personal information and to develop and update responses to such risks.

1.2.5   **Consistency of Commitments With Privacy Policies and Procedures**

Internal personnel or advisers review contracts for consistency with privacy policies and procedures and address any inconsistencies.

1.2.6   **Infrastructure and Systems Management**

The potential privacy impact is assessed when new processes involving personal information are implemented, and when changes are made to such processes (including any such activities outsourced to third parties or contractors), and personal information continues to be protected in accordance with the privacy policies. For this purpose, processes involving personal information include the design, acquisition, development, implementation, configuration, modification and management of the following:
- Infrastructure
- Systems
- Applications
- Websites
- Procedures
- Products and services
- Data bases and information repositories
- Mobile computing and other similar electronic devices

The use of personal information in process and system test and development is prohibited unless such information is anonymized or otherwise protected in accordance with the entity's privacy policies and procedures.

1.2.7   **Privacy Incident and Breach Management**

A documented privacy incident and breach management program has been implemented that includes, but is not limited to, the following:
- Procedures for the identification, management, and resolution of privacy incidents and breaches
- Defined responsibilities
- A process to identify incident severity and determine required actions and escalation procedures

Ref.	*Management Principle and Criteria*
	• A process for complying with breach laws and regulations, including stakeholders breach notification, if required
	• An accountability process for employees or third parties responsible for incidents or breaches with remediation, penalties, or discipline as appropriate
	• A process for periodic review (at least on an annual basis) of actual incidents to identify necessary program updates based on the following:
	— Incident patterns and root cause
	— Changes in the internal control environment or external requirements (regulation or legislation)
	• Periodic testing or walkthrough process (at least on an annual basis) and associated program remediation as needed

1.2.8 **Supporting Resources**

Resources are provided by the entity to implement and support its privacy policies.

1.2.9 **Qualifications of Internal Personnel**

The entity establishes qualifications for personnel responsible for protecting the privacy and security of personal information and assigns such responsibilities only to those personnel who meet these qualifications and have received needed training.

1.2.10 **Privacy Awareness and Training**

A privacy awareness program about the entity's privacy policies and related matters, and specific training for selected personnel depending on their roles and responsibilities, are provided.

1.2.11 **Changes in Regulatory and Business Requirements**

For each jurisdiction in which the entity operates, the effect on privacy requirements from changes in the following factors is identified and addressed:
- Legal and regulatory
- Contracts, including service-level agreements
- Industry requirements
- Business operations and processes
- People, roles, and responsibilities
- Technology

Privacy policies and procedures are updated to reflect changes in requirements.

Notice

Ref.	*Notice Principle and Criteria*
2.0	**The entity provides notice about its privacy policies and procedures and identifies the purposes for which personal information is collected, used, retained, and disclosed.**

(continued)

Ref.	Notice Principle and Criteria

2.1   **Policies and Communications**

2.1.0   **Privacy Policies**

The entity's privacy policies address providing notice to individuals.

2.1.1   **Communication to Individuals**

Notice is provided to individuals regarding the following privacy policies:

    a. Purpose for collecting personal information

    b. Choice and consent (See 3.1.1)

    c. Collection (See 4.1.1)

    d. Use, retention, and disposal (See 5.1.1)

    e. Access (See 6.1.1)

    f. Disclosure to third parties (See 7.1.1)

    g. Security for privacy (See 8.1.1)

    h. Quality (See 9.1.1)

    i. Monitoring and enforcement (See 10.1.1)

If personal information is collected from sources other than the individual, such sources are described in the notice.

2.2   **Procedures and Controls**

2.2.1   **Provision of Notice**

Notice is provided to the individual about the entity's privacy policies and procedures (*a*) at or before the time personal information is collected, or as soon as practical thereafter, (*b*) at or before the entity changes its privacy policies and procedures, or as soon as practical thereafter, or (*c*) before personal information is used for new purposes not previously identified.

2.2.2   **Entities and Activities Covered**

An objective description of the entities and activities covered by the privacy policies and procedures is included in the entity's privacy notice.

2.2.3   **Clear and Conspicuous**

The entity's privacy notice is conspicuous and uses clear language.

Choice and Consent

Ref.	Choice and Consent Principle and Criteria
3.0	**The entity describes the choices available to the individual and obtains implicit or explicit consent with respect to the collection, use, and disclosure of personal information.**
3.1	**Policies and Communications**
3.1.0	**Privacy Policies**
	The entity's privacy policies address the choices available to individuals and the consent to be obtained.
3.1.1	**Communication to Individuals**
	Individuals are informed about (a) the choices available to them with respect to the collection, use, and disclosure of personal information, and (b) that implicit or explicit consent is required to collect, use, and disclose personal information, unless a law or regulation specifically requires or allows otherwise.
3.1.2	**Consequences of Denying or Withdrawing Consent**
	When personal information is collected, individuals are informed of the consequences of refusing to provide personal information or of denying or withdrawing consent to use personal information for purposes identified in the notice.
3.2	**Procedures and Controls**
3.2.1	**Implicit or Explicit Consent**
	Implicit or explicit consent is obtained from the individual at or before the time personal information is collected or soon after. The individual's preferences expressed in his or her consent are confirmed and implemented.
3.2.2	**Consent for New Purposes and Uses**
	If information that was previously collected is to be used for purposes not previously identified in the privacy notice, the new purpose is documented, the individual is notified, and implicit or explicit consent is obtained prior to such new use or purpose.
3.2.3	**Explicit Consent for Sensitive Information**
	Explicit consent is obtained directly from the individual when sensitive personal information is collected, used, or disclosed, unless a law or regulation specifically requires otherwise.
3.2.4	**Consent for Online Data Transfers To or From an Individual's Computer or Other Similar Electronic Devices**
	Consent is obtained before personal information is transferred to or from an individual's computer or other similar device.

Collection

Ref.	Collection Principle and Criteria
4.0	**The entity collects personal information only for the purposes identified in the notice.**
4.1	**Policies and Communications**
4.1.0	**Privacy Policies**
	The entity's privacy policies address the collection of personal information.
4.1.1	**Communication to Individuals**
	Individuals are informed that personal information is collected only for the purposes identified in the notice.
4.1.2	**Types of Personal Information Collected and Methods of Collection**
	The types of personal information collected and the methods of collection, including the use of cookies or other tracking techniques, are documented and described in the privacy notice.
4.2	**Procedures and Controls**
4.2.1	**Collection Limited to Identified Purpose**
	The collection of personal information is limited to that necessary for the purposes identified in the notice.
4.2.2	**Collection by Fair and Lawful Means**
	Methods of collecting personal information are reviewed by management before they are implemented to confirm that personal information is obtained (a) fairly, without intimidation or deception, and (b) lawfully, adhering to all relevant rules of law, whether derived from statute or common law, relating to the collection of personal information.
4.2.3	**Collection From Third Parties**
	Management confirms that third parties from whom personal information is collected (that is, sources other than the individual) are reliable sources that collect information fairly and lawfully.
4.2.4	**Information Developed about Individuals**
	Individuals are informed if the entity develops or acquires additional information about them for its use.

Use, Retention, and Disposal

Ref.	Use, Retention, and Disposal Principle and Criteria
5.0	The entity limits the use of personal information to the purposes identified in the notice and for which the individual has provided implicit or explicit consent. The entity retains personal information for only as long as necessary to fulfill the stated purposes or as required by law or regulations and thereafter appropriately disposes of such information.

5.1 Policies and Communications

5.1.0 Privacy Policies

The entity's privacy policies address the use, retention, and disposal of personal information.

5.1.1 Communication to Individuals

Individuals are informed that personal information is (a) used only for the purposes identified in the notice and only if the individual has provided implicit or explicit consent, unless a law or regulation specifically requires otherwise, (b) retained for no longer than necessary to fulfill the stated purposes, or for a period specifically required by law or regulation, and (c) disposed of in a manner that prevents loss, theft, misuse, or unauthorized access.

5.2 Procedures and Controls

5.2.1 Use of Personal Information

Personal information is used only for the purposes identified in the notice and only if the individual has provided implicit or explicit consent, unless a law or regulation specifically requires otherwise.

5.2.2 Retention of Personal Information

Personal information is retained for no longer than necessary to fulfill the stated purposes unless a law or regulation specifically requires otherwise.

5.2.3 Disposal, Destruction and Redaction of Personal Information

Personal information no longer retained is anonymized, disposed of, or destroyed in a manner that prevents loss, theft, misuse, or unauthorized access.

Access

Ref.	Access Principle and Criteria
6.0	The entity provides individuals with access to their personal information for review and update.

(continued)

Ref.	Access Principle and Criteria
6.1	**Policies and Communications**

6.1.0   **Privacy Policies**

The entity's privacy policies address providing individuals with access to their personal information.

6.1.1   **Communication to Individuals**

Individuals are informed about how they may obtain access to their personal information to review, update, and correct that information.

6.2   **Procedures and Controls**

6.2.1   **Access by Individuals to Their Personal Information**

Individuals are able to determine whether the entity maintains personal information about them and, upon request, may obtain access to their personal information.

6.2.2   **Confirmation of an Individual's Identity**

The identity of individuals who request access to their personal information is authenticated before they are given access to that information.

6.2.3   **Understandable Personal Information, Time Frame, and Cost**

Personal information is provided to the individual in an understandable form, in a reasonable timeframe, and at a reasonable cost, if any.

6.2.4   **Denial of Access**

Individuals are informed, in writing, of the reason a request for access to their personal information was denied, the source of the entity's legal right to deny such access, if applicable, and the individual's right, if any, to challenge such denial, as specifically permitted or required by law or regulation.

6.2.5   **Updating or Correcting Personal Information**

Individuals are able to update or correct personal information held by the entity. If practical and economically feasible to do so, the entity provides such updated or corrected information to third parties that previously were provided with the individual's personal information.

6.2.6   **Statement of Disagreement**

Individuals are informed, in writing, about the reason a request for correction of personal information was denied, and how they may appeal.

Disclosure to Third Parties

Ref.	Disclosure to Third Parties Principle and Criteria
7.0	The entity discloses personal information to third parties only for the purposes identified in the notice and with the implicit or explicit consent of the individual.
7.1	**Policies and Communications**
7.1.0	**Privacy Policies**
	The entity's privacy policies address the disclosure of personal information to third parties.
7.1.1	**Communication to Individuals**
	Individuals are informed that personal information is disclosed to third parties only for the purposes identified in the notice and for which the individual has provided implicit or explicit consent unless a law or regulation specifically allows or requires otherwise.
7.1.2	**Communication to Third Parties**
	Privacy policies or other specific instructions or requirements for handling personal information are communicated to third parties to whom personal information is disclosed.
7.2	**Procedures and Controls**
7.2.1	**Disclosure of Personal Information**
	Personal information is disclosed to third parties only for the purposes described in the notice, and for which the individual has provided implicit or explicit consent, unless a law or regulation specifically requires or allows otherwise.
7.2.2	**Protection of Personal Information**
	Personal information is disclosed only to third parties who have agreements with the entity to protect personal information in a manner consistent with the relevant aspects of the entity's privacy policies or other specific instructions or requirements. The entity has procedures in place to evaluate that the third parties have effective controls to meet the terms of the agreement, instructions, or requirements.
7.2.3	**New Purposes and Uses**
	Personal information is disclosed to third parties for new purposes or uses only with the prior implicit or explicit consent of the individual.
7.2.4	**Misuse of Personal Information by a Third Party**
	The entity takes remedial action in response to misuse of personal information by a third party to whom the entity has transferred such information.

Security for Privacy

Ref.	Security for Privacy Principle and Criteria
8.0	**The entity protects personal information against unauthorized access (both physical and logical).**

8.1	**Policies and Communications**

8.1.0   **Privacy Policies**

The entity's privacy policies (including any relevant security policies), address the security of personal information.

8.1.1   **Communication to Individuals**

Individuals are informed that precautions are taken to protect personal information.

8.2   **Procedures and Controls**

8.2.1   **Information Security Program**

A security program has been developed, documented, approved, and implemented that includes administrative, technical, and physical safeguards to protect personal information from loss, misuse, unauthorized access, disclosure, alteration, and destruction. The security program should address, but not be limited to, the following areas[1] insofar as they relate to the security of personal information:

    a. Risk assessment and treatment [1.2.4]

    b. Security policy [8.1.0]

    c. Organization of information security [sections 1, 7, and 10]

    d. Asset management [section 1]

    e. Human resources security [section 1]

    f. Physical and environmental security [8.2.3 and 8.2.4]

    g. Communications and operations management [sections 1, 7, and 10]

    h. Access control [sections 1, 8.2, and 10]

    i. Information systems acquisition, development, and maintenance [1.2.6]

    j. Information security incident management [1.2.7]

    k. Business continuity management [section 8.2]

    l. Compliance [sections 1 and 10]

---

[1] These areas are drawn from ISO/IEC 27002:2005, Information technology—Security techniques—Code of practice for information security management. Permission is granted by the American National Standards Institute (ANSI) on behalf of the International Organization for Standardization (ISO). Copies of ISO/IEC 27002 can be purchased from ANSI in the United States at http://webstore.ansi.org/ and in Canada from the Standards Council of Canada at www.standardsstore.ca/eSpecs/index.jsp. It is not necessary to meet all of the criteria of

Ref.	Security for Privacy Principle and Criteria

8.2.2 **Logical Access Controls**

Logical access to personal information is restricted by procedures that address the following matters:

a. Authorizing and registering internal personnel and individuals

b. Identifying and authenticating internal personnel and individuals

c. Making changes and updating access profiles

d. Granting privileges and permissions for access to IT infrastructure components and personal information

e. Preventing individuals from accessing anything other than their own personal or sensitive information

f. Limiting access to personal information to only authorized internal personnel based upon their assigned roles and responsibilities

g. Distributing output only to authorized internal personnel

h. Restricting logical access to offline storage, backup data, systems, and media

i. Restricting access to system configurations, superuser functionality, master passwords, powerful utilities, and security devices (for example, firewalls)

j. Preventing the introduction of viruses, malicious code, and unauthorized software

8.2.3 **Physical Access Controls**

Physical access is restricted to personal information in any form (including the components of the entity's system(s) that contain or protect personal information).

8.2.4 **Environmental Safeguards**

Personal information, in all forms, is protected against accidental disclosure due to natural disasters and environmental hazards.

8.2.5 **Transmitted Personal Information**

Personal information is protected when transmitted by mail or other physical means. Personal information collected and transmitted over the Internet, over public and other nonsecure networks, and wireless networks is protected by deploying industry standard encryption technology for transferring and receiving personal information.

(continued)

(footnote continued)

ISO/IEC 27002:2005 to satisfy *Generally Accepted Privacy Principles'* criterion 8.2.1. The references associated with each area indicate the most relevant *Generally Accepted Privacy Principles'* criteria for this purpose.

Ref.	Security for Privacy Principle and Criteria
8.2.6	**Personal Information on Portable Media**
	Personal information stored on portable media or devices is protected from unauthorized access.
8.2.7	**Testing Security Safeguards**
	Tests of the effectiveness of the key administrative, technical, and physical safeguards protecting personal information are conducted at least annually.

Quality

Ref.	Quality Principle and Criteria
9.0	**The entity maintains accurate, complete, and relevant personal information for the purposes identified in the notice.**
9.1	**Policies and Communications**
9.1.0	**Privacy Policies**
	The entity's privacy policies address the quality of personal information.
9.1.1	**Communication to Individuals**
	Individuals are informed that they are responsible for providing the entity with accurate and complete personal information, and for contacting the entity if correction of such information is required.
9.2	**Procedures and Controls**
9.2.1	**Accuracy and Completeness of Personal Information**
	Personal information is accurate and complete for the purposes for which it is to be used.
9.2.2	**Relevance of Personal Information**
	Personal information is relevant to the purposes for which it is to be used.

Monitoring and Enforcement

Ref.	Monitoring and Enforcement Principle and Criteria
10.0	**The entity monitors compliance with its privacy policies and procedures and has procedures to address privacy related inquiries, complaints and disputes.**
10.1	**Policies and Communications**

Ref.	Monitoring and Enforcement Principle and Criteria
10.1.0	**Privacy Policies**

The entity's privacy policies address the monitoring and enforcement of privacy policies and procedures.

10.1.1 Communication to Individuals

Individuals are informed about how to contact the entity with inquiries, complaints and disputes.

10.2 Procedures and Controls

10.2.1 Inquiry, Complaint, and Dispute Process

A process is in place to address inquiries, complaints, and disputes.

10.2.2 Dispute Resolution and Recourse

Each complaint is addressed, and the resolution is documented and communicated to the individual.

10.2.3 Compliance Review

Compliance with privacy policies and procedures, commitments and applicable laws, regulations, service-level agreements, and other contracts is reviewed and documented, and the results of such reviews are reported to management. If problems are identified, remediation plans are developed and implemented.

10.2.4 Instances of Noncompliance

Instances of noncompliance with privacy policies and procedures are documented and reported and, if needed, corrective and disciplinary measures are taken on a timely basis.

10.2.5 Ongoing Monitoring

Ongoing procedures are performed for monitoring the effectiveness of controls over personal information, based on a risk assessment [1.2.4], and for taking timely corrective actions where necessary.

Appendix C

Illustrative Management Assertions and Related Service Auditor's Reports on Controls at a Service Organization Relevant to Security, Availability, Processing Integrity, Confidentiality, and Privacy

This appendix presents two examples of management's assertion, each followed by the related service auditor's report. The following table summarizes how these examples differ:

	Example 1	*Example 2*
Principles covered by management's assertion and the service auditor's report	Security, availability, processing integrity, and confidentiality.	Privacy.
Need for complementary user-entity controls at the user entities	Complementary user-entity controls are needed to meet certain applicable trust services criteria. Modifications to the report are shown in boldface italics.	Complementary user-entity controls are not needed to meet certain applicable trust services criteria.
Placement of the description criteria in management's assertion	The description criteria are presented immediately after management's assertion about the fairness of the presentation of the description of the service organization's system.	The description criteria are presented after all of management's assertions.

Example 1: Illustrative Management Assertion on Controls at a Service Organization Relevant to the Security, Availability, Processing Integrity, and Confidentiality Principles

Management of XYZ Service Organization's Assertion
Regarding Its Accurate Claims Processing System Throughout
the Period January 1, 20X1, to December 31, 20X1

We have prepared the attached description titled "Description of XYZ Service Organization's Accurate Claims Processing System Throughout the Period January 1, 20X1, to December 31, 20X1" (the description), based on the criteria in items (a)(i)–(ii) below, which are the criteria for a description of a service organization's system in paragraphs 1.34–.35 of the AICPA Guide *Reporting on Controls at a Service Organization Relevant to Security, Availability, Processing Integrity, Confidentiality, or Privacy (SOC 2^{SM})* (the description criteria). The description is intended to provide users with information about the Accurate Claims Processing System, particularly system controls intended to meet the criteria for the security, availability, processing integrity, and confidentiality principles set forth in TSP section 100, *Trust Services Principles, Criteria, and Illustrations for Security, Availability, Processing Integrity, Confidentiality, and Privacy* (AICPA, *Technical Practice Aids*) (applicable trust services criteria). We confirm, to the best of our knowledge and belief, that

    a. the description fairly presents the [*type or name of*] system throughout the period [*date*] to [*date*], based on the following description criteria:

        i. The description contains the following information:

            (1) The types of services provided

            (2) The components of the system used to provide the services, which are the following:

- *Infrastructure.* The physical and hardware components of a system (facilities, equipment, and networks).

- *Software.* The programs and operating software of a system (systems, applications, and utilities).

- *People.* The personnel involved in the operation and use of a system (developers, operators, users, and managers).

- *Procedures.* The automated and manual procedures involved in the operation of a system.

- *Data.* The information used and supported by a system (transaction streams, files, databases, and tables).

            (3) The boundaries or aspects of the system covered by the description

            (4) How the system captures and addresses significant events and conditions

            (5) The process used to prepare and deliver reports and other information to user entities or other parties

(6) If information is provided to, or received from, subservice organizations or other parties, how such information is provided or received; the role of the subservice organization or other parties; and the procedures performed to determine that such information and its processing, maintenance, and storage are subject to appropriate controls

(7) For each principle being reported on, the applicable trust services criteria and the related controls designed to meet those criteria, including, as applicable, complementary user-entity controls contemplated in the design of the service organization's system

(8) For subservice organizations presented using the carve-out method, the nature of the services provided by the subservice organization; each of the applicable trust services criteria that are intended to be met by controls at the subservice organization, alone or in combination with controls at the service organization, and the types of controls expected to be implemented at carved-out subservice organizations to meet those criteria; and for privacy, the types of activities that the subservice organization would need to perform to comply with our privacy commitments

(9) Any applicable trust services criteria that are not addressed by a control at the service organization or a subservice organization and the reasons therefore

(10) Other aspects of the service organization's control environment, risk assessment process, information and communication systems, and monitoring of controls that are relevant to the services provided and the applicable trust services criteria

(11) Relevant details of changes to the service organization's system during the period covered by the description

ii. The description does not omit or distort information relevant to the service organization's system while acknowledging that the description is prepared to meet the common needs of a broad range of users and may not, therefore, include every aspect of the system that each individual user may consider important to his or her own particular needs.

b. the controls stated in description were suitably designed throughout the specified period to meet the applicable trust services criteria.

c. the controls stated in the description operated effectively throughout the specified period to meet the applicable trust services criteria.

Example 1: Illustrative Service Auditor's Report on Controls at a Service Organization Relevant to Security, Availability, Processing Integrity, and Confidentiality

(Language shown in boldface italics represents modifications that would be made to the service auditor's report if complementary user-entity controls are needed to meet certain applicable trust services criteria.)

Independent Service Auditor's Report

To: XYZ Service Organization

Scope

We have examined the attached description titled "Description of XYZ Service Organization's Accurate Claims Processing System Throughout the Period January 1, 20X1, to December 31, 20X1"[1] (the description) and the suitability of the design and operating effectiveness of controls to meet the criteria for the security, availability, processing integrity, and confidentiality principles set forth in TSP section 100, *Trust Services Principles, Criteria, and Illustrations for Security, Availability, Processing Integrity, Confidentiality, and Privacy* (AICPA, *Technical Practice Aids*) (applicable trust services criteria), throughout the period January 1, 20X1, to December 31, 20X1. *The description indicates that certain applicable trust services criteria specified in the description can be achieved only if complementary user-entity controls contemplated in the design of XYZ Service Organization's controls are suitably designed and operating effectively, along with related controls at the service organization. We have not evaluated the suitability of the design or operating effectiveness of such complementary user-entity controls.*

Service organization's responsibilities

XYZ Service Organization has provided the attached assertion titled "Management of XYZ Service Organization's Assertion Regarding Its Accurate Claims Processing System Throughout the Period January 1, 20X1, to December 31, 20X1,"[2] which is based on the criteria identified in management's assertion. XYZ Service Organization is responsible for (1) preparing the description and assertion; (2) the completeness, accuracy, and method of presentation of both the description and assertion; (3) providing the services covered by the description; (4) specifying the controls that meet the applicable trust services criteria and stating them in the description; and (5) designing, implementing, and documenting the controls to meet the applicable trust services criteria.

Service auditor's responsibilities

Our responsibility is to express an opinion on the fairness of the presentation of the description based on the description criteria set forth in XYZ Service Organization's assertion and on the suitability of the design and operating effectiveness of the controls to meet the applicable trust services criteria, based on our examination. We conducted our examination in accordance with attestation standards established by the American Institute of Certified Public Accountants. Those standards require that we plan and perform our examination to obtain reasonable assurance about whether, in all material respects,

---

[1] The title of the description of the service organization's system in the service auditor's report is the same as the title used by management of the service organization in its description of the service organization's system.

[2] The title of the assertion in the service auditor's report is the same as the title used by management of the service organization in its assertion.

(1) the description is fairly presented based on the description criteria, and (2) the controls were suitably designed and operating effectively to meet the applicable trust services criteria throughout the period January 1, 20X1, to December 31, 20X1.

Our examination involved performing procedures to obtain evidence about the fairness of the presentation of the description based on the description criteria and the suitability of the design and operating effectiveness of those controls to meet the applicable trust services criteria. Our procedures included assessing the risks that the description is not fairly presented and that the controls were not suitably designed or operating effectively to meet the applicable trust services criteria. Our procedures also included testing the operating effectiveness of those controls that we consider necessary to provide reasonable assurance that the applicable trust services criteria were met. Our examination also included evaluating the overall presentation of the description. We believe that the evidence we obtained is sufficient and appropriate to provide a reasonable basis for our opinion.

Inherent limitations

Because of their nature and inherent limitations, controls at a service organization may not always operate effectively to meet the applicable trust services criteria. Also, the projection to the future of any evaluation of the fairness of the presentation of the description or conclusions about the suitability of the design or operating effectiveness of the controls to meet the applicable trust services criteria is subject to the risks that the system may change or that controls at a service organization may become inadequate or fail.

Opinion

In our opinion, in all material respects, based on the description criteria identified in XYZ Service Organization's assertion and the applicable trust services criteria

     a. the description fairly presents the system that was designed and implemented throughout the period January 1, 20X1, to December 31, 20X1.

     b. the controls stated in the description were suitably designed to provide reasonable assurance that the applicable trust services criteria would be met if the controls operated effectively throughout the period January 1, 20X1 to December 31, 20X1, *and user entities applied the complementary user-entity controls contemplated in the design of XYZ Service Organization's controls throughout the period January 1, 20X1, to December 31, 20X1.*

     c. the controls tested, which *together with the complementary user-entity controls referred to in the scope paragraph of this report, if operating effectively,* were those necessary to provide reasonable assurance that the applicable trust services criteria were met, operated effectively throughout the period January 1, 20X1, to December 31, 20X1.

Description of tests of controls

The specific controls we tested and the nature, timing, and results of our tests are presented in the section of our report titled "Description of Test of Controls and Results Thereof."

Restricted use

This report and the description of tests of controls and results thereof are intended solely for the information and use of XYZ Service Organization; user entities of XYZ Service Organization's Accurate Claims Processing System during some or all of the period January 1, 20X1, to December 31, 20X1; and prospective user entities, independent auditors and practitioners providing services to such user entities, and regulators who have sufficient knowledge and understanding of the following:

- The nature of the service provided by the service organization
- How the service organization's system interacts with user entities, subservice organizations, or other parties
- Internal control and its limitations
- Complementary user-entity controls and how they interact with related controls at the service organization to meet the applicable trust services criteria
- The applicable trust services criteria
- The risks that may threaten the achievement of the applicable trust services criteria and how controls address those risks

This report is not intended to be and should not be used by anyone other than these specified parties.

[Service auditor's signature]

[Date of the service auditor's report]

[Service auditor's city and state]

Example 2: Illustrative Management Assertion Regarding a Description of a Service Organization's System, the Suitability of the Design and Operating Effectiveness of Its Controls Relevant to the Privacy Principle, and Its Compliance With Commitments in Its Statement of Privacy Practices

Management of XYZ Service Organization's Assertion

We have prepared the attached description titled [*title of the description*][3] (the description) of XYZ Service Organization's [*type or name of*] system and our statement of privacy practices[4] related to XYZ Service Organization's [*type or name of*] service. The description is intended to provide users with information about our system, particularly system controls intended to meet the criteria for the privacy principle set forth in TSP section 100, *Trust Services Principles, Criteria, and Illustrationsfor Security, Availability, Processing Integrity, Confidentiality, and Privacy* (AICPA, *Technical Practice Aids*)[5] (applicable trust services criteria). We confirm, to the best of our knowledge and belief, that

- the description fairly presents the [*type or name of*] system throughout the period [*date*] to [*date*]. The criteria for the description are identified below under the heading "Description Criteria."

- the controls stated in the description were suitably designed and operating effectively throughout the period [*date*] to [*date*] to meet the applicable trust services criteria.

- we complied with the commitments in our statement of privacy practices, in all material respects, throughout the period [*date*] to [*date*].

Description Criteria

In preparing our description and making our assertion regarding the fairness of the presentation of the description, we used the criteria in items (a)–(b) below, which are the criteria in paragraphs 1.34–.35 of the AICPA Guide *Reporting on Controls at a Service Organization Relevant to Security, Availability, Processing Integrity, Confidentiality, or Privacy (SOC 2^{SM})*:

  a. The description contains the following information:

    i. The types of services provided.

    ii. The components of the system used to provide the services, which are the following:

---

[3] Insert the title of the description of the service organization's system used by management of the service organization in its description (for example, "Description of XYZ Service Organization's Claims-Processing System Throughout the Period January 1, 20X1, to December 31, 20X1, Including its Statement of Privacy Practices").

[4] In many cases, the user entities provide a privacy notice to the individuals about whom information is collected. In such cases, the service organization would prepare a statement of privacy practices for use by the user entities to describe its practices and commitments to user entities related to the matters typically included in a privacy notice to individuals. If the service organization is responsible for providing the privacy notice directly to individuals, such notice may be a suitable substitute for a statement of privacy practices.

[5] The criteria for privacy are also set forth in *Generally Accepted Privacy Principles* issued by the AICPA and the Canadian Institute of Chartered Accountants, which could be referenced here instead of TSP section 100, *Trust Services Principles, Criteria, and Illustrations for Security, Availability, Processing Integrity, Confidentiality, and Privacy* (AICPA, *Technical Practice Aids*).

(1) *Infrastructure* . The physical and hardware components of a system (facilities, equipment, and networks).

(2) *Software*. The programs and operating software of a system (systems, applications, and utilities).

(3) *People*. The personnel involved in the operation and use of a system (developers, operators, users, and managers).

(4) *Procedures*. The automated and manual procedures involved in the operation of a system.

(5) *Data*. The information used and supported by a system (transaction streams, files, databases, and tables).

iii. The boundaries or aspects of the system covered by the description. As it relates to the privacy of information, a system includes, at a minimum, all system components directly or indirectly related to the collection, use, retention, disclosure, and disposal or anonymization of personal information throughout its personal information life cycle.

iv. The types of personal information collected from individuals or obtained from user entities or other parties and how such information is collected and, if collected by user entities, how it is obtained by the service organization.

v. The process for (1) identifying specific requirements in agreements with user entities and laws and regulations applicable to personal information and (2) implementing controls and practices to meet those requirements.

vi. If the service organization provides the privacy notice to individuals about whom personal information is collected, used, retained, disclosed, and disposed of or anonymized, the privacy notice prepared in conformity with the relevant criteria for a privacy notice set forth in TSP section 100.

vii. If the user entities, rather than the service organization, are responsible for providing the privacy notice to individuals, a statement regarding how the privacy notice is communicated to individuals, that the user entities are responsible for communicating such notice to the individuals, and that the service organization is responsible for communicating its privacy practices to the user entities in its statement of privacy practices, which includes the following information:

(1) A summary of the significant privacy and related security requirements common to most agreements between the service organization and its user entities and any requirements in a user-entity agreement that the service organization meets for all or most user entities

(2) A summary of the significant privacy and related security requirements mandated by law, regulation, an industry, or a market that the service organization meets for all or most user entities that are not included in user-entity agreements

(3) The purposes, uses, and disclosures of personal information as permitted by user-entity agreements and beyond those permitted by such agreements but not prohibited by such agreements and the service organization's commitments regarding the purpose, use, and disclosure of personal information that are prohibited by such agreements

(4) A statement that the information will be retained for a period no longer than necessary to fulfill the stated purposes or contractual requirements, or for the period required by law or regulation, as applicable, or a statement describing other retention practices

(5) A statement that the information will be disposed of in a manner that prevents loss, theft, misuse, or unauthorized access to the information

(6) If applicable, how the service organization supports any process permitted by user entities for individuals to obtain access to their information to review, update, or correct it

(7) If applicable, a description of the process to determine that personal information is accurate and complete and how the service organization implements correction processes permitted by user entities

(8) If applicable, how inquiries, complaints, and disputes from individuals (whether directly from the individual or indirectly through user entities) regarding their personal information are handled by the service organization

(9) A statement regarding the existence of a written security program and what industry or other standards it is based on

(10) Other relevant information related to privacy practices deemed appropriate for user entities by the service organization

viii. If the user entities, rather than the service organization, are responsible for providing the privacy notice to individuals, the service organization's statement of privacy practices.

ix. How the system captures and addresses significant events and conditions.

x. The process used to deliver services, reports, and other information to user entities or other parties.

xi. If information is provided to, or received from, subservice organizations or third parties

(1) how such information is provided or received and the role of the subservice organizations or other parties.

(2) the procedures performed to determine that such information is protected in conformity with the service organization's statement of privacy practices.

   xii. For each principle being reported on, the applicable trust services criteria and the related controls designed to meet those criteria, including, as applicable, complementary user-entity controls contemplated in the design of the service organization's system.

   xiii. For subservice organizations presented using the carve-out method

      (1) the nature of the services provided by the subservice organization.

      (2) any aspects of the personal information life cycle for which responsibility has been delegated to the subservice organization, if applicable.

      (3) each of the applicable trust services criteria that are intended to be met by controls at the subservice organization, alone or in combination with controls at the service organization, and the types of controls expected to be implemented at carved-out subservice organizations to meet those criteria.

      (4) the types of activities that the subservice organization would need to perform to comply with the service organization's privacy commitments.

   xiv. Any applicable trust services criteria that are not addressed by a control at the service organization or subservice organization and the reasons therefore.

   xv. Other aspects of the service organization's control environment, risk assessment process, information and communication systems, and monitoring of controls that are relevant to the services provided, the personal information life cycle, and the applicable trust services criteria.

   xvi. Relevant details of changes to the service organization's system during the period covered by the description.

  b. The description does not omit or distort information relevant to the service organization's system and personal information life cycle while acknowledging that the description is presented to meet the common needs of a broad range of users and may not, therefore, include every aspect of the system and personal information life cycle that each individual user may consider important to his or her own particular needs.

Example 2: Illustrative Service Auditor's Report on a Description of a Service Organization's System, the Suitability of the Design and Operating Effectiveness of Its Controls Relevant to the Privacy Principle, and Its Compliance With Commitments in Its Statement of Privacy Practices

Independent Service Auditor's Report

To: XYZ Service Organization

Scope

We have examined (1) the accompanying description titled [*title of the description*];[6] (2) the suitability of the design and operating effectiveness of controls to meet the criteria for the privacy principle set forth in TSP section 100, *Trust Services Principles, Criteria, and Illustrations for Security, Availability, Processing Integrity, Confidentiality, and Privacy* (AICPA, *Technical Practice Aids*) (applicable trust services criteria); and (3) XYZ Service Organization's compliance with the commitments in its statement of privacy practices throughout the period January 1, 20X1, to December 31, 20X1. Our examination does not provide a legal determination on XYZ Service Organization's compliance with laws and regulations related to privacy or its compliance with the commitments in its statement of privacy practices throughout the period January 1, 20X1, to December 31, 20X1.

Service organization's responsibilities

XYZ Service Organization has provided the accompanying assertion titled [*title of assertion*].[7] XYZ Service Organization is responsible for (1) preparing the description and assertion; (2) the completeness, accuracy, and method of presentation of both the description and assertion; (3) providing the services covered by the description; (4) specifying the controls that meet the applicable trust services criteria and stating them in the description; (5) designing, implementing, maintaining, and documenting controls to meet the applicable trust services criteria; and (6) complying with the commitments in its statement of privacy practices that is included in the description.

Service auditor's responsibilities

Our responsibility is to express an opinion on (1) the fairness of the presentation of the description based on the description criteria identified in management's assertion; (2) the suitability of the design and operating effectiveness of the controls to meet the applicable trust services criteria; and (3) XYZ Service Organization's compliance with the commitments in its statement of privacy practices, based on our examination. We conducted our examination in accordance with attestation standards established by the American Institute of Certified Public Accountants. Those standards require that we plan and perform our examination to obtain reasonable assurance about whether, in all

---

[6] Insert the title of the description used by management of the service organization (for example, "Description of XYZ Service Organization's Claims Processing System Throughout the Period January 1, 20X1, to December 31, 20X1, Including Its Statement of Privacy Practices").

[7] Insert the title of the assertion used by management of the service organization (for example, "Management of XYZ Service Organization's Assertion Regarding Its Description of the Claims-Processing System, the Suitability of the Design and Operating Effectiveness of Controls, and Compliance With the Commitments in Its Statement of Privacy Practices Throughout the Period January 1, 20X1, to December 31, 20X1").

material respects, (1) the description is fairly presented based on the description criteria, (2) the controls were suitably designed and operating effectively to meet the applicable trust services criteria throughout the period from [date] to [date], and (3) XYZ Service Organization complied with the commitments in its statement of privacy practices throughout the period from [date] to [date].

Our examination involved performing procedures to obtain evidence about the fairness of the presentation of the description based on the description criteria, the suitability of the design and operating effectiveness of the controls to meet the applicable trust services criteria, and XYZ Service Organization's compliance with the commitments in its statement of privacy practices. Our procedures included assessing the risks that the description is not fairly presented, that the controls were not suitably designed or operating effectively to meet the applicable trust services criteria, and that XYZ Service Organization did not comply with the commitments in its statement of privacy practices. Our procedures also included testing the operating effectiveness of those controls that we consider necessary to provide reasonable assurance that the applicable trust services criteria were met and testing XYZ Service Organization's compliance with the commitments in its statement of privacy practices. Our examination also included evaluating the overall presentation of the description. We believe that the evidence we obtained is sufficient and appropriate to provide a reasonable basis for our opinion.

Inherent limitations

Because of their nature and inherent limitations, controls at a service organization may not always protect personal information against unauthorized access or use nor do they ensure compliance with applicable laws and regulations. For example, fraud or unauthorized access to personal information or unauthorized use or disclosure of personal information by persons authorized to access it may not be prevented or detected, or service organization personnel may not always comply with the commitments in the statement of privacy practices. Also, the projection of any conclusions, based on our findings, to future periods is subject to the risk that any changes or future events may alter the validity of such conclusions.

Opinion

In our opinion, in all material respects, based on the description criteria identified in XYZ Service Organization's assertion and the applicable trust services criteria

> a. the description fairly presents XYZ Service Organization's [type or name of] system and related privacy practices that were designed and implemented throughout the period [date] to [date].
>
> b. the controls stated in the description were suitably designed to provide reasonable assurance that the applicable trust services criteria would be met if the controls operated effectively throughout the period [date] to [date].
>
> c. the controls we tested, which were those necessary to provide reasonable assurance that the applicable trust services criteria were met, operated effectively throughout the period [date] to [date].
>
> d. XYZ Service Organization complied with the commitments in its statement of privacy practices throughout the period [date] to [date].

Description of tests of controls

The specific controls and privacy commitments tested and the nature, timing, and results of those tests are listed on pages [*yy–zz*].

Restricted use

This report and the description of tests of controls, tests of privacy commitments, and results thereof in section X of this report are intended solely for the information and use of XYZ Service Organization; user entities of XYZ Service Organization's [type or name of] system during some or all of the period [date] to [date]; and those prospective user entities, independent auditors and practitioners providing services to such user entities, and regulators who have sufficient knowledge and understanding of the following:

- The nature of the service provided by the service organization
- How the service organization's system interacts with user entities, subservice organizations, or other parties
- Internal control and its limitations
- Complementary user-entity controls and how they interact with related controls at the service organization to meet the applicable trust services criteria
- The applicable trust services criteria
- The risks that may threaten the achievement of the applicable trust services criteria and how controls address those risks

This report is not intended to be and should not be used by anyone other than these specified parties.

[*Service auditor's signature*]

[*Date of the service auditor's report*]

[*Service auditor's city and state*]

Appendix D

Illustrative Type 2 Service Organization Controls Report

Although the AICPA Guide *Reporting on Controls at a Service Organization Relevant to Security, Availability, Processing Integrity, Confidentiality, or Privacy (SOC 2^{SM})* specifies the components of a service organization controls (SOC) 2 report and the information to be included in each component, it is not specific about the format for these reports. Service organizations and service auditors may organize and present the required information in a variety of formats. The format of the illustrative type 2 SOC 2^{SM} report presented in this appendix is not meant to be prescriptive but rather illustrative. The illustrative report contains all of the components of a type 2 SOC 2 report; however, for brevity, it does not include everything that might be described in a type 2 SOC 2 report. Ellipses (...) or notes to readers indicate places where detail has been omitted.

The trust services principle(s) being reported on, the controls specified by the service organization, and the tests performed by the service auditor are presented for illustrative purposes only. They are not intended to represent the principles that would be addressed in every type 2 SOC 2 engagement or the controls, or tests of controls, that would be appropriate for all service organizations. The trust services principles to be reported on, the controls a service organization would include in its description, and the tests of controls a service auditor would perform for a specific type 2 SOC 2 engagement will vary based on the specific facts and circumstances of the engagement. Accordingly, it is expected that actual type 2 SOC 2 reports will address different principles and include different controls and tests of controls that are tailored to the service organization that is the subject of the engagement.

Report on Example Service Organization's Description of Its Transportation Management System and on the Suitability of the Design and Operating Effectiveness of Its Controls Relevant to Security Throughout the Period January 1, 20X1, to December 31, 20X1

CONTENTS

Section 1 — Management of Example Service Organization's Assertion Regarding Its Transportation Management System Throughout the Period January 1, 20X1, to December 31, 20X1

We have prepared the description in section 3 titled "Example Service Organization's Description of its Transportation Management System Throughout the Period January 1, 20X1, to December 31, 20X1" (description), based on the criteria for a description of a service organization's system identified in paragraphs 1.34–.35 of AICPA Guide *Reporting on Controls at a Service Organization Relevant to Security, Availability, Processing Integrity, Confidentiality, or Privacy (SOC 2^{SM})* (description criteria). The description is intended to provide users with information about the transportation management system, particularly system controls intended to meet the criteria for the security principle set forth in TSP section 100, *Trust Services Principles, Criteria, and Illustrations for Security, Availability, Processing Integrity, Confidentiality, and Privacy* (AICPA, *Technical Practice Aids*). We confirm, to the best of our knowledge and belief, that

a. the description fairly presents the transportation management system throughout the period January 1, 20X1, to December 31, 20X1, based on the following description criteria:

 i. The description contains the following information:

 (1) The types of services provided.

 (2) The components of the system used to provide the services, which are the following:

 (a) *Infrastructure.* The physical and hardware components of a system (facilities, equipment, and networks).

 (b) *Software.* The programs and operating software of a system (systems, applications, and utilities).

 (c) *People.* The personnel involved in the operation and use of a system (developers, operators, users, and managers).

 (d) *Procedures.* The automated and manual procedures involved in the operation of a system.

 (e) *Data.* The information used and supported by a system (transaction streams, files, databases, and tables).

 (3) The boundaries or aspects of the system covered by the description.

 (4) How the system captures and addresses significant events and conditions.

 (5) The process used to prepare and deliver reports and other information to user entities or other parties.

 (6) If information is provided to, or received from, subservice organizations or other parties, (a) how such information is provided or received and the role of the subservice organization or other parties and (b) the procedures

performed to determine that such information and its processing, maintenance, and storage are subject to appropriate controls.[1]

(7) For each principle being reported on, the applicable trust services criteria and the related controls designed to meet those criteria, including, as applicable, (a) complementary user-entity controls contemplated in the design of the service organization's system and (b) when the inclusive method is used to present a subservice organization, controls at the subservice organization.[2]

(8) For subservice organizations presented using the carve-out method, the nature of the services provided by the subservice organization; each of the applicable trust services criteria that are intended to be met by controls at the subservice organization, alone or in combination with controls at the service organization, and the types of controls expected to be implemented at carved-out subservice organizations to meet those criteria; and for privacy, the types of activities that the subservice organization would need to perform to comply with our privacy commitments.[3]

(9) Any applicable trust services criteria that are not addressed by a control at the service organization and the reasons therefore.

(10) Other aspects of the service organization's control environment, risk assessment process, information and communication systems, and monitoring of controls that are relevant to the services provided and the applicable trust services criteria.

(11) Relevant details of changes to the service organization's system during the period covered by the description.

ii. The description does not omit or distort information relevant to the service organization's system while acknowledging that the description is prepared to meet the common needs of a broad range of users and may not, therefore, include every aspect of the system that each individual user may consider important to his or her own particular needs.

---

[1] Certain description criteria may not be pertinent to a particular service organization or system, for example, a service organization may not use any subservice organizations or other parties to operate its system. Because the criteria in paragraphs 1.34–.35 of this guide may not be readily available to report users, management of a service organization should include in its assertion all of the description criteria in paragraphs 1.34–.35 of this guide. For description criteria that are not pertinent to a particular service organization or system, report users generally find it useful if management presents all of the description criteria and indicates which criteria are not pertinent to the service organization and the reasons therefore. Management may do so either in its system description or in a note to the specific description criteria. The following is illustrative language for a note to criteria that are not pertinent to the service organization or its system:

Example Service Organization does not use subservice organizations or other parties to operate its transportation management system. Accordingly, our description does not address the criteria in items (a)(i)(6) and (a)(i)(8).

[2] See footnote 1.

[3] See footnote 1.

b. the controls stated in the description were suitably designed throughout the period January 1, 20X1, to December 31, 20X1, to meet the applicable trust services criteria.

c. the controls stated in the description operated effectively throughout the period January 1, 20X1, to December 31, 20X1, to meet the applicable trust services criteria.

Section 2 — Independent Service Auditor's Report

To Management of Example Service Organization

Scope

We have examined the description in section 3 titled "Example Service Organization's Description of its Transportation Management System Throughout the Period January 1, 20X1, to December 31, 20X1" (description) and the suitability of the design and operating effectiveness of controls to meet the criteria for the security principle set forth in TSP section 100, *Trust Services Principles, Criteria, and Illustrations for Security, Availability, Processing Integrity, Confidentiality, and Privacy* (AICPA, *Technical Practice Aids*) (applicable trust services criteria), throughout the period January 1, 20X1, to December 31, 20X1. The description indicates that certain applicable trust services criteria specified in the description can be achieved only if complementary user entity controls contemplated in the design of Example Service Organization's controls are suitably designed and operating effectively, along with related controls at Example Service Organization. We have not evaluated the suitability of the design or operating effectiveness of such complementary user entity controls.

Service organization's responsibilities

In section 1, Example Service Organization has provided its assertion titled "Management of Example Service Organization's Assertion Regarding its Transportation Management System Throughout the Period January 1, 20X1, to December 31, 20X1," which is based on the criteria identified in management's assertion. Example Service Organization is responsible for (1) preparing the description and the assertion; (2) the completeness, accuracy, and method of presentation of both the description and assertion; (3) providing the services covered by the description; (4) specifying the controls that meet the applicable trust services criteria and stating them in the description; and (5) designing, implementing, and documenting the controls to meet the applicable trust services criteria.

Service auditor's responsibilities

Our responsibility is to express an opinion on the

- fairness of the presentation of the description based on the description criteria set forth in Example Service Organization's assertion.
- suitability of the design and operating effectiveness of the controls to meet the applicable trust services criteria, based on our examination.

We conducted our examination in accordance with attestation standards established by the American Institute of Certified Public Accountants. Those standards require that we plan and perform our examination to obtain reasonable assurance about whether, in all material respects, (1) the description is fairly presented based on the description criteria, and (2) the controls were suitably designed and operating effectively to meet the applicable trust services criteria throughout the period January 1, 20X1, to December 31, 20X1.

Our examination involved performing procedures to obtain evidence about the fairness of the presentation of the description based on the description criteria and the suitability of the design and operating effectiveness of those controls to meet the applicable trust services criteria. Our procedures included assessing the risks that the description is not fairly presented and that the controls were not suitably designed or operating effectively to meet the applicable trust services criteria. Our procedures also included testing the operating effectiveness of those controls that we consider necessary to provide reasonable assurance that the applicable trust services criteria were met. Our examination also included evaluating the overall presentation of the description. We believe that the evidence we obtained is sufficient and appropriate to provide a reasonable basis for our opinion.

Inherent limitations

Because of their nature and inherent limitations, controls at a service organization may not always operate effectively to meet the applicable trust services criteria. Also, the projection to the future of any evaluation of the fairness of the presentation of the description or conclusions about the suitability of the design or operating effectiveness of the controls to meet the applicable trust services criteria is subject to risks that the system may change or that controls at a service organization may become inadequate or fail.

Opinion

In our opinion, in all material respects, based on the description criteria identified in Example Service Organization's assertion and the applicable trust services criteria

a. the description fairly presents the system that was designed and implemented throughout the period January 1, 20X1, to December 31, 20X1.

b. the controls stated in the description were suitably designed to provide reasonable assurance that the applicable trust services criteria would be met if the controls operated effectively throughout the period January 1, 20X1, to December 31, 20X1, and user entities applied the complementary user entity controls contemplated in the design of Example Service Organization's controls throughout the period January 1, 20X1, to December 31, 20X1.

c. the controls tested, which together with the complementary user-entity controls referred to in the scope paragraph in this section, if operating effectively, were those necessary to provide reasonable assurance that the applicable trust services criteria were met, operated effectively throughout the period January 1, 20X1, to December 31, 20X1.

Description of tests of controls

The specific controls we tested, the tests we performed, and the results of our tests are presented in section 4, "Trust Services Security Principle, Criteria, Related Controls, and Tests of Controls," of this report in columns 2, 3, and 4, respectively.

The information in section 5 titled "Other Information Provided by Example Service Organization That Is Not Covered by the Service Auditor's Report" describes the service organization's future plans for new systems. It is presented by the management of Example Service Organization to provide additional information and is not a part of the service organization's description of its transportation management system made available to user entities during the period from January 1, 20X1, to December 31, 20X1. Information about Example Service Organization's future plans for new systems has not been subjected to the procedures applied in the examination of the description of the transportation management system and the suitability of the design and operating effectiveness of controls to meet the related criteria stated in the description of the transportation management system.

Restricted use

This report and the description of tests of controls and results thereof are intended solely for the information and use of Example Service Organization; user entities of Example Service Organization's transportation management system during some or all of the period January 1, 20X1, to December 31, 20X1; and prospective user entities, independent auditors and practitioners providing services to such user entities, and regulators who have sufficient knowledge and understanding of the following:

- The nature of the service provided by the service organization
- How the service organization's system interacts with user entities or other parties
- Internal control and its limitations
- Complementary user-entity controls and how they interact with related controls at the service organization to meet the applicable trust services criteria
- The applicable trust services criteria
- The risks that may threaten the achievement of the applicable trust services criteria and how controls address those risks

This report is not intended to be and should not be used by anyone other than these specified parties.

[*Service auditor's signature*]

[*Date of the service auditor's report*]

[*Service auditor's city and state*]

Section 3 — Example Service Organization's Description of its Transportation Management System Throughout the Period January 1, 20X1, to December 31, 20X1

> *Note to Readers:* The following system description is for illustrative purposes only and is not meant to be prescriptive. For brevity, the illustration does not include everything that might be described in management's description of the service organization's system. Ellipses (...) or notes to readers indicate places where detail has been omitted from the illustration.

System Overview

Background

Example Service Organization provides medical transportation (MT) throughout the United States. The company was founded in 19XX to provide MT services to Medicaid recipients.

Example Service Organization's core application, XYZ Transportation Management System (XYZ), is a multiuser, transaction-based application suite that enables the processing and delivery of transportation and logistics services. XYZ enables processing of the following tasks related to MT trips:

- Capturing data for transportation providers, governments and managed care providers (user entities), treating facilities, and riders
- Determining rider eligibility
- Providing gate keeping and ride authorization
- Managing complaints and verifying compliance with transportation agreements
- Managing transportation providers
- Reconciling billing to competed rides
- Providing operational, management, and ad hoc reports
- Providing data reporting in a variety of formats

Trips are tracked through the order cycle, from initial ride assignment to completion or reassignment of the ride, and by payments. Transportation providers send Example Service Organization daily trip information including information about trips completed or cancelled (or no-shows) and weekly driver logs, which are entered into XYZ. System-generated reports provide supporting documentation for trips, including date, transportation provider, rider, and actual trip via a unique job number.

Information is shared with user entities by telephone, fax, secure electronic exchange (FTP [file transfer protocol], e-mail, and EDI [electronic data interchange]), and secured websites.

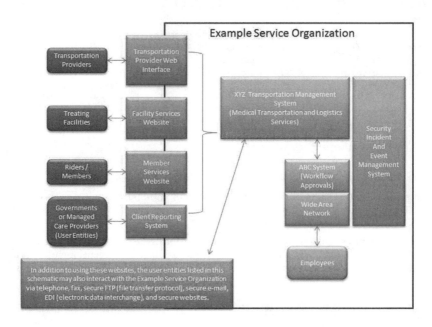

Infrastructure

XYZ runs on Microsoft Windows file servers using a wide area network.

Employees access the application either through their desktop on company-supplied computers or through a Citrix Access Gateway. Data communications between offices are encrypted with Cisco virtual private networking (VPN) technology using Advanced Encryption Standard 256-bit encryption to protect data and intra-company communications.

XYZ uses the IBM DB2 relational database management system. These database servers and file servers are housed in Example Service Organization's secured network operations centers (NOCs).

Software

XYZ is a Microsoft Windows client-server application developed and maintained by Example Service Organization's in-house software engineering group. The software engineering group enhances and maintains XYZ to provide service for the company's transportation providers, governments and managed care providers (user entities), treating facilities, and riders. Example Service Organization's software is not sold on the open market.

XYZ tracks information in real-time. The information is immediately stored in the database and is accessible for daily operations, service authorization, trip scheduling, provider reimbursement, agency monitoring, and report generation. The information can be retrieved, reviewed, and reported as needed to create the history of approvals and denials for any rider. Information can be retrieved by rider identification number, rider name, trip date, facility attended, and transportation provider.

External websites are supplied to supplement Example Service Organization's ability to communicate and exchange information with transportation providers, governments and managed care providers (user entities), treating facilities, and riders. Each website targets a specific audience and is designed to address their business needs. These include a site for the transportation providers, governments and managed care providers, treating facilities, and riders.

The Example Service Organization transportation provider Web interface is a multiuser, Web-based application that helps to manage the flow of information between Example Service Organization and the transportation providers. This website allows transportation providers to enter and retrieve certain information about trips they were assigned by Example Service Organization. It also provides some specific performance reports to help them manage their work with Example Service Organization. To access the site, transportation providers must sign up for the site and fill out certain EDI forms.

The Example Service Organization facility services website supports transportation requests from treating facilities on behalf of their clients. The purpose of the site is to provide a means to request trips and to manage trip requests online without the need to call an Example Service Organization call center. The facility services website allows a treating facility to enter a single trip or standing order request for review and approval by an Example Service Organization facility representative, look up and view trip requests, modify or update pending requests, and withdraw pending requests.

The Example Service Organization member services website is similar to the facility services website except its focus is on the riders. After a rider has successfully logged in, he or she is able to request new trip reservations, view pending requests and processed reservations, edit pending requests, withdraw pending requests, and cancel existing reservations. Requests are placed in a request queue within the XYZ database for review by call center personnel through the XYZ.

The Example Service Organization client reporting interface is provided as a service to Example Service Organization's governments or managed care providers (user entities). This interface allows them to monitor basic statistics of their business and resolve simple questions and complaints. Summary reports of trip volume, complaints, and utilization are available as well as detailed reports for single trips, single complaints, and rider eligibility.

People

Example Service Organization has a staff of approximately 500 employees organized in the following functional areas:

- *Corporate.* Executives, senior operations staff, and company administrative support staff, such as legal, training, contracting, accounting, finance, human resources, and transportation provider relations. These individuals use XYZ primarily as a tool to measure performance at an overall corporate level. This includes reporting done for internal metrics as well as for Example Service Organization's user entities.

- *Operations.* Staff that administers the scheduling and administration of transportation providers and riders. They provide the direct day-to-day services such as transportation reservation intake, trip distribution to transportation providers, quality assurance monitoring, medical facility support, service claims adjudication, transportation network support, and reporting.

— Customer service representatives take phone calls directly from riders to arrange transportation. These requests are entered into XYZ and initiate the lifecycle of a trip.

— Transportation coordinators use XYZ to assign trips to transportation providers. They also manage rerouting and dispensing work from XYZ to the transportation providers on daily trip lists via fax. Transportation managers maintain the transportation provider network database, including updates for training, violations, screenings, and other compliance measures.

— Quality assurance (or utilization review) employees use reports generated by XYZ to select samples of trips that are tested for contractual compliance and to monitor for fraud and abuse. They also take complaints from riders, facilities, and transportation providers and work them to resolution, using tools within XYZ.

— The facility staff manages the facility database for XYZ. They also maintain the transportation standing orders within the system and take single trip requests from facilities only.

— The claims staff receives requests for payment and adjudicates these claims in the software. This includes invoice management, trip verification, and billing support.

— A reports manager typically uses XYZ to produce contract-level specific reports for Example Service Organization's user entities.

- *IT.* Help desk, IT infrastructure, IT networking, IT system administration, software systems development and application support, information security, and IT operations personnel manage electronic interfaces and business implementation support and telecom.

— The help desk group provides technical assistance to XYZ users.

— The infrastructure, networking, and systems administration staff typically has no direct use of XYZ. Rather, it supports the Example Service Organization IT infrastructure relied upon by the software. A systems administrator will deploy the releases of XYZ and other software into the production environment.

— The software development staff develops and maintains the custom software for Example Service Organization. This includes XYZ, supporting utilities, and the external websites that interact with the XYZ. The staff includes software developers, database administration, software quality assurance, and technical writers.

— The information security staff supports XYZ indirectly by monitoring internal and external security threats and maintaining current antivirus software.

— The information security staff maintain the inventory of IT assets.

— IT operations manages the user interfaces for XYZ. This includes processing user entity supplied membership and eligibility files, producing encounter claims files, and other user oriented data (capitation files, error reports, remittance advice, and so on).

— Telecom personnel maintain the voice communications environment, provide user support to Example Service Organization, and resolve communication problems. This group does not directly use XYZ, but it provides infrastructure support as well as disaster recovery assistance.

Procedures

Management has developed and communicated to transportation providers, governments and managed care providers, treating facilities, and riders' procedures to restrict logical access to XYZ. Changes to these procedures are performed annually and authorized by senior management. These procedures cover the following key security lifecycle areas:

- Data classification (data at rest, in motion and output)
- Categorization of information
- Assessment of the business impact resulting from proposed security approaches
- Selection, documentation, and implementation of security controls
- Performance of annual management self-assessments to assess security controls
- Authorization, changes to, and termination of information system access
- Monitoring security controls
- Management of access and roles
- Maintenance and support of the security system and necessary back-ups and offline storage
- Incident response
- Maintenance of restricted access to system configurations, superuser functionality, master passwords, powerful utilities, and security devices (for example, firewalls)
- …

Data

Data as defined by XYZ constitutes the following:

- Master transportation file data
- Transaction data
- Electronic interface files
- Output reports
- Input reports
- System files
- Error logs

Transaction processing is initiated by the receipt of a trip or standing order request. This request typically comes directly from a rider or treating facility by telephone or via the websites, or it may arrive by fax from a treating facility. After the trip is completed, the transportation providers sends Example Service Organization paper documents with daily trip information, including information about completed trips, cancellations or no-shows, and weekly driver logs, all of which is entered into the system's verification module; a portion of this trip completion information may be entered on the Example Service Organization transportation provider Web interface.

Output reports are available in electronic PDF, comma-delimited value file exports, or electronically from the various websites. The availability of these reports is limited by job function. Reports delivered externally will only be sent using a secure method—encrypted e-mail, secure FTP, or secure websites—to transportation providers, treating facilities, and governments or managed care providers using Example Service Organization developed websites or over connections secured by trusted security certificates.

Relevant Aspects of the Control Environment, Risk Assessment Process, Information and Communication Systems, and Monitoring of Controls

Control Environment

Management Philosophy

Example Service Organization's control environment reflects the philosophy of senior management concerning the importance of security of medical transportation and logistics data and information. Example Service Organization's Security Steering Committee meets quarterly and reports to the board annually. The committee, under the direction of the Example Service Organization board, oversees the security activities of Example Service Organization. The committee members are from each of the business lines. The committee is charged with establishing overall security policies and procedures for Example Service Organization. The importance of security is emphasized within Example Service Organization through the establishment and communication of policies and procedures and is supported by investment in resources and people to carry out the policies. In designing its controls, Example Service Organization has taken into consideration the relevance of controls to meet the relevant trust criteria.

Security Management

Example Service Organization has a dedicated information security team, consisting of a security officer and a senior security specialist, responsible for management of information security throughout the organization. They hold positions on the Security Steering Committee and maintain security credentials and are required to annually sign and acknowledge their review of the information security policies. They are responsible for developing, maintaining, and enforcing Example Service Organization's information security policies. The information security policy is reviewed annually by the security officer, CIO, and vice president of operations, and it is approved by the Security Steering Committee.

As the information security team maintains security, it monitors, for example, known incidents and patches as well as results from recent vulnerability assessments and address necessary changes to the policies and procedures. Such changes can include a reclassification of data, a reassessment of risk, changes in incident response plans, and a verification of responsibilities for authorizing and monitoring accesses. Changes are reviewed and communicated during weekly IT maintenance meetings or through system alerts.

During annual security training and awareness programs, management ensures communication of the latest security policies as well as written job descriptions for security management.

Additionally, management is responsible for ensuring business associate agreements are current for third parties and for updating the annual IT risk assessment.

Security Policies

The following security policies and related processes are in place for XYZ:

- Data classification and business impact assessment
- Selection, documentation, and implementation of security controls
- Assessment of security controls
- User access authorization and provisioning
- Removal of user access
- Monitoring of security controls
- Security management

In December 20X1, application ABC was installed to enhance the workflow and approval process in support of the policies. This application enables tracking of

- changes to data classification;
- additions, modifications, or deletions of users;
- changes to authority levels in access approvals;
- tests of new security components prior to installation; and
- reviews of significant security monitoring events.

Personnel Security

Background checks are performed on new information security employees, who are also required to review and acknowledge their receipt of relevant security policies. The new positions are supported by job descriptions. Once employed, employees are subject to Example Service Organization procedures for accessing systems, violating Example Service Organization's information security policy, and related disciplinary action. Employees are instructed to report potential security incidents to the help desk.

Example Service Organization's business associate agreement instructs user entities and transportation providers to notify their respective account representative if they become aware of a possible security breach.

Physical Security and Environmental Controls

XYZ is located in Example Service Organization's NOCs. NOC access is monitored by video surveillance and on-site personnel, and it is controlled through the use of card reader systems. Access to the NOC is limited to authorized personnel based on job function, and physical security access permissions are reviewed quarterly by the security administration team.

Example Service Organization's NOC employ UPS power systems, air conditioning systems, fire detection and suppression systems, and environmental monitoring and alert notification systems.

Change Management

Example Service Organization has a formalized change management process in place which requires identification and recording of significant changes, assessment of risk and potential effect of such changes, approval of proposed changes, and testing of changes to verify operational functionality. Proposed changes are evaluated to determine if they present a security risk and what mitigating actions, including employee and user entity notifications, must be performed. The IT management team meets weekly to review and schedule changes to the IT environment.

Emergency changes follow the formalized change management process, but at an accelerated timeline. Prior to initiating an emergency change, necessary approvals are obtained and documented.

Changes to infrastructure and software are developed and tested in a separate development or test environment before implementation. Additionally, developers do not have the ability to migrate changes into production environments.

Example Service Organization has a formalized security and systems development methodology that includes project planning, design, testing, implementation, maintenance, and disposal or decommissioning.

Example Service Organization uses a standardized server build checklist to help secure its servers, as well as conducts monthly vulnerability assessments to identify potential system vulnerabilities. Patches are applied regularly in accordance with Example Service Organization's patch management process.

System Monitoring

The security administration team uses a variety of security utilities to identify and detect possible security threats and incidents. These utilities include, but are not limited to, firewall notifications, HP Tipping Point IDS or IPS alerts, vulnerability assessment reports, and operating system event logs. These alerts and notifications are reviewed daily by the security administration team using RSA enVision, a security incident and event monitoring (SIEM) product. Additionally, the security administration team has developed and will review the following SIEM reports:

- Failed object level access
- Daily intrusion detection system (IDS) or intrusion prevention system (IPS) attacks
- Critical IDS or IPS alerts
- Devices not reporting in the past 24 hours
- Failed login detail
- Firewall configuration changes
- Windows policy changes
- Windows system shutdowns and restarts
- Security events requiring further investigation are tracked using a help desk ticket and monitored until resolved.

Problem Management

Security incidents and other IT-related problems are reported to the help desk. Issues are tracked using a help desk ticket and monitored until resolved.

Data Backup and Recovery

Example Service Organization uses data replication and tapes to backup its data files and software. Access to backup devices, scheduling utilities, systems, and media is restricted to authorized personnel.

System Account Management

Example Service Organization has implemented role-based security to limit and control access within XYZ. Employees are granted logical and physical access to in-scope systems based on documented approvals by appropriate management personnel. Example Service Organization's transportation providers, governments and managed care providers (user entities), treating facilities, and riders are approved for access by an authorized user. The ability to create or modify user access accounts and user access privileges is limited to authorized personnel. User access is reviewed quarterly to verify whether individuals' access is necessary for their job functions and to identify the existence of inappropriate accounts.

The human resources (HR) department provides IT personnel with an employee termination report every two weeks. IT reconciles the termination report with current access privileges to determine if access has been appropriately removed or disabled. Dormant network accounts are disabled after 90 days of inactivity, and dormant XYZ accounts are disabled after 45 days of inactivity.

Administrative access to Active Directory, Unix, and XYZ servers and databases is restricted to authorized employees.

Unique user identification numbers, names, and passwords are required to authenticate all users to XYZ, as well as to the facility services, transportation provider, member services, and client reporting websites. Password parameters consist of the following:

- Passwords contain a minimum of 6 characters including 1 nonalphanumeric character.
- Passwords expire every 120 days for nonprivileged accounts and 60 days for privileged accounts.
- Logon sessions are terminated after 3 failed logon attempts.
- Users cannot reuse last 3 passwords (5 passwords for privileged accounts).

Risk Assessment Process

Example Service Organization regularly reviews the risks that may threaten the achievement of the criteria for the security principle set forth in TSP section 100, *Trust Services Principles, Criteria, and Illustrations for Security, Availability, Processing Integrity, Confidentiality, and Privacy* (AICPA, *Technical Practice Aids*).

The information security team assesses security risks on an ongoing basis. This is done through regular management meetings with IT personnel, reviewing and acting upon security event logs, performing vulnerability assessments, and conducting a formal annual IT risk assessment in conjunction with the company-wide risk assessment.

An IT strategic plan is developed annually by the CIO and is communicated to and approved by senior management and the Security Steering Committee. As part of this plan, strategic IT risks affecting the organization and recommended courses of action are identified and discussed.

Senior management, as part of its annual information security policy review, considers developments in technology and the impact of applicable laws and regulations on Example Service Organization's security policies.

Changes in security threats and risks are reviewed by Example Service Organization and updates to existing control activities and information security policies are performed as necessary.

Information and Communication Systems

Example Service Organization has an information security policy to help ensure that employees understand their individual roles and responsibilities concerning processing and controls to ensure significant events are communicated in a timely manner. These include formal and informal training programs and the use of e-mail to communicate time sensitive information and processes for security and system availability purposes that notify key personnel in the event of problems.

Example Service Organization uses checklists to help facilitate the upload of user (rider or member) information, such as encounter data, trip report, and client complaints, to the appropriate repository (for example, a portal or secure FTP folder) in accordance with the user's instructions.

Monitoring Controls

In addition to the daily oversight, monthly vulnerability assessments, and use of SIEM, management provides further security monitoring through the internal audit department, which performs periodic audits to include information security assessments.

Trust Services Criteria and Related Controls

Although the trust services criteria and related controls are presented in section 4, "Trust Services Security Principles, Criteria, Related Controls, and Tests of Controls," they are an integral part of Example Service Organization's system description.

Complementary User-Entity Controls

Example Service Organization's services were designed with the assumption that certain controls would be implemented by user entities. These controls should be in operation at user entities to complement Example Service Organization's controls. The user entity controls subsequently presented should not be regarded as a comprehensive list of all controls that should be employed by user entities.

User entities of Example Service Organization's transportation management system should maintain controls to provide reasonable assurance that

- access to Example Service Organization's websites (transportation provider, facility services, member services, and client reporting system) is restricted to authorized employees and that user names and passwords are kept confidential.

- user access to Example Service Organization's websites (transportation provider, facility services, member services, and client reporting system) is periodically reviewed.

- password and user access modification requests are submitted timely to Example Service Organization.

- communications are sent securely via secure FTP, VPN, or encrypted files.

- changes to the user reporting process, as well as changes in authorized user personnel, should be communicated to Example Service Organization timely.

Section 4 — Trust Services Security Principle, Criteria, Related Controls, and Tests of Controls

Column 1: Trust Service Criteria for the Security Principle

Column 2: Description of Example Service Organization's Controls

Column 3: Service Auditor's Tests of Controls

Column 4: Results of Service Auditor's Tests of Controls

Note to Readers: Although the applicable trust services criteria and related controls are presented in this section, they are, nevertheless, an integral part of Example Service Organization's description of its transportation management system throughout the period January 31, 20X1, to December 31, 20X1. The following type 2 service organization control 2 report is for illustrative purposes only and is not meant to be prescriptive. Example Service Organization controls and test of controls presented in this section are for illustrative purposes and accordingly are not all inclusive and may not be suitable for all service organizations and examinations.

Security Principle and Criteria

The system is protected against unauthorized access (both physical and logical).

1.0 Policies
The entity defines and documents its policies for the security of its system.

Trust Services Criteria for the Security Principle	Description of Example Service Organization's Controls	Service Auditor's Tests of Controls	Results of Service Auditor's Tests of Controls
1.1 The entity's security policies are established and periodically reviewed and approved by a designated individual or group.	Example Service Organization's information security policy addresses both IT and physical security, and it is reviewed and approved annually by the CIO, vice president of operations, and security officer, as well as the Security Steering Committee.	Inspected the security policies to ascertain whether procedures governing IT and physical security for the in-scope technology and locations are included. Inspected documentation for annual IT and physical security policy review by the CIO, vice president of operations, and security officer.	No exceptions noted.

1.0 Policies
The entity defines and documents its policies for the security of its system.

Trust Services Criteria for the Security Principle	Description of Example Service Organization's Controls	Service Auditor's Tests of Controls	Results of Service Auditor's Tests of Controls
1.2 The entity's security policies include, but may not be limited to, the following matters:	Example Service Organization's information security policy addresses the following:	Inspected the security policies to ascertain whether they include section headings that address the areas noted in the Example Service Organization's description of controls (*a*)–(*n*) for the in-scope technology and locations.	No exceptions noted.
a. Identifying and documenting the security requirements of authorized users	*a.* Identifying and documenting the security requirements of authorized users.		
b. Classifying data based on its criticality and sensitivity and that classification is used to define protection requirements, access rights and access restrictions, and retention and destruction requirements	*b.* Classifying data based on its criticality and sensitivity and using the assigned classification to define protection requirements, access rights and access restrictions, and retention and destruction requirements.		
c. Assessing risks on a periodic basis	*c.* Assessing risks on a periodic basis.		
d. Preventing unauthorized access	*d.* Preventing unauthorized access.		
e. Adding new users, modifying the access levels of existing users, and removing users who no longer need access	*e.* Adding new users, modifying the access levels of existing users, and removing users who no longer need access		
f. Assigning responsibility and accountability for system security	*f.* Assigning responsibility and accountability for system security		
g. Assigning responsibility and accountability for system changes and maintenance	*g.* Assigning responsibility and accountability for system changes and maintenance		

(continued)

AAG-SOP APP D

1.0 Policies
The entity defines and documents its policies for the security of its system.

Trust Services Criteria for the Security Principle	Description of Example Service Organization's Controls	Service Auditor's Tests of Controls	Results of Service Auditor's Tests of Controls
h. Testing, evaluating, and authorizing system components before implementation	*h.* Testing, evaluating, and authorizing system components before implementation		
i. Addressing how complaints and requests relating to security issues are resolved	*i.* Addressing how complaints and requests relating to security issues are resolved		
j. Identifying and mitigating security breaches and other incidents	*j.* Identifying and mitigating security breaches and other incidents		
k. Providing for training and other resources to support its system security policies	*k.* Providing for training and other resources to support its system security policies		
l. Providing for the handling of exceptions and situations not specifically addressed in its system security policies	*l.* Providing for the handling of exceptions and situations not specifically addressed in its system security policies		
m. Providing for the identification of and consistency with applicable laws and regulations, defined commitments, service level agreements, and other contractual requirements	*m.* Providing for the identification of and consistency with applicable laws and regulations, defined commitments, service-level agreements, and other contractual requirement		
n. Providing for sharing information with third parties	*n.* Providing for sharing information with third parties		

1.0 Policies
The entity defines and documents its policies for the security of its system.

Trust Services Criteria for the Security Principle	Description of Example Service Organization's Controls	Service Auditor's Tests of Controls	Results of Service Auditor's Tests of Controls
1.3 Responsibility and accountability for developing and maintaining the entity's system security policies, and changes and updates to those policies, are assigned.	Responsibility and accountability for the maintenance and enforcement of Example Service Organization's information security policy has been assigned to Example Service Organization's security administration team.	Inspected the job descriptions for members of the Example Service Organization's security administration team to determine whether the description identifies the responsibilities of the security administration team for the maintenance and enforcement of the organization's security policy.	No exceptions noted.

2.0 Communications
The entity communicates its defined system security policies to responsible parties and authorized users.

Trust Services Criteria for Security Principle	Description of Example Service Organization's Controls	Service Auditor's Tests of Controls	Results of Service Auditor's Tests of Controls
2.1 The entity has prepared an objective description of the system and its boundaries and communicated such description to authorized users.	Example Service Organization posts a description of its system, system boundaries, and system processes that includes infrastructure, software, people, procedures, and data on its intranet for internal users and on the Internet for external users.	Inspected intranet and Internet descriptions of Example Service Organization's system, system boundaries, and system processes to determine whether the description addresses infrastructure, software, people, procedures, and data for the in-scope technology and locations.	No exceptions noted.

(continued)

2.0 Communications
The entity communicates its defined system security policies to responsible parties and authorized users.

Trust Services Criteria for Security Principle	*Description of Example Service Organization's Controls*	*Service Auditor's Tests of Controls*	*Results of Service Auditor's Tests of Controls*
2.2 The security obligations of users and the entity's security commitments to users are communicated to authorized users.	Example Service Organization provides annual security training, as well as quarterly security compliance updates, to its employees.	Obtained the dates of and attendance sheets for the annual security training, as well as the quarterly security compliance updates, for employees. Determined whether employees had signed the attendance sheet for training sessions and updates on the specified dates.	No exceptions noted.
	Example Service Organization's IT employees are required to annually sign and acknowledge their review of the information security policy.	For a sample of IT employees, inspected their employee acknowledgement forms to determine whether the employees in the sample had provided annual signatures acknowledging their review of the information security policy.	One of 50 employees sampled had not signed the security policy acknowledgement.
	Example Service Organization's policies relating to security are reviewed with new employees as part of their orientation, and new employees are required to sign and acknowledge their review of the employee manual.	For a sample of new hires (employees), inspected the new hire employee acknowledgement forms to determine whether they had signed and acknowledged their review of the employee manual, which includes the security policies, at the time of orientation.	No exceptions noted.

	2.0 Communications		
	The entity communicates its defined system security policies to responsible parties and authorized users.		
Trust Services Criteria for Security Principle	*Description of Example Service Organization's Controls*	*Service Auditor's Tests of Controls*	*Results of Service Auditor's Tests of Controls*
	The security commitments and obligation of transportation providers, governments and managed care providers (user entities), treating facilities, and riders are posted on Example Service Organization's websites and the Web interface and included in business associate agreements.	Inspected Example Service Organization's websites, Web interface, and business associate agreements for communication regarding security commitments and obligations.	No exceptions noted.
2.3 Responsibility and accountability for the entity's system security policies and changes and updates to those policies are communicated to entity personnel responsible for implementing them.	Example Service Organization's security administration team receives an annual communication from the CIO that identifies their responsibility and accountability for the day-to-day maintenance and implementation of the entity's security policies.	Inspected the annual communication to security administration team from the CIO identifying their responsibility and accountability for the security policies and changes to those policies.	No exceptions noted.
	Written job descriptions have been defined and communicated to the security administration team.	Inspected the job descriptions for members of the Example Service Organization's security administration team to determine whether the description indicates that the security administration team is responsible for the custody and maintenance of the organization's	No exceptions noted.

(continued)

2.0 Communications
The entity communicates its defined system security policies to responsible parties and authorized users.

Trust Services Criteria for Security Principle	Description of Example Service Organization's Controls	Service Auditor's Tests of Controls	Results of Service Auditor's Tests of Controls
		security policy. Inspected a sample of annual human resources reviews of security administration team members to determine whether those reviews indicate that these team members' are accountable for the custody and maintenance of the Example Service Organization's security policy.	
2.4 The process for informing the entity about breaches of the system security and for submitting complaints is communicated to authorized users.	Example Service Organization's security awareness program trains employees how to identify and report possible security breaches.	Inspected attendance sheets for the annual security training for employees and determined whether employees had signed the attendance sheet for the training session on those dates. Inspected the presentation material for relevant training sessions during 20X1 and determined whether that material described how to identify and report possible security breaches.	No exceptions noted.
	Governments or managed care providers and transportation providers, via the business associate	For a sample of governments or managed care providers and transportation providers,	No exceptions noted.

2.0 Communications
The entity communicates its defined system security policies to responsible parties and authorized users.

Trust Services Criteria for Security Principle	Description of Example Service Organization's Controls	Service Auditor's Tests of Controls	Results of Service Auditor's Tests of Controls
	agreement, are instructed to contact their account representative if they become aware of a possible security breach.	inspected the related business associate agreements for user entities and third-party transportation providers to determine whether they • were signed and on file. • included in-structions to contact the ac-count repre-sentative if the user en-tity becomes aware of a possible secu-rity breach.	
	System alerts, including planned outages and known issues, are displayed on the login website of Example Service Organization's government or managed care providers, treating facility providers, and transportation providers.	Observed twice during the period that system alerts are being displayed on Example Service Organization's website.	No exceptions noted.
2.5 Changes that may affect system security are communicated to management and users who will be affected.	Planned changes to system components are reviewed, scheduled, and communicated to management as part of the weekly IT maintenance process.	Inspected a sample of weekly IT maintenance schedules and communications to determine whether planned system changes were included and had been reviewed and signed off by IT management.	No exceptions noted.

3.0 Procedures
The entity placed in operation procedures to achieve its documented system security objectives in accordance with its defined policies.

Trust Services Criteria for Security Principle	Description of Example Service Organization Controls	Service Auditor's Tests of Controls	Results of Service Auditor's Tests of Controls
3.1 Procedures exist to *a.* identify potential threats of disruption to systems operation that would impair system security commitments and *b.* assess the risks associated with the identified threats.	The Example Service Organization maintains records of information technology assets (for example, hardware, operating systems, applications, and data). The records are updated as part of the change management process. On an annual basis, the information technology asset records are compared to system reports and fixed asset records for completeness and accuracy.	For a sample of changes, inspected information technology asset records noting changes in information technology assets recorded, if applicable. Inspected comparison of information technology asset records to system reports and fixed asset records and noted that differences were investigated and corrected.	No exceptions noted
	A company-wide risk assessment is performed annually by management and includes the following: • Determining business objectives including security commitments • Evaluating the effect of environmental, regulatory, and technological changes on Example Service Organization's system security • Identifying threats to operations, including security threats, using information technology asset records • Analyzing risks associated with the threats	Inspected the annual risk assessment documentation to determine whether it included the specified procedures.	No exceptions noted

3.0 Procedures
The entity placed in operation procedures to achieve its documented system security objectives in accordance with its defined policies.

Trust Services Criteria for Security Principle	Description of Example Service Organization Controls	Service Auditor's Tests of Controls	Results of Service Auditor's Tests of Controls
	• Determining a risk mitigation strategy • Developing or modifying and deploying controls consistent with the risk mitigation strategy.		
3.2 Procedures exist to restrict logical access to the defined system including, but not limited to, the following matters: *a.* Logical access security measures to restrict access to information resources not deemed to be public	Access to XYZ and the client reporting, member services, facility services, and transportation provider websites is restricted through the use of defined application and database user roles. Access granted to users is authorized by the department manager.	Obtained an access list for client reporting, member services, facility services, and transportation provider websites and XYZ. Selected a sample of users and determined whether access was authorized and consistent with their role.	No exceptions noted
	XYZ user role assignments are reviewed quarterly by department manager.	Inspected a sample of quarterly reviews noting the date the review had been performed to determine whether the reviews had occurred timely.	No exceptions noted
b. Identification and authentication of users	Unique user identification numbers, names, and passwords are required to authenticate all users to XYZ and to the client reporting, member services, facility services, and transportation provider websites. Password parameters consist of the following:	Inspected the password parameters for the system to determine whether the following password parameters were configured with the following specifications: • Passwords have a minimum of 6	No exceptions noted

(continued)

AAG-SOP APP D

3.0 Procedures
The entity placed in operation procedures to achieve its documented system security objectives in accordance with its defined policies.

Trust Services Criteria for Security Principle	Description of Example Service Organization Controls	Service Auditor's Tests of Controls	Results of Service Auditor's Tests of Controls
	• Passwords have a minimum of 6 characters including 1 nonalphanumeric character. • Passwords expire every 120 days for nonprivileged accounts and 60 days for privileged accounts. • Logon sessions terminate after 3 failed logon attempts. • The last 3 passwords cannot be reused (5 passwords for privileged accounts).	characters including 1 nonalphanumeric character. • Passwords expire every 120 days for nonprivileged accounts and 60 days for privileged accounts. • Logon sessions terminate after 3 failed logon attempts. • The last 3 passwords cannot be re-used (5 passwords for privileged accounts).	
c. Registration and authorization of new users	In order for Example Service Organization employees to obtain system and application access, the employee's manager or supervisor must submit a help desk ticket authorizing such assess. Proper segregation of duties is considered in granting access privileges based on the user's job role.	Inspected the help desk tickets for a sample of employees requiring access to the system to determine whether access was authorized by the employee's manager or supervisor. Determined whether the access granted provided for the proper segregation of duties.	No exceptions noted
	New user access requests from Example Service Organization's government or managed care providers, facility providers, and transportation	For a sample of Example Service Organization's government or managed care providers, facility providers, and transportation providers	No exceptions noted

AAG-SOP APP D

3.0 Procedures
The entity placed in operation procedures to achieve its documented system security objectives in accordance with its defined policies.

Trust Services Criteria for Security Principle	Description of Example Service Organization Controls	Service Auditor's Tests of Controls	Results of Service Auditor's Tests of Controls
	providers must be submitted and approved by an authorized individual.	inspected new user access requests to determine whether the requests were approved by an authorized individual.	
	Only authorized Example Service Organization personnel are able to create or modify user access and user access privileges.	Inspected a report identifying individuals with access to create or modify user access privileges to determine whether the access is limited to authorized personnel.	No exceptions noted
d. The process to make changes and updates to user profiles	Approved changes to internal user accounts and profiles are submitted to the help desk and updates are made by the security administration team.	Observed system security configurations and determined that only security administration team is authorized to make changes to user accounts and profiles.	No exceptions noted
	Access change requests from Example Service Organization's government or managed care providers, facility providers, and transportation providers must be submitted and approved by an authorized individual. A list of authorized access approvers for government or managed care providers, facility providers, and transportation	Inspected a sample of change request by Example Service Organization's government or managed care providers, facility providers, and transportation providers and determined that the requests were approved by an individual on the authorized access approver list.	No exceptions noted

(continued)

AAG-SOP APP D

3.0 Procedures *The entity placed in operation procedures to achieve its documented* *system security objectives in accordance with its defined policies.*			
Trust Services Criteria for Security Principle	**Description of Example Service Organization Controls**	**Service Auditor's Tests of Controls**	**Results of Service Auditor's Tests of Controls**
	providers is maintained by Example Service Organization and updated annually.		
	The human resources department provides IT personnel with a termination report every two weeks. IT reconciles the report against current system privileges to determine if access has been appropriately removed or disabled.	Inspected a sample of bi-weekly termination reconciliations to determine whether IT had performed the reconciliation.	No exceptions noted
	Dormant XYZ accounts are disabled after 45 days of inactivity, and dormant network accounts are disabled after 90 days of inactivity.	Inspected the system configurations to determine whether they are configured to disable user accounts after 45 days of inactivity and dormant network accounts after 90 days of inactivity.	No exceptions noted
e. Distribution of output restricted to authorized users	Example Service Organization uses checklists to help facilitate the upload of client information, such as trip reports and client complaints, to the appropriate client repository (for example, a portal or secure FTP [file transfer protocol] folder) in accordance with the user entity's instructions.	Inspected the client checklist for a sample of uploads to the client repository to determine if the checklist was used and completed for the upload of client data and signed-off by the person performing the upload.	No exceptions noted
	Clients accessing the client-reporting portal can only view reports for their assigned riders.	Observed an associate attempt to view reports for riders not assigned to the	No exceptions noted

3.0 Procedures
The entity placed in operation procedures to achieve its documented system security objectives in accordance with its defined policies.

Trust Services Criteria for Security Principle	Description of Example Service Organization Controls	Service Auditor's Tests of Controls	Results of Service Auditor's Tests of Controls
		client to determine if the client-reporting portal prevented the associate from accessing the reports.	
f. Restriction of access to offline storage, backup data, systems, and media	A key card system restricts access to offline storage, backup data, and media located at the data centers for supporting the XYZ system.	Observed that access to the data center is restricted by use of a key card system.	No exceptions noted
	Example Service Organization performs quarterly data center access reviews to determine if key card security permissions are appropriate.	Inspected the access reviews for evidence of review by IT.	No exceptions noted
g. Restriction of access to system configurations, superuser functionality, master passwords, powerful utilities, and security devices (for example, firewalls)	Administrative access to Example Service Organization's firewall is restricted to network engineering personnel. All firewall configuration changes are logged by Example Service Organization's security incident and event management (SIEM) utility and are reviewed by the security administration team.	Inspected the firewall access listing to determine whether access is restricted to network engineering personnel. Inspected system configuration parameter and determined that firewall configuration changes are logged. Inspected a sample of firewall configuration change logs for evidence of review by the security administration team.	No exceptions noted

(continued)

3.0 Procedures The entity placed in operation procedures to achieve its documented system security objectives in accordance with its defined policies.			
Trust Services Criteria for Security Principle	*Description of Example Service Organization Controls*	*Service Auditor's Tests of Controls*	*Results of Service Auditor's Tests of Controls*
	Administrative access to Active Directory, Unix, and XYZ servers and databases is restricted to authorized employees.	Inspected the Active Directory, UNIX, and servers' access listings to determine whether access is restricted to appropriate employees based on their job responsibilities.	No exceptions noted
	A list of all master passwords is maintained in a password-encrypted database. Additionally, a hard copy of the master passwords is maintained in a sealed envelope inside a locked case in the possession of the CIO.	Observed the database configurations to determine whether master passwords are maintained in an encrypted database. Observed the hard copy master password envelope to determine whether the envelope was sealed and stored in a locked case.	No exceptions noted
3.3 Procedures exist to restrict physical access to the defined system including, but not limited to, facilities, backup media, and other system components, such as firewalls, routers, and servers.	Physical access to the data centers which house Example Service Organization's IT resources, servers, backup media, and related hardware, such as firewalls and routers, is restricted to authorized individuals by card key systems and monitored by video surveillance.	Observed entrances to the data center to determine whether key card systems restricted access. Observed the video surveillance system to determine whether security guards monitor the activity.	No exceptions noted
	Requests for physical access privileges to Example Service Organization's computer facilities require approval from	For a sample of new hires and transfers, inspected access requests to determine	No exceptions noted

3.0 *Procedures* *The entity placed in operation procedures to achieve its documented* *system security objectives in accordance with its defined policies.*			
Trust Services Criteria for Security Principle	*Description of Example Service Organization Controls*	*Service Auditor's Tests of Controls*	*Results of Service Auditor's Tests of Controls*
	authorized IT management personnel.	whether the request was approved by authorized IT management personnel.	
	Physical access to Example Service Organization's data centers is key card controlled and reviewed quarterly.	Inspected entrances to the data center to determine whether key card systems restricted access. Inspected a sample of management's quarterly access reviews and ascertained that access was appropriate and any inappropriate access was removed.	No exceptions noted
	Documented procedures exist for the identification and escalation of potential physical security breaches.	Inspected written security policies and ascertained the policies address the identification and escalation of potential physical security breaches.	No exceptions noted
3.4 Procedures exist to protect against unauthorized access to system resources.	Virtual private networking (VPN) software is used to restrict remote access. Users are authenticated by the VPN server through specific client software and user identification numbers, names, and passwords.	Observed the remote access process to determine whether VPN software is used. Inspected the VPN configurations to determine whether user identification numbers, names, and passwords are required.	No exceptions noted

(continued)

AAG-SOP APP D

3.0 Procedures
The entity placed in operation procedures to achieve its documented system security objectives in accordance with its defined policies.

Trust Services Criteria for Security Principle	Description of Example Service Organization Controls	Service Auditor's Tests of Controls	Results of Service Auditor's Tests of Controls
	Example Service Organization uses firewalls to prevent unauthorized network access.	Inspected the network diagram to determine whether the design of the system includes firewalls to prevent unauthorized network access.	No exceptions noted
	Example Service Organization uses a standard server build checklist to help secure each server.	For a sample of new server installations, inspected installations documentation to determine whether the standard server build checklist was used.	No exceptions noted
	Example Service Organization contracts with third-party security providers to conduct monthly security reviews and vulnerability assessments. Results and recommendations are communicated to and addressed by management.	For a sample of months, inspected the security review and vulnerability assessment reports and list of action items resulting from the review and assessment. Determined whether the assessments were performed and communicated and whether action items were addressed by management through system change requests.	No exceptions noted
3.5 Procedures exist to protect against infection by computer viruses, malicious code, and unauthorized software.	Example Service Organization uses antivirus software on all Windows-based desktops, laptops, and servers. These systems are	Inspected a sample of desktops, laptops, and servers to determine whether antivirus software was	No exceptions noted

3.0 Procedures
The entity placed in operation procedures to achieve its documented system security objectives in accordance with its defined policies.

Trust Services Criteria for Security Principle	Description of Example Service Organization Controls	Service Auditor's Tests of Controls	Results of Service Auditor's Tests of Controls
	configured to query the antivirus repository daily to retrieve the latest antivirus definitions.	installed. Inspected the antivirus software configurations to determine whether the software was configured to retrieve the latest antivirus definitions on a daily basis.	
	Example Service Organization uses a SIEM utility to identify and record any computer viruses identified on the Example Service Organization network.	Observed the SIEM utility to determine whether management had recorded any identified computer viruses.	No exceptions noted
3.6 Encryption or other equivalent security techniques are used to protect user authentication information and the corresponding session transmitted over the Internet or other public networks.	Example Service Organization employees have the ability to encrypt e-mails using a secure Web messaging server.	Inspected active system setting on the Web messaging server to determine whether e-mails can be encrypted when required.	No exceptions noted
	Example Service Organization's remote access VPN uses Secure Socket Layer (SSL), and connections are automatically timed out after 20 minutes of inactivity.	Inspected the VPN configurations to determine whether SSL is used and whether connections automatically timed out after 20 minutes of inactivity.	No exceptions noted
	Dynamic VPN sessions are established on demand between Example Service Organization's sites using Advanced Encryption Standard (AES) 256-bit encryption.	Inspected the VPN configurations to determine whether AES 256-bit encryption is used.	No exceptions noted

(continued)

3.0 Procedures
The entity placed in operation procedures to achieve its documented system security objectives in accordance with its defined policies.

Trust Services Criteria for Security Principle	Description of Example Service Organization Controls	Service Auditor's Tests of Controls	Results of Service Auditor's Tests of Controls
	Example Service Organization's government or managed care provider, facility provider, and transportation provider logon pages use SSL to encrypt logon sessions.	Observed the provider logon process to determine whether SSL encrypt logon sessions were used.	No exceptions noted
3.7 Procedures exist to identify, report, and act upon system security breaches and other incidents.	User entities are provided with instructions for communicating potential security breaches to the information security team.	Inspected the instructions provided to user entities to determine whether they include protocols for communicating potential security breaches.	No exceptions noted
	When a potential security incident is detected, a defined incident management process is initiated by authorized personnel. Corrective actions are implemented in accordance with defined policies and procedures.	Inspected the written incident management procedures to determine whether the procedures include a process for handling the security incident.	No exceptions noted
	All reported or detected security incidents are tracked via a help desk ticket until resolved. Closed security incidents are reviewed and approved by management weekly.	Observed the help desk ticketing system to determine whether security incidents are tracked. Inspected closed security incident tickets to determine whether the tickets were reviewed and approved by management.	No exceptions noted
3.8 Procedures exist to classify data in accordance with	Example Service Organization has a defined information	Inspected the data classification policy to	No exceptions noted

3.0 Procedures
The entity placed in operation procedures to achieve its documented system security objectives in accordance with its defined policies.

Trust Services Criteria for Security Principle	Description of Example Service Organization Controls	Service Auditor's Tests of Controls	Results of Service Auditor's Tests of Controls
classification policies and periodically monitor and update such classifications as necessary	classification scheme for the labeling and handling of data. Example Service Organization classifies data into four levels: public, internal use, confidential, and protected.	determine whether there is a documented classification scheme for labeling and handling data.	
3.9 Procedures exist to provide that issues of noncompliance with security policies are promptly addressed and that corrective measures are taken on a timely basis.	Security incidents are reported to the help desk and tracked through to resolution. Incidents that may affect security compliance are reported to the security compliance officer.	Selected a sample of security incidents logged in the incident tracking system and inspected documentation to determine whether the incident was tracked within a help desk ticket until resolution. Inspected a sample of security incidents logged in the incident tracking system and associated communications to the security officer that may affect security compliance to determine whether the incidents were reported to the security officer.	No exceptions noted
	Employees found to be in violation of Example Service Organization's information security policy are subject to disciplinary action up to and including termination of employment.	Inspected the security policy to determine whether the policy includes procedures for employees in violation of the policy.	No exceptions noted

(continued)

3.0 Procedures
The entity placed in operation procedures to achieve its documented system security objectives in accordance with its defined policies.

Trust Services Criteria for Security Principle	Description of Example Service Organization Controls	Service Auditor's Tests of Controls	Results of Service Auditor's Tests of Controls
3.10 Design, acquisition, implementation, configuration, modification, and management of infrastructure and software are consistent with defined system security policies to enable authorized access and to prevent unauthorized access.	Example Service Organization has a formalized security and systems development methodology that includes project planning, design, testing, implementation, maintenance, and disposal or decommissioning.	Inspected the security and systems methodology policy to determine whether it includes project planning, design, testing, implementation, maintenance, and disposal or decommissioning.	No exceptions noted
3.11 Procedures exist to provide that personnel responsible for the design, development, implementation, and operation of systems affecting security have the qualifications and resources to fulfill their responsibilities.	Example Service Organization has written job descriptions specifying the responsibilities and academic and professional requirements for key job positions.	For a sample of positions, inspected written job descriptions to determine whether the job descriptions include responsibilities and academic and professional requirements.	No exceptions noted
	Hiring procedures include a comprehensive screening of candidates for key positions and consideration of whether the candidate's credentials are commensurate with the position. New personnel are offered employment subject to background checks.	For a sample of new employees, inspected the results of background checks to determine whether a background check was performed.	No exceptions noted
3.12 Procedures exist to maintain system components, including configurations consistent with the defined system security policies.	Example Service Organization maintains a documented change management and patch management process.	Inspected the change and patch management policies to determine whether there are documented procedures.	No exceptions noted

3.0 Procedures The entity placed in operation procedures to achieve its documented system security objectives in accordance with its defined policies.			
Trust Services Criteria for Security Principle	*Description of Example Service Organization Controls*	*Service Auditor's Tests of Controls*	*Results of Service Auditor's Tests of Controls*
	Servers are reviewed monthly by the security administration team to determine if required vendor security patches have been applied.	For a sample of months, inspected management's server review documentation to determine whether the security administration team had completed the review.	No exceptions noted
	Example Service Organization contracts with third parties to conduct monthly security reviews and vulnerability assessments. Results and recommendations for improvement are reported to management. Management develops a plan of action for each recommendation and follows up on open recommendations on a monthly basis.	For a sample of months, inspected the security review and vulnerability assessment reports to determine whether the assessments were performed, communicated, and addressed by management.	No exceptions noted
3.13 Procedures exist to provide that only authorized, tested, and documented changes are made to the system.	Example Service Organization maintains a formally documented change management process. Changes to hardware, operating system, and system software are authorized, tested (when applicable), and approved by appropriate personnel prior to implementation.	Inspected the change management policy for hardware, operating system, and system software to determine whether procedures are documented to include authorization, tested (when applicable), and approved prior to implementation.	No exceptions noted

(continued)

3.0 Procedures
The entity placed in operation procedures to achieve its documented system security objectives in accordance with its defined policies.

Trust Services Criteria for Security Principle	Description of Example Service Organization Controls	Service Auditor's Tests of Controls	Results of Service Auditor's Tests of Controls
	Changes to system infrastructure and software are developed and tested in a separate development or test environment before implementation. Additionally, developers do not have the ability to migrate changes into production environments.	Inspected documentation of the system infrastructure architecture to determine whether a separate development or test environment existed from the production environment. Inspected the access list to the change management tools to determine whether access to migrate changes to production was appropriate based on job responsibilities and that developers did not have the ability to migrate changes into production.	No exceptions noted
3.14 Procedures exist to provide that emergency changes are documented and authorized timely.	Emergency changes follow the standard change management process, but at an accelerated timeline. Prior to initiating an emergency change, all necessary approvals are obtained and documented.	Inspected change documentation from system generated list of program changes for a sample of emergency changes to determine whether the changes were approved.	No exceptions noted

4.0 Monitoring *The entity monitors the system and takes action to maintain compliance with its defined system security policies.*			
Trust Services Criteria for the Security Principle	*Description of Example Service Organization Controls*	*Service Auditor's Tests of Controls*	*Results of Service Auditor's Tests of Controls*
4.1 The entity's system security is periodically reviewed and compared with the defined system security policies.	External vulnerability assessments are performed on a monthly basis, and management initiates corrective actions for identified vulnerabilities.	Inspected a sample of vulnerability assessments noting monthly performance. Selected a sample of logged corrective actions as a result of the vulnerability assessments, noting when corrective actions were initiated.	No exceptions noted
	Example Service Organization performs quarterly user access reviews.	Obtained a sample of quarterly user access reviews, noting review by management.	No exceptions noted
4.2 There is a process to identify and address potential impairments to the entity's ongoing ability to achieve its objectives in accordance with its defined system security policies.	Example Service Organization uses a security incident and event management (SIEM) utility to capture the following critical security events: • Failed object level access • Daily intrusion detection system (IDS) or intrusion prevention system (IPS) attacks • Critical IDS or IPS alerts • Devices not reporting in the past 24 hours • Failed login detail • Firewall configuration changes • Windows policy changes • Windows system shutdowns and restarts	Selected a sample of SIEM logs, noting evidence of review by the security administration team.	No exceptions noted

(continued)

4.0 Monitoring The entity monitors the system and takes action to maintain compliance with its defined system security policies.			
Trust Services *Criteria for the* *Security Principle*	*Description of* *Example Service* *Organization* *Controls*	*Service Auditor's* *Tests of Controls*	*Results of* *Service* *Auditor's* *Tests of* *Controls*
	Reports are logged and reviewed daily by the security administration team.		
	On a weekly basis, the security administration team meets and discusses vulnerability assessment results with system administrators who are responsible for addressing critical vulnerabilities.	Reviewed a sample of minutes from weekly security administration team meetings, noting discussion on critical vulnerabilities.	No exceptions noted
4.3 Environmental, regulatory, and technological changes are monitored and their effect on system security is assessed on a timely basis and policies are updated for that assessment.	Example Service Organization, through its ongoing and annual risk assessment processes (see criteria 3.1), evaluates the effect of environmental, regulatory, and technological changes on Example Service Organization's system security. Updates to Example Service Organization's information security policies are communicated regularly to employees (see criteria 2.2) and documented in the appropriate information security policy.	Inspected the documentation of the annual risk assessment noting management addressed environmental, regulatory, and technological changes.	No exceptions noted

Section 5 — Other Information Provided by Example Service Organization That Is Not Covered by the Service Auditor's Report

Note to Readers: *The service organization may wish to attach to the description of the service organization's system, or include in a document containing the service auditor's report, information in addition to its description. The following are examples of such information:*

- *Future plans for new systems*
- *Other services provided by the service organization that are not included in the scope of the engagement*
- *Qualitative information, such as marketing claims, that may not be objectively measurable*
- *Responses from management to deviations identified by the service auditor when such responses have not been subject to procedures by the service auditor*

For brevity an example is not provided.

Appendix E

Service Auditor Considerations in Performing SOC 2^{SM} or SOC 3^{SM} Engagements for Cloud Computing Service Organizations

Introduction

The National Institute of Standards and Technology (NIST) is a nonregulatory federal agency within the U.S. Department of Commerce (www.commerce.gov/). Its mission is to promote U.S. innovation and industrial competitiveness by advancing measurement science, standards, and technology in ways that enhance economic security and improve quality of life. The NIST publication, *The NIST Definition of Cloud Computing: Recommendations of the National Institute of Standards and Technology* (NIST publication),[1] defines *cloud computing* as a model for enabling ubiquitous, convenient, on-demand network access to a shared pool of configurable computing resources (for example, networks, servers, storage, applications, and services) that can be rapidly provisioned and released with minimal management effort or service provider interaction. This cloud model is composed of five essential characteristics, three service models, and four deployment models.

In general, the requirements and implementation guidance for performing a service organization controls (SOC) 2 or SOC 3^{SM} engagement for a cloud computing service organization (CCSO) is the same as it is for any other SOC 2^{SM} or SOC 3 engagement. However, when performing such engagements, a service auditor may face unique issues related to the technology that is an integral part of a CCSO's services.

Objective of the Appendix

When performing a SOC 2 or 3 engagement for a CCSO, a service auditor will likely encounter engagement issues that present unique challenges and risks. The objective of this appendix is to assist practitioners in understanding the typical risks, controls, and other related considerations associated with performing a SOC 2 or 3 engagement for a CCSO. The appendix is not meant to be an alternative to the requirements and guidance for performing and reporting on SOC 2 and SOC 3 engagements, which are included in the following professional standards and interpretive guidance:

- *SOC 2 engagements.* AT section 101, *Attest Engagements* (AICPA, *Professional Standards*), and the AICPA Guide *Reporting on Controls at a Service Organization Relevant to Security, Availability, Processing Integrity, Confidentiality, or Privacy (SOC 2^{SM})*

- *SOC 3 engagements.* AT section 101 and appendix C, "Practitioner Guidance on Scoping and Reporting Issues," of TSP section 100, *Trust*

---

[1] National Institute of Standards and Technology, U.S. Department of Commerce, *The NIST Definition of Cloud Computing: Recommendations of the National Institute of Standards and Technology*, (Special Publication 800-145) (Gaithersburg, Maryland, 2011), 2–3.

Services Principles, Criteria, and Illustrations for Security, Availability, Processing Integrity, Confidentiality, and Privacy (AICPA, *Technical Practice Aids*)

This appendix is not meant to provide comprehensive guidance for performing SOC 2 or SOC 3 engagements for a CCSO but rather to highlight the unique aspects of these engagements. The appendix does not necessarily prescribe solutions because the best approach may vary depending on the specific facts and circumstances.

Definitions of Terms From the National Institute of Standards and Technology

The NIST publication provides the following additional information about the essential characteristics of cloud computing and the service and deployment models used.

Essential Characteristics:

On-demand self-service. A consumer can unilaterally provision computing capabilities, such as server time and network storage, as needed automatically without requiring human interaction with each service provider.

Broad network access. Capabilities are available over the network and accessed through standard mechanisms that promote use by heterogeneous thin or thick client platforms (e.g., mobile phones, tablets, laptops, and workstations).

Resource pooling. The provider's computing resources are pooled to serve multiple consumers using a multi-tenant model, with different physical and virtual resources dynamically assigned and reassigned according to consumer demand. There is a sense of location independence in that the customer generally has no control or knowledge over the exact location of the provided resources but may be able to specify location at a higher level of abstraction (e.g., country, state, or data center). Examples of resources include storage, processing, memory, and network bandwidth.

Rapid elasticity. Capabilities can be elastically provisioned and released, in some cases automatically, to scale rapidly outward and inward commensurate with demand. To the consumer, the capabilities available for provisioning often appear to be unlimited and can be appropriated in any quantity at any time.

Measured service. Cloud systems automatically control and optimize resource use by leveraging a metering capability[2] at some level of abstraction appropriate to the type of service (e.g., storage, processing, bandwidth, and active user accounts). Resource usage can be monitored, controlled, and reported, providing transparency for both the provider and consumer of the utilized service.

Service Models:

Software as a Service (SaaS). The capability provided to the consumer is to use the provider's applications running on a cloud infrastructure.[3] The applications are accessible from various client devices through either a thin

---

[2] Typically this is done on a pay-per-use or charge-per-use basis.

[3] A *cloud infrastructure* is the collection of hardware and software that enables the five essential characteristics of cloud computing. The cloud infrastructure can be viewed as containing both a physical layer and an abstraction layer. The physical layer consists of the hardware resources that are necessary to support the cloud services being provided and

client interface, such as a web browser (e.g., web-based email), or a program interface. The consumer does not manage or control the underlying cloud infrastructure, including network, servers, operating systems, storage, or even individual application capabilities, with the possible exception of limited user-specific application configuration settings.

Platform as a Service (PaaS). The capability provided to the consumer is to deploy onto the cloud infrastructure consumer-created or acquired applications created using programming languages, libraries, services, and tools supported by the provider.[4] The consumer does not manage or control the underlying cloud infrastructure, including network, servers, operating systems, or storage, but has control over the deployed applications and possibly configuration settings for the application-hosting environment.

Infrastructure as a Service (IaaS). The capability provided to the consumer is to provision processing, storage, networks, and other fundamental computing resources where the consumer is able to deploy and run arbitrary software, which can include operating systems and applications. The consumer does not manage or control the underlying cloud infrastructure but has control over operating systems, storage, and deployed applications; and possibly limited control of select networking components (e.g., host firewalls).

Deployment Models:

Private cloud. The cloud infrastructure is provisioned for exclusive use by a single organization comprising multiple consumers (e.g., business units). It may be owned, managed, and operated by the organization, a third party, or some combination of them, and it may exist on or off premises.

Community cloud. The cloud infrastructure is provisioned for exclusive use by a specific community of consumers from organizations that have shared concerns (e.g., mission, security requirements, policy, and compliance considerations). It may be owned, managed, and operated by one or more of the organizations in the community, a third party, or some combination of them, and it may exist on or off premises.

Public cloud. The cloud infrastructure is provisioned for open use by the general public. It may be owned, managed, and operated by a business, academic, or government organization, or some combination of them. It exists on the premises of the cloud provider.

Hybrid cloud. The cloud infrastructure is a composition of two or more distinct cloud infrastructures (private, community, or public) that remain unique entities but are bound together by standardized or proprietary technology that enables data and application portability (e.g., cloud bursting for load balancing between clouds).

(footnote continued)

typically includes server, storage, and network components. The abstraction layer consists of the software deployed across the physical layer, which manifests the essential cloud characteristics. Conceptually the abstraction layer sits above the physical layer.

[4] This capability does not necessarily preclude the use of compatible programming languages, libraries, services, and tools from other sources.

Unique Considerations Related to CCSOs

Automated Provisioning, Virtualization, and Transparency

Although not exclusive to CCSOs, two technologies are fundamental to most cloud technologies: automated provisioning and infrastructure virtualization. Automated provisioning permits a user entity to order, configure, and deploy CCSO services in real time without human involvement by the CCSO's personnel. An automated process is designed to generate and implement selected configurations.

Virtualization involves creating a virtual version of infrastructure resources, such as servers, operating system instances, or other system or network resources. Most CCSOs are operated in the virtual environment, and there may be qualitative differences in the level of virtualization at individual CCSOs. For example, in an IaaS model, virtual servers may be moved among different physical servers. Consequently, the service auditor needs to understand both how the virtual server was originally provisioned and how the CCSO maintains the virtual server throughout its existence.

The user entities' need for transparency is another consideration for service auditors. In describing their procedures, applications, and services, CCSOs are often reluctant to disclose those aspects of their system they consider proprietary or a competitive advantage. Consequently, the CCSO's description of its system may not provide the transparency that certain user entities need. The service auditor needs to consider these factors in assessing the fairness of the presentation of the CCSO's description of its system. In certain cases, a user entity's risk management team or a practitioner performing an engagement for the user entity may require a level of detail that goes beyond what is provided in the CCSO's system description. In these situations, the user entity may contact the CCSO to request such information. For example, a user entity may ask the CCSO for detailed information about the procedures for sanitizing production hardware decommissioned from a storage area network. Generally it is best if the CCSO identifies such information needs when negotiating the contract with the user entity so that it can be stipulated in the service level or other contractual agreement (hereinafter referred to as SLA).

Virtualization may create challenges for the service auditor in evaluating the suitability of the design and testing the operating effectiveness of controls. In a physical environment, the service auditor can obtain network diagrams and visual representations of system infrastructure relationships among the system components. However, depending on the level of virtualization, that may not be possible for a CCSO's system, which uses a combination of physical and virtualized solutions. To gain an adequate level of understanding of the risks associated with the architecture, the service auditor needs to understand the degree to which virtualization has been implemented, including

- how the virtual system components are managed and
- the interfaces between the components and management software.

The service auditor also needs to understand the controls used to obtain logical segregation, such as controls that separate physical resources in nonvirtualized environments, and apply this understanding to other aspects of the examination.

Service Level Terms and Agreements

To understand the CCSO's system and to determine if the CCSO's description of its system is fairly stated, the service auditor will need to obtain an understanding of the CCSO's process for providing services, including aspects of the process that are applicable to all user entities, and aspects that may be customized for certain user entities. Reading SLAs and other contracts with user entities will enable the service auditor to obtain an understanding of the nature and scope of the services provided by the CCSO as well as the CCSO's contractual obligations to user entities. Matters that generally are covered in SLAs include customer commitments, roles and responsibilities, service support requirements, and quantitative and qualitative metrics for measuring the service signed off on by the stakeholders. The SLA may also stipulate the boundaries of the system or specific information to be included in the CCSO's description of its system. An understanding of the CCSO's commitments to user entities will assist the service auditor in evaluating the suitability of the design of controls in meeting the applicable trust services criteria.[5] In an engagement that addresses the privacy principle, for example, the user entity may require that the CCSO make commitments regarding the source from which the user entity's data is acquired and where it may reside, meaning not just where it is stored but also how it is processed and what systems it moves through. Consider a case in which a CCSO with five locations has a breach in one. It may be difficult to determine if any one user entity's data was in that location at the time of the breach or where it was from the time it was input to the time it was moved to a secondary server.

Regulatory requirements and the terms that the CCSO establishes on how it will address such requirements would also be expected to be covered in the SLA. A CCSO providing IaaS, for example, may establish that user entities are responsible for meeting privacy regulations. However, if the user entity places specific limitations on the geographical data location, based on the user entity's legal obligations, the CCSO will also be responsible for meeting these legal obligations and will need to establish controls that address compliance with this requirement. An example of a situation in which the user entity takes on greater responsibility for identifying and complying with stipulated privacy requirements is a payment processor that operates merchant terminals in a SaaS environment. A CCSO may commit to providing varying levels of service to different user entities, for example, varying system availability and downtime commitments. This potential variability between commitments to different user entities at a single CCSO underscores the importance of reading and understanding the CCSO's SLAs.

Other Unique Considerations

Dynamic Use of Available Resources

Many special considerations will have to be addressed in a CCSO's system description. A main concern here is one of scope. Because cloud computing is usually elastic, automated, and virtualized, the cloud technology will change based on the user entities' ongoing processing needs, and user entities may be using equipment and other resources that reside in a variety of locations. User entity needs, the data involved, and the resources the user entity is using may be in a constant state of flux. This feature of cloud computing represents a challenge for the service auditor beyond what is seen in traditional IT service

---

[5] TSP section 100, *Trust Services Principles, Criteria, and Illustrations for Security, Availability, Processing Integrity, Confidentiality, and Privacy* (AICPA, *Technical Practice Aids*).

organization models. In traditional models, the service organization may be managing customer-specific hardware (computer and data storage) or software data centers that are 100 percent dedicated to an individual user entity. With cloud computing, one system and the data it uses may be serving multiple customers simultaneously and the data may be offloaded to different locations or to subservice organizations as necessary. All of these characteristics can complicate the range of issues a service auditor needs to consider.

In addition to the information that ordinarily is included in a system description, such as system boundaries and system components, other aspects of the system may need to be included in a CCSO's description of its system, such as the operating model, the use of internal versus external resources, and the geographic location of the data centers.

Although cloud systems are often touted as having "unlimited" capacity, realistically there are limits to bandwidth, processing power, response time, system and data backup, and system recovery capabilities (especially during system outages). Such information about system capacity should be covered in the system description (for guidance on system descriptions, refer to paragraphs 1.25, 1.34–.35, and 3.01–.33 and appendix A, "Information for Management of a Service Organization," of this guide).

Processing

A key characteristic of cloud environments is that the CCSO typically has the ability to switch processing between hardware and physical locations, bringing new facilities online quickly, or migrating portions of processing to infrastructure located in the facility of an outside subservice organization. This permits the CCSO to respond to changes in demand and infrastructure availability. As a result, there can be multiple CCSOs supporting user entities. A key concern for user entities and the service auditor, then, is in understanding where processing may occur, under what conditions various locations might be used, the process for migrating processing to the new environments, contractual relationships with subservice organizations, and any commitments to user entities that may be affected by such changes.

Data Storage

In a multi-tenancy cloud environment, CCSO customer data is usually stored in storage systems that are shared among the customers. Absent proper access controls and management processes, this sharing of resources means that it is possible for customers or a third party to gain unauthorized access, either inadvertently or intentionally, to another user entity's data. This may result in a breach of the CCSO's commitment to user entities to maintain the privacy of the data or a violation of a law or regulation (for example, the Health Insurance Portability and Accountability Act of 1996) by the CCSO, the user entity, or both. In a sales and billing system, for example, a regulator who receives access to one user entity's data in that system may inadvertently gain access to the data of other customers. The CCSO's system description would be expected to include controls that cover this risk to appropriately address user entity concerns, particularly when the description addresses the confidentiality or privacy principle. The service auditor should evaluate whether the CCSO's controls are suitably designed and operating effectively to meet the criteria related to this risk, particularly after giving consideration to the CCSO's commitments and laws and regulations that are relevant to the services provided.

Encryption of user entity data (discussed in more detail subsequently) is often an important control to mitigate the risk of unauthorized access, for example, to protect electronic communications and data transfer traffic. Transport encryption using the Transport Layer Security (TLS) protocol/SSL (secure sockets layer) protocol is commonly used for encrypting traffic between entities. However, in some instances, the data may be so sensitive that the sender and the recipient may want to protect the data from being accessed by the CCSO. In these situations, securing the data may require the sender and the recipient to implement full end-to-end encryption.

Depending on the risks, the encryption may be performed by the user entity, the CCSO, or both. Encryption may be required by laws or regulations, particularly for sensitive personal information for which privacy laws mandate its use as a basic protection mechanism.

Encryption and Key Management

The cloud environment frequently requires a more secure level of encryption than other technology environments. Encryption occurs in different stages of the data life cycle or transaction process (for example, data in transit, physical access, and data at rest). Encryption can occur at the hardware level or in software; each of these technologies has its own risks and controls that need to be operating effectively for the encryption to be effective. The service auditor may consider whether the description provides sufficient information about the use of encryption and its supporting processes to meet user needs.

For the description of the encryption process to be useful, the description needs to address controls related to the creation, storage, and use of the associated encryption keys for data at rest and in transport. The service auditor should determine whether such controls are suitably designed and operating effectively to meet the encryption key management requirements. The CCSO also needs controls that protect encryption keys during key generation, storage, use, change, and destruction. For some services, users may require unique encryption keys when there are multiple system users; however, unique keys may not be feasible in some deployment models. The service auditor may need to consider whether such unique keys are needed in order to meet user needs.

Control Considerations Regarding Resource Sharing With Subservice Organizations

A CCSO that requires added capacity to meet user entity needs or that seeks to offer user entities a greater variety of options may outsource some of its work to a subservice organization. If the CCSO uses a subservice organization, the service auditor will need to identify data life cycle flow as well as the transaction flow to determine where the data resides and how applications are processed. If the subservice organization is carved out of the engagement,[6] it may be challenging for the service auditor to understand the exact nature of the carve-out and what systems, processes, or timeframes are included or excluded from the system on which the service auditor is reporting. Issues to be considered will include, for example, various aspects of privacy, such as onward

---

[6] In order for a practitioner to issue an unqualified practitioner's report for a service organization controls (SOC) 3 engagement, all of the criteria in TSP section 100 that are applicable to the principle(s) being reported on (applicable trust services criteria) must be met. If a service organization engages a practitioner to perform a SOC 3 engagement in which subservice organizations have been carved out of the engagement and one or more controls necessary to meet one or more of the criteria have been carved out (excluded from the scope of the engagement), the service auditor will be unable to issue an unqualified practitioner's report.

transfer and secondary use of information and confidentiality. Because of ongoing data exchange between the cloud and a subservice organization, a system description in which the subservice organization is carved out may not provide user entities with sufficiently useful information. Exclusion of the subservice organization through a carve-out may result in a gap in information about controls that is necessary for the system to be understood by user entities, especially as it relates to privacy. The service auditor can attempt to identify the boundaries of what is being reported on but may be challenged to do this in a meaningful way. When the risk of misunderstanding is high, the service auditor needs to consider whether it is appropriate to perform an engagement using the carve-out method. If use of the carve-out method is appropriate, the service auditor should evaluate whether the system description appropriately identifies the services provided by the carved-out subservice organization, the criteria that would need to be either completely or partially met by controls at the subservice organization, and the types of controls that the CCSO expects the subservice organization to have in place to meet the criteria. When a service organization uses the carve-out method to present a subservice organization, the service auditor should look to the guidance in paragraphs 3.37–.38 of this guide, which describe considerations in determining whether the use of the carve-out method prevents the description of the service organization's system from being fairly presented.

Engagement Timing

Because of the highly virtual and dynamic nature of cloud technology, the service auditor faces testing and timing challenges, especially when virtualization means that some systems or data are temporary in nature and may not exist at the time the service auditor plans to perform testing. The scope and timing of testing will be affected when the CCSO uses multiple locations and data flows between the locations at peak times or during scheduled maintenance. All potential processing locations need to be considered for inclusion in the scope of the engagement, and the service auditor needs to consider whether the locations are in scope for the entire reporting period or only a portion of the period. Also, when certain locations or infrastructure are used only for a portion of the period, it may not be possible to obtain historical audit logs, access lists, or configuration files once processing has migrated back to the original location or to a new location or infrastructure. As a result, the service auditor needs to consider such factors in determining the scope and timing of procedures. In addition, the service auditor needs to understand the CCSO's system operational and security logging (for example, outages, initial program loading, system patching, and operation management activities) and make inquiries about the retention of logs. The absence of such information could affect the ability to obtain sufficient appropriate evidence regarding the effectiveness of the CCSO's controls.

As an example, consider a situation in which privacy and confidentiality are particular concerns. If the CCSO has a secondary location but no data is processed there, this location may be out of scope at the beginning and end of the examination period and may not appear to require inclusion in the scope of the examination. However, if data is moved to the secondary location during the period covered by the engagement, then the secondary location will need to be included in the scope of the engagement. The service auditor would need to determine whether the information from the secondary location will be available for testing during the planned testing period and may need to alter the timing of the testing.

Rights and Obligations

Matters for the service auditor to consider include the rights and obligations of user entities and which rights and obligations have been imposed upon or ceded to the CCSO. There may be disagreements between the user entities and the CCSO in this area and a need for controls at the CCSO that work in conjunction with user entity or other third-party controls. In these situations, the location of data throughout the user entity's process may need to be understood and addressed in scoping and planning the engagement.

Confidentiality and Privacy

The following definitions of *confidentiality* and *privacy* are based on the definitions in TSP section 100:

> **Confidentiality**. Information designated as confidential is protected as committed or agreed. (Under TSP section 100, *confidentiality* ordinarily applies to information that is not personal information.)

> **Privacy**. Personal information is collected, used, retained, disclosed, and destroyed in conformity with the commitments in the entity's privacy notice and with criteria set forth in generally accepted privacy principles (GAPP). (The term *privacy* ordinarily applies to personal information or personally identifiable information.)

However, other definitions of these terms may be included in laws, regulations, or contractual agreements.

Contracts and service level agreements may set forth many privacy and confidentiality commitments and obligations. Some special considerations in the cloud environment include the following:

- *The kinds of data the CCSO is handling.* Data definitions may vary based on the client location, industry, or user entity. For example, data may be subject to different definitions of *private* or *confidential* based on whether it is sourced from the United States versus the European Union (EU). As an industry example, an entity in the health care industry may have specific definitions of privacy or confidentiality based on existing laws or regulations. Various companies and contractual agreements may also have their own specific definitions of protected classes of data that the service auditor needs to understand, for example, the difference between *sensitive personal information* and other types of personal information. The definitions may be subject to various layers of complexity. For example, cross border data restrictions may apply to EU-sourced personal information or to sensitive personal information, but not to other types of information. As a result, the service auditor will need to gain an understanding of the particular kinds of data being acquired, processed, stored, and destroyed and how such data is affected by applicable laws, regulations, or contractual agreements.

- *How data is obtained, retained, and destroyed.* The handling and disposal of the data may be subject to various laws, regulations, or contract terms.

- *The need to address contractual, legal, or regulatory obligations.* The Massachusetts Data Privacy Law (201 CMR 17.00: "Standards for the Protection of Personal Information of Residents of the Commonwealth") is an example of a legal requirement applicable to CCSOs that receive, store, maintain, process, or have access to personal information as a result of providing services to anyone subject to that specific law (that is, residents of the Commonwealth of Massachusetts) regardless of where the data is obtained, processed, and stored.

- *Secondary use issues.* Many contracts with CCSOs establish that the CCSO has a right to use the data in its possession for testing or other purposes. The service auditor would need to determine whether the CCSO has effective controls that ensure that any secondary use of information is consistent with the commitments in its contracts, service-level agreements, and relevant statements of privacy practices.

- *Ownership of the data.* At issue would be not only ownership of the data but also how user entities can secure and retrieve data at the end of the relationship with the CCSO. Some CCSO contracts stipulate that the CCSO retains ownership of the data if the user entity fails to meet the contract terms and conditions. In some cases ownership rights may be ceded to the CCSO as a result of law or regulation. These considerations will have an effect on the CCSO's ability to move data, access it, and archive it and could have a material effect on the user entity's ability to comply with its privacy obligations. Such examples highlight the scoping questions a service auditor may face in approaching the engagement. The service auditor may have to understand how data is defined, accessed, used, and managed (how it can be leveraged, moved, or manipulated).

- *Unique user specifications and requirements.* At its most basic level, these specifications and requirements address who has the right to access and use the data, although other considerations may arise based on the specific circumstances of the user entity and the CCSO.

- *Location of data and related privacy regulations.* Use of private data is generally governed by the law of the jurisdiction in which it is held, but it may also be subject to laws of other jurisdictions based on the data subject, where the data was acquired, or the residency of the person to which the data relates. As a result, there are numerous potential sources of privacy laws and regulations (such as governing law, data subject, and data source or location). It is important that the service auditor understand the CCSO's mechanism for recognizing the applicable rules and complying with them. Compliance with laws and regulations in the CCSO's home country may not be sufficient if the CCSO is operating in or has possession of data of a resident in another country that is subject to regulation there. As a result, it is important to understand not only where the data is stored and processed, but also where the data was acquired.

Examination Considerations in a Cloud Environment

Service Auditor Considerations

In performing a SOC 2 or SOC 3 engagement, a service auditor needs to consider a number of matters, particularly given the variety of deployment models and service models that may be used in various combinations. Issues for the service auditor include how to

- gain an understanding of the information life cycle, the system, and their boundaries.

- establish the boundaries of the system that the practitioner is reporting on.

- understand who is responsible for controls and the nature and effect of complementary user entity controls.

- develop a testing approach for virtual processing environments, particularly nonpersistent (ephemeral) environments.

The service auditor's considerations may vary based on the type of deployment model (private, public, hybrid, or community cloud) and service model (SaaS, PaaS, or IaaS) or the various combinations of deployment or service models. The practitioner may need to consider additional matters depending on which of the trust services principles the service auditor is reporting on. The following are the five trust services principles and examples of the related matters:

- Security (unauthorized access)

- Availability (interdependency of various CCSOs)

- Processing integrity (replication of processing environments across cloud instances)

- Confidentiality (understanding all uses and locations of confidential information)

- Privacy (understanding all uses and locations of personally identifiable information)

Considering Subservice Organizations in a Cloud Environment

CCSOs may outsource some of their functions to other service organizations (subservice organizations). As a result, the service auditor needs to consider all of the service organizations involved with respect to the principle the service auditor is reporting on. Considerable service auditor judgment is necessary to identify the boundaries of the system based on the services provided by the subservice organization.

To some extent, the considerations are the same as in any SOC 2 or SOC 3 engagement. However, in the cloud environment, other concerns arise from the dynamic nature of the architecture itself. The ability of the CCSO to rapidly expand, through the use of subservice organizations, or contract, by decommissioning virtualized components, may present the service auditor with unique challenges. In evaluating the boundaries of the system, the service auditor should begin by considering the broadest boundaries of the system. Although the effect on user entities of aspects of the system within the broader boundaries of the system may not be obvious, they may have a downstream or indirect effect on the services provided to user entities. These broad limits may incorporate multiple subservice organizations or the subservice organizations of a subservice organization. If the boundaries of the system are defined too narrowly, the service auditor should consider whether the report will be meaningful and useful to user entities. Due to the complexity of cloud services, the challenge of defining the boundaries of the CCSO's system often goes beyond the usual considerations in a SOC 2 or SOC 3 engagement that does not involve a CCSO.

To deliver a useful report, the service auditor would have to understand the architectures involved. The risks to the service auditor or the CCSO include failure to identify all the third parties that have potential access to client data or subservice organizations that share responsibility for controls necessary to support the applicable trust services principles. A SaaS provider, for example, may itself use services from an IaaS, which may sometimes outsource its overflow to a subservice organization. These multiple levels of providers would be a particular concern if, for example, the CCSO is contractually or otherwise bound to limit access to protected information to a contractually identified group of personnel.

Assessing the Applicability of the Trust Services Principles to a CCSO Engagement

Scoping is critical in any SOC engagement, and that is certainly true with engagements in the cloud environment. Ordinarily, any or all of the trust services principles may be applicable to a CCSO's system. In discussing the scope of the engagement with management of the CCSO, the service auditor may discuss the relevance of the various principles to the CCSO's system, such as the availability principle in relation to various deployment models used and the system's ability to meet the volume demands placed on it by multiple users. The industry involved may also dictate the kind of engagement performed. CPAs will find extensive information on defining the scope of a SOC 2 engagement in chapter 2, "Planning a Service Auditor's Engagement," of this guide.

Cloud Considerations Affecting the Examination

The cloud environment presents several unique scope and testing considerations.

Scope

Describing the system and understanding its unique aspects are important in a SOC engagement for a CCSO. The very term *cloud* implies that the system's boundaries are difficult to define. Unique cloud attributes that affect the engagement include the cloud's virtual and dynamic nature, which may make it hard to determine the location and timing of processes or to examine them after they occur. Locating data storage sites may also present a challenge. Multi-tenancy and the use of subservice organizations represent added difficulties in identifying who has access to the system. For the service auditor, it may be challenging to determine whether appropriate access restrictions are in place, underscoring the importance of understanding the different levels of access controls.

The CCSO provides the system description that the service auditor uses to perform the engagement. The service auditor may need to work with the CCSO to refine the description, because it may be challenging to arrive at a realistic set of boundaries.

Testing

The service auditor should inform the CCSO about the nature of the evidence and audit trails that are needed. Thus, when there are significant changes in the system, the CCSO will know what evidence should be retained. Consider a CCSO that offloaded data to a secondary location for one month during scheduled maintenance. That secondary location is later converted or upgraded and its servers are decommissioned. If the CCSO is not aware that the service auditor will need documented evidence from that period of time, that evidence may be destroyed or unavailable.

Another challenge for service auditors is the virtualized environment. The service auditor is only able to examine either artifacts—information left over after a process has been performed—or the monitoring and activity logs that were created at the time the processes occurred (for example, the creation or decommissioning of a virtualized environment). Unless the CCSO maintains audit trails for the service auditor (such as logs or access lists), there can be no direct testing of ephemeral environments because they no longer exist the time service auditor performs testing. As a result, it probably will be necessary to test the processes over the creation, configuration, and decommissioning of the virtual environments or to test continuously throughout the examination period, rather than testing a sample of the environments that exist at a point in time. Standardized processes should exist for the creation, configuration, management, and decommissioning of virtual environments and effective change management standards should be followed. Such steps are important in addressing data rights and obligations in the case of a breach when an effort is being made to determine how data was leaked or how an unauthorized user gained access to it. The service auditor at this point may have to turn to certain controls, such as those over the process that creates the virtual environment, to understand an environment that is no longer live.

Type 1 Versus Type 2 Report Considerations Unique to CCSOs

A type 1 SOC 2 report enables user entities to understand CCSO controls, but it does not offer assurance about the effectiveness of those controls. In the cloud environment, a great deal of concern exists about not only the design of controls but also their operating effectiveness due to the risk involved in this environment. The service auditor can help management of the CCSO in assessing the needs of user entities and explain that a type 2 report may add valuable assurance. Service auditors are reminded that, from a regulatory standpoint, even though data may be outsourced to a CCSO, risk management, liability, and accountability cannot be. In other words, although the CCSO has its own responsibilities for legal and regulatory requirements, the user entities retain responsibility for meeting all legal and regulatory requirements regarding data that has been outsourced to a cloud. The service auditor should understand the aspects of laws or regulations relevant to the service provided by the CCSO.

Questions for Service Auditors to Consider

The following list provides an overview of some of the questions a service auditor might consider related to a SOC 2 engagement for a CCSO. It is not meant to be exhaustive and is not entirely cloud specific, but it offers an introduction to issues that may be helpful to service auditors in accepting, planning, conducting, and reporting on the engagement:

- What is the cloud deployment model: public, private, hybrid, community?
- Which service models are provided by the CCSO: IaaS, PaaS, or SaaS?
- Are controls over the functions performed by a CCSO's vendor needed to meet the applicable trust services criteria? Is the vendor a subservice organization?
- What controls have been implemented to address the requirements included in SLAs?
- Are controls at subservice organizations adequate? How does the CCSO determine that?
- Are controls in place to deliver the services agreed upon in SLAs? Is the effectiveness of these controls monitored?

- What kinds of accountability and responsibility have been assigned to the CCSO and the user entities?
- What complementary user entity controls are required, and have they been identified in the description of the CCSO's system?
- How does configuration management protect against accidental changes that could affect security?
- Where is the data stored? Does location hinder availability in any way or raise other concerns?
- How is data storage and movement of data between storage devices or locations handled? What is the CCSO's process for encrypting and protecting the integrity of data at rest; in transit; and when backed-up, archived, and removed from storage? What are the controls over data stored on media devices and the handling of physical media devices?
- What opportunities are available to monitor cloud performance? Can the service auditor gain a realistic understanding of the CCSO's virtual environments, particularly those of ephemeral nature?
- What controls over system performance have been implemented to provide reasonable assurance that service levels are achieved during periods of increased—or decreased—network traffic or system processing?
- What are the user entity's rights and obligations if the CCSO is acquired or undergoes a significant structural change?
- How scalable and agile is the cloud model? Is the system reassessed when new technologies are introduced to identify or anticipate issues related to security, privacy, confidentiality, processing integrity, and availability?
- What is covered in the subservice organization agreement? Issues to consider include the following:
  — Who is liable if there is a security breach, if data is leaked, or in any other event that could prove a liability for the user entity?
  — Based on the contract, who is responsible for protecting the data? What assurances are there that the data will be protected and available as needed?
  — What options are available if there is a service interruption?
  — Under what circumstances can the contract be terminated?
  — What happens to the applications and data if the contract is terminated?
- If the data is housed in another jurisdiction, does the CCSO comply with the privacy or other laws to which the user entities are subject?
- What is the skill level of CCSO and subservice organization employees? Are they adequate to meet user entity needs now and in the future?
- Who owns the user entity data? What happens to that data at the end of its life cycle or the end of the user entity and CCSO relationship? Can the user entity retrieve the data at that point? If not, how is it handled? What steps are taken to address previous comingling of data when the relationship ends?

- How are the input, loading, and update of application standing data or master file data performed when the data is the responsibility of the CCSO? For example, if the CCSO provides standing data such as updates to sales tax tables, how is this data managed and maintained if it is a critical part of the application system calculations or other functionalities?

- How long is data retained, and in what location? How is it disposed of? What steps are taken to ensure it is deleted or destroyed across various data stores?

- What kind of comingling of data or systems takes place? What steps are taken to prevent comingling from allowing unauthorized access to client data?

- Do controls appropriately prevent CCSO personnel or others from accessing encryption keys?

- Are security systems continually reviewed and updated to ensure they meet user expectations and any possible legal or regulatory challenges?

- Does multi-tenancy present any security threats not appropriately addressed?

- Do security controls take into account the fact that different data controls may be used in different locations?

- What physical or other kinds of security does the CCSO have?

- How would a disaster or breach in service at a subservice organization affect the user entity?

- How quickly can the CCSO realistically be expected to address breaches or failures or get the system running again? In which order will customer problems be addressed? (In other words, what priority will be given to specific needs of user entities?)

- How does the CCSO investigate or plan to investigate breaches or service failures?

- What steps would be taken to isolate problems affecting one tenant or one section of the cloud?

- What data loss prevention steps are taken by the CCSO? Does the CCSO's description of its system include complementary user entity controls that address data loss prevention?

- What kind of assessment is made of the security or vulnerability of subservice organizations, vendors, and others involved in the system?

- What standards and types of controls are subservice organizations or vendors expected to maintain?

- In the case of SaaS, who owns the applications? Where are they located? Who is responsible for updating and maintaining them?

- Are security upgrades made for software in use?

- How is application security protected?

Appendix F

Guidance Updates—Clarified Auditing Standards

This appendix includes information about how the clarified Statement on Auditing Standards (SAS) Nos. 122–125 may affect an auditor's practice or methodology. These clarified standards are effective for periods ending on or after December 15, 2012. Early adoption is not permitted. Any references to or excerpts from auditing guidance in this guide will be conformed to reflect the guidance in SAS Nos. 122–125 in the next edition, which is when these clarified SASs are effective.

As a result of the Auditing Standards Board's (ASB's) Clarity Project, all extant[1] AU sections have been modified. In some cases, individual AU sections have been revised into individual clarified standards. In other cases, some AU sections have been grouped together and revised as one or more clarified standards. In addition, the ASB revised the AU section number order established by SAS No. 1, *Responsibilities and Functions of the Independent Auditor* (AICPA, *Professional Standards*, AU sec. 110), to follow the same number order used in International Standards on Auditing (ISAs) for all clarified AU sections for which there are comparable ISAs.

Although the Clarity Project was not intended to create additional requirements, some revisions have resulted in substantive changes (primarily clarifying) changes that may require auditors to make adjustments in their practices.

Substantive Changes

Substantive changes are considered likely to affect the firms' audit methodology and engagements because they contain *substantive* or *other changes*, defined as having one or both of the following characteristics:

- A change or changes to an audit methodology that may require effort to implement
- A number of small changes that, although not individually significant, may affect audit engagements

Primarily Clarifying Changes

Primarily clarifying changes are intended to explicitly state what may have been implicit in the extant standards, which, over time, resulted in diversity in practice.

The preface of this guide and the Financial Reporting Center at www.aicpa.org/InterestAreas/FRC/Pages/FRC.aspx provide more information about the Clarity Project. You can also visit www.aicpa.org/InterestAreas/FRC/AuditAttest/Pages/ImprovingClarityASBStandards.aspx.

---

[1] The term *extant* is used throughout this appendix in reference to the standards that are superseded by the clarified standards

Audit Updates—Clarified Auditing Standards

Part I: Substantive Changes

The AU-C sections in this part are considered likely to affect the firms' audit methodology and engagements because they contain *substantive* or *other changes*, defined as having one or both of the following characteristics:

- A change or changes to an audit methodology that may require effort to implement
- A number of small changes that, although not individually significant, may affect audit engagements

The auditor may need to address the changes in these AU-C sections early in the audit process. Some of the requirements may affect decisions to accept an engagement, and some will need to be communicated early in the planning process. The clarified standards are effective for periods ending on or after December 15, 2012, and may require the auditor to apply certain of the substantive changes as early as the planning stage for 2012 year-end audits. The auditor needs to review these AU-C sections to identify areas that apply to his or her practice.

F.01 Consideration of Laws and Regulations

AU-C section 250, *Consideration of Laws and Regulations in an Audit of Financial Statements* (AICPA, *Professional Standards*), requires the performance of procedures to identify instances of noncompliance with those laws and regulations that may have a material effect on the financial statements. Specifically, it requires the auditor to inspect correspondence, if any, with the relevant licensing or regulatory authorities. Because the extant standard did not require the auditor to perform procedures to identify such instances of noncompliance, unless specific information concerning possible illegal acts came to the auditor's attention, this requirement is expected to affect current practice.

Additionally, AU-C section 250 makes explicit several requirements for the auditor that were implicit in the extant standard and, accordingly, are not expected to change current practice, including the following:

- Obtain an understanding of the legal and regulatory framework.
- Obtain an understanding of how the entity is complying with that framework.
- Determine whether the auditor has a responsibility to report suspected noncompliance to parties outside the entity.
- Document identified or suspected noncompliance, including the results of any discussions about such items.

AU-C section 250 states that because of the inherent limitations of an audit, some material misstatements in the financial statements may not be detected, even though the audit is properly planned and performed in accordance with generally accepted auditing standards (GAAS). The concept described as "inherent limitations of an audit" is different from the concept of "no assurance" in the extant standard, which, in relation to indirect illegal acts, states that an audit performed in accordance with GAAS provides no assurance that noncompliance with laws and regulations will be detected or that any contingent liabilities that may result will be disclosed. The differing descriptions of these concepts are not expected to affect current practice.

The requirement in the extant standard to obtain a written representation from management concerning the absence of noncompliance with laws or regulations is included in AU-C section 580, *Written Representations* (AICPA, *Professional Standards*).

AU-C section 250 supersedes AU section 317, *Illegal Acts by Clients* (AICPA, *Professional Standards*).

F.02 Communicating Internal Control Related Matters

AU-C section 265, *Communicating Internal Control Related Matters Identified in an Audit* (AICPA, *Professional Standards*), adds two new requirements for communication of internal control matters and makes explicit two requirements that were implicit in the extant standards.

AU-C section 265 adds the following two new requirements:

- It requires the auditor to communicate in writing or orally, only to management, other deficiencies in internal control identified during the audit that have not been communicated to management by other parties and that, in the auditor's professional judgment, are of sufficient importance to merit management's attention. The ASB does not view this new requirement as a difference from the extant standard because auditor judgment is the sole determinant regarding whether a deficiency, other than a material weakness or significant deficiency, is of sufficient importance to communicate to management. Likewise, the extant standard does not preclude the auditor from communicating other internal control matters to management if the auditor believes that it is important to do so.

- It requires the auditor to include in the written communication an explanation of the potential effects of the significant deficiencies and material weaknesses identified. The ASB believes that management and those charged with governance need this information to enable them to take appropriate remedial action. Further, the ASB does not believe that this requires additional effort by the auditor because the potential effects would have been considered as part of the evaluation of the severity of the deficiency. The potential effects of this requirement do not need to be quantified.

For audits in which the auditor was engaged to report on the effectiveness of an entity's internal control over financial reporting under AT section 501, *An Examination of an Entity's Internal Control Over Financial Reporting That Is Integrated With an Audit of Its Financial Statements* (AICPA, *Professional Standards*), the preceding items are not required because they are already included within the examination requirements.

AU-C section 265 also makes explicit two requirements that were implicit in the extant standards and, accordingly, are not expected to change current practice:

- It requires the auditor to determine whether, on the basis of the audit work performed, the auditor has identified one or more deficiencies in internal control.

- It requires the auditor to include specific matters in the optional written communication stating that no material weaknesses were identified during the audit. The new language is similar to that used in the written communication of significant deficiencies and material weaknesses presented in an illustrative example in the extant standard but not explicitly required.

AU-C section 265 supersedes AU section 325, *Communicating Internal Control Related Matters Identified in an Audit* (AICPA, *Professional Standards*).

F.03 Related Parties

AU-C section 550, *Related Parties* (AICPA, *Professional Standards*), shifts the focus of the audit to looking at the risk of material misstatements from related parties, regardless of which financial reporting framework is used. The shift to a risk-based approach to auditing-related parties may be significant for audits of financial statements prepared in accordance with an other comprehensive basis of accounting (OCBOA). AU-C section 550 is framework neutral, encompassing financial reporting frameworks, in addition to accounting principles generally accepted in the United States of America (GAAP), such as International Financial Reporting Standards, as promulgated by the International Accounting Standards Board, as well as special purpose frameworks described in AU-C section 800, *Special Considerations—Audits of Financial Statements Prepared in Accordance With Special Purpose Frameworks* (AICPA, *Professional Standards*). Note that the objectives, requirements, and definitions in AU-C section 550 are applicable irrespective of whether the applicable financial reporting framework establishes requirements for related-party disclosures.

AU-C section 550 supersedes AU section 334, *Related Parties* (AICPA, *Professional Standards*). The extant standard focuses on auditing the amounts and disclosures pursuant to GAAP and centers on the provisions of Financial Accounting Standards Board *Accounting Standards Codification* 850, *Related Party Disclosures.*

F.04 Group Audits

AU-C section 600, *Special Considerations—Audits of Group Financial Statements (Including the Work of Component Auditors)* (AICPA, *Professional Standards*), specifically articulates the procedures necessary for a group engagement team to perform when auditing group financial statements. The requirements of AU-C section 600 may affect a firm's decision whether to accept or continue an engagement. In addition, a major area of change addresses effective communication with, and supervision of, the component auditor.

The clarified standard identifies a *group audit* as the audit of group financial statements (that is, financial statements that include the financial information of more than one component). A group audit exists, for example, when management prepares financial information that is included in the group financial statements related to a function, process, product or service, or geographical location (subsidiary in a foreign country). Group audits usually, but not always, include the work of component auditors. A component auditor performs work on financial information related to a component of the group that the group engagement team will use for the group audit and can be an auditor within the same audit firm (member office firm in another city or country) or a different audit firm. A component auditor would include, for example, another auditor or an audit team from another office that performs inventory testing in remote locations for the group auditor.

AU-C section 600 is significantly broader in scope than the extant standard. It shifts the focus of the audit from how to conduct an audit that involves other auditors to how to conduct an effective audit of group financial statements (see the subsequent section, "Terminology"). AU-C section 600 includes requirements of GAAS established in other standards that are applied in audits of group financial statements. AU-C section 600 strengthens existing standards by making it easier for auditors to understand and apply the requirements of

GAAS, such as those contained in the risk assessment standards, in the context of an audit of group financial statements. The extant standard was written in 1972 and, thus, does not take into consideration the risk assessment standards.

Differences in Focus and Approach

Because AU-C section 600 is based on ISA 600, *Special Considerations—Audits of Group Financial Statements (Including the Work of Component Auditors)*, the scope of AU-C section 600, including its objective, requirements, and guidance, has been significantly expanded from the scope of the extant standard. AU-C section 600 specifically articulates the procedures necessary for the group engagement team to perform in order to be involved with component auditors to the extent necessary for an effective audit and, compared with the extant standard, better articulates the degree of involvement required when reference is made to component auditors in the auditor's report.

The requirements of AU-C section 600 address the following:

- Acceptance and continuance considerations
- The group engagement team's process to assess risk
- The determination of materiality to be used to audit the group financial statements
- The determination of materiality to be used to audit components
- The selection of components and account balances for audit testing
- Communications between the group engagement team and component auditors
- Assessing the adequacy and appropriateness of audit evidence by the group engagement team in forming an opinion on the financial statements

In situations when the group engagement partner does not make reference to a component auditor in the auditor's report on the group financial statements, all the requirements of AU-C section 600 apply, when relevant, in the context of the specific group audit engagement. Highlights of the requirements, particularly those that represent a change from existing standards, follow.

In situations when the group engagement partner decides to make reference to a component auditor in the audit report on the group financial statements, certain of the requirements of AU-C section 600 do not apply. Note that, although AU-C section 600 is based on ISA 600, ISA 600 does not permit reference to a component auditor in the auditor's report on the group financial statements. This is the most significant area of divergence between the clarified standards and the ISAs.

Terminology

As previously mentioned, AU-C section 600 includes several new terms, as well as certain revised terms, from the extant standard. The term *group* is introduced, which is defined as "all the components whose financial information is included in the group financial statements. A group always has more than one component." *Component* is defined as "an entity or business activity for which group or component management prepares financial information that is required by the applicable financial reporting framework to be included in the group financial statements." *Group financial statements* are defined as "financial statements that include the financial information of more than one component."

The term *principal auditor*, which is used in the extant standard, is not used in AU-C section 600 and has been replaced by the terms *group engagement partner, group engagement team,* or *auditor of the group financial statements.*

The definition of *group engagement partner* is aligned with the definition of *engagement partner* provided in AU-C section 220, *Quality Control for an Engagement Conducted in Accordance With Generally Accepted Auditing Standards* (AICPA, *Professional Standards*), as follows: "The partner or other person in the firm who is responsible for the group audit engagement and its performance and for the auditor's report on the group financial statements that is issued on behalf of the firm."

The group engagement partner is the individual responsible for

- the direction, supervision, and performance of the group audit engagement in compliance with professional standards and regulatory and legal requirements and

- determining whether the auditor's report that is issued is appropriate in the circumstances.

However, the group engagement partner may be assisted in fulfilling his or her responsibilities by the group engagement team or, as appropriate in the circumstances, by the firm. To help distinguish when such assistance is permitted, AU-C section 600 uses the terms *group engagement partner, group engagement team,* and *auditor of the group financial statements.*

Requirements to be undertaken by the group engagement partner are addressed to the group engagement partner. When the group engagement team may assist the group engagement partner in fulfilling a requirement, the requirement is addressed to the group engagement team. When it may be appropriate in the circumstances for the firm to fulfill a requirement, the requirement is addressed to the auditor of the group financial statements.

Group engagement team is defined as "partners, including the group engagement partner, and staff who establish the overall group audit strategy, communicate with component auditors, perform work on the consolidation process, and evaluate the conclusions drawn from the audit evidence as the basis for forming an opinion on the group financial statements." Note that auditors who do not meet the definition of a *member of the group engagement team* are considered to be component auditors. Thus, a component auditor may work for a network firm of the group engagement partner's firm or may even work for a different office of the same firm.

Acceptance and Continuance

An overall difference between AU-C section 600 and the extant standard is the change in focus when determining whether to accept or continue the engagement. AU-C section 600 bases that determination on whether the auditor believes that he or she will be able to obtain sufficient appropriate audit evidence over the group financial statements, including whether the group engagement team will have appropriate access to information. The extant standard bases that determination on whether the auditor would be able to sufficiently participate in the group audit in order to be the principal auditor.

Note that this approach means a change in the mindset of the group engagement partner from considering the group engagement team's coverage of the principal amounts and reliance on other (component) auditors to considering the sufficiency of the group engagement team's involvement in the performance of the audit, including involvement in the work of the component auditors.

Link to the Risk Assessment Standards

In aligning with ISA 600, AU-C section 600 focuses on the application of the risk assessment standards to the performance of the group audit, including references and discussion of their specific application in group audit situations.

Involvement With, and Understanding of, Component Auditors

The clarified standard requires the group engagement team to gain an understanding of the component auditor. This understanding includes certain aspects that are already covered by the extant standard, such as competence and independence, as well as additional areas, such as a determination of the extent to which the group engagement team will be able to be involved in the work of the component auditor.

Once an understanding of the component auditor has been gained, the group engagement partner may choose to either

- assume responsibility for, and, thus, be required to be involved in, the work of component auditors, insofar as that work relates to the expression of an opinion on the group financial statements or

- not assume responsibility for, and, accordingly, make reference to, the audit of a component auditor in the auditor's report on the group financial statements.

Involvement in the work performed by a component auditor will involve the group engagement team undertaking the following actions:

- Establishing component materiality to be used by the component auditor.

- Performing risk assessment procedures and participating in the assessment of risks of material misstatement and the planned audit response. These may be performed together with the component auditor or by the group engagement team.

Materiality

The clarified standard requires the group engagement team to determine materiality and performance materiality for the group as a whole, as well as component materiality (that is, the materiality to be used to audit the financial information of a component for purposes of the group audit). The extant standard does not provide guidance on the application of materiality in the audit of group financial statements. Component materiality is determined by the group engagement team, regardless of whether the group engagement partner is making reference to the audit of a component auditor. For purposes of the group audit, component materiality is required to be lower than group materiality in order to reduce the risk that the aggregate of detected and undetected misstatements in the group financial statements exceeds the materiality for the group financial statements as a whole.

Responding to Assessed Risks

AU-C section 600 builds on the principle in the extant standard that, in order to achieve a proper review of matters affecting the consolidating or combining of accounts in the financial statements, the principal auditor should adopt appropriate measures to assure the coordination of activities with those of the other auditor. AU-C section 600 includes requirements and guidance relating to work to be performed on all components for which the group engagement partner is assuming responsibility for the work of the component auditor, regardless of whether that work is performed by the group engagement team or component auditors. It includes requirements and guidance specifying the nature, timing, and extent of the group engagement team's involvement in the work of the component auditors, particularly when performing work on significant components.

A *significant component* is defined in AU-C section 600 as "a component identified by the group engagement team that

- is of individual financial significance to the group or
- due to its specific nature or circumstances, is likely to include significant risks of material misstatement of the group financial statements."

For components that are financially significant, an audit of the component's financial information is performed. For components considered significant due to their likelihood of including significant risks of material misstatements, an audit or other audit procedures are performed. For components that are not significant, the group engagement team performs analytical procedures at the group level.

AU-C section 600 also includes requirements and guidance related to the group wide internal controls, the consolidation process, and subsequent events.

Communication With Others and Documentation

The clarified standard requires the group engagement team to communicate specific items to the component auditor and to request that the component auditor also communicate with the group engagement team about certain matters. Specific items are also required to be communicated to group management or those charged with governance of the group, or both.

The clarified standard also requires explicit documentation, including an analysis of the group's components indicating the significant components and type of work performed on the components.

Other Changes

In order for reference to the component auditor to be made in the auditor's report on the group financial statements, the component financial statements need to be prepared using the same financial reporting framework as the group financial statements, and the component auditor has to have performed an audit on the financial statements of the component in accordance with GAAS or, when required by law or regulation, auditing standards promulgated by the Public Company Accounting Oversight Board. The ASB believes that this requirement makes explicit what is implicit in the extant standard.

The AICPA is developing an Audit Risk Alert, *Group Audits*, which will be available in 2012 and will provide additional guidance for implementing this standard.

AU-C section 600 supersedes AU section 543, *Part of Audit Performed by Other Independent Auditors* (AICPA, *Professional Standards*).

F.05 Auditor's Reports

The following clarified standards include auditor report changes describing management's responsibility; the use of headings; and the introduction of the two new terms *emphasis-of-matter* and *other-matter paragraphs*, replacing the term *explanatory paragraph*:

- AU-C section 700, *Forming an Opinion and Reporting on Financial Statements* (AICPA, *Professional Standards*)

- AU-C section 705, *Modifications to the Opinion in the Independent Auditor's Report* (AICPA, *Professional Standards*)

- AU-C section 706, *Emphasis-of-Matter Paragraphs and Other-Matter Paragraphs in the Independent Auditor's Report* (AICPA, *Professional Standards*)

These clarified standards include close integration with AU-C sections 210, *Terms of Engagement* (AICPA, *Professional Standards*) and 580. AU-C section 700 includes a requirement to describe management's responsibility for the preparation and fair presentation of the financial statements in more detail than what was required in the extant standards. The description includes an explanation that management is responsible for the preparation and fair presentation of the financial statements in accordance with the applicable financial reporting framework and that this responsibility includes the design, implementation, and maintenance of internal control relevant to the preparation and fair presentation of financial statements that are free from material misstatement, whether due to fraud or error. This clarified standard also includes the use of headings throughout the auditor's report to clearly distinguish each section of the report.

AU-C section 706 introduces and describes

- an *emphasis-of-matter* as a paragraph included in the auditor's report that refers to a matter appropriately presented or disclosed in the financial statements. An emphasis-of-matter paragraph would refer to any paragraph added to the auditor's report that relates to a matter that is appropriately presented or disclosed in the financial statements. Some of these paragraphs are required by certain standards, whereas others are added at the discretion of the auditor, consistent with current practice. However, all such paragraphs are to be considered emphasis-of-matter paragraphs because they are intended to draw the users' attention to a particular matter.

- an *other-matter* as a paragraph included in the auditor's report that refers to a matter other than those presented or disclosed in the financial statements that, in the auditor's judgment, is relevant to the users' understanding of the audit, the auditor's responsibilities, or the auditor's report.

Accordingly, the term *explanatory paragraph* is no longer to be included in GAAS. Instead, additional communications in the auditor's report are labeled as either emphasis-of-matter or other-matter paragraphs. AU-C section 706 requires an emphasis-of-matter or other-matter paragraph to always follow the opinion paragraph and to be included in a separate section of the auditor's report under the heading "Emphasis of Matter" or "Other Matter."

AU-C section 705 has no significant changes from the extant standard.[2]

AU-C section 700, 705, and 706 supersede AU section 410, *Adherence to Generally Accepted Accounting Principles* (AICPA, *Professional Standards*); paragraphs .01–.02 of AU section 530, *Dating of the Independent Auditor's Report* (AICPA, *Professional Standards*); and paragraphs .01–.11, .14–.15,

---

[2] Although AU-C section 705, *Modifications to the Opinion in the Independent Auditor's Report* (AICPA, *Professional Standards*), is discussed here with the other AU-C section 700, *Forming an Opinion and Reporting on Financial Statements* (AICPA, *Professional Standards*), reporting sections, it primarily contains formatting changes and, thus, if separately categorized, would not be included in part I.

.19–.32, .35–.52, .58–.70, and .74–.76 of AU section 508, *Reports on Audited Financial Statements* (AICPA, *Professional Standards*).

Part II: Primarily Clarifying Changes

The AU-C sections discussed in this part have primarily clarifying changes that are intended to explicitly state what may have been implicit in the extant standards, which, over time, resulted in diversity in practice. Certain of these clarified standards address management responsibilities that may need to be communicated to clients early in the planning stage. Some of these requirements may already be performed in practice, although not explicitly required by the extant standards. Most notably, certain of the new requirements shift the timing of certain requirements from the reporting stage of an audit to the planning stage. The new requirements in this section may not have a substantial impact but may result in adjustments to the timing and responsibilities of the auditor and his or her clients and will need to be reviewed by the auditor to ensure that all requirements have been properly addressed.

F.06 Terms of Engagement

AU-C section 210 requires the auditor to establish an understanding regarding services to be performed for each engagement (new and continuing) and to document that understanding through a written communication with the client.

Financial Reporting Framework

The clarified standard requires the auditor to determine whether the financial reporting framework to be applied in the preparation of the financial statements is acceptable. The auditor's responsibility for determining the acceptability of the applicable financial reporting framework, which is necessary in order to express an opinion on the financial statements, has been implicit in GAAS. It is appropriate that this determination be performed in conjunction with accepting the engagement.

The clarified standard requires the auditor to obtain management's agreement that it acknowledges and understands its responsibility for selecting the appropriate financial reporting framework, establishing and maintaining internal control, and providing access and information to the auditor. The extant standard requires the auditor to establish an understanding with management that includes management's responsibilities, including the selection and application of financial reporting, establishing and maintaining internal control, and making all financial records and related information available to the auditor as matters that may be included in the understanding established with the client. Thus, a level of detail that is suggested in the extant standard is now a requirement. The ASB believes that it is appropriate to require that management's responsibilities be explicit in the engagement letter because there is no point in starting an audit if management won't acknowledge its responsibilities.

Imposed Limitation on the Scope

If management or those charged with governance of an entity that is not required by law or regulation to have an audit impose a limitation on the scope of the auditor's work in the terms of a proposed audit engagement such that the auditor believes that the limitation will result in the auditor disclaiming an opinion on the financial statements as a whole, the auditor should not accept such a limited engagement as an audit engagement unless the audit is required by law or regulation. AU-C section 210 requires that, unless required by law or regulation to do so, the auditor should not accept the engagement if the auditor has determined that the applicable financial reporting framework is not acceptable or if the agreement with management that it acknowledges and understands its responsibility for selecting the appropriate financial reporting framework has not been obtained. Existing GAAS does not contain these requirements. Thus, these changes in requirements will affect current practice.

Recurring Audits

For recurring audits, the clarified standard requires the auditor to assess whether circumstances require the terms of the audit engagement to be revised. If the auditor concludes that the terms of the engagement need not be revised, the auditor should remind the entity of the terms of the engagement by means of a new engagement letter or a reminder, either written or oral, that the responsibilities in the previous terms of engagement still apply. The extant standard requires that the auditor should establish an understanding with the client for each engagement, which, in practice, may not result in a reminder each year for recurring audits. AU-C section 210 also requires that the reminder, which may be written or oral, should be documented. These requirements may affect current practice, depending on how the extant standard has been interpreted.

Changing Level of Assurance

AU-C section 210 addresses situations in which the auditor is requested to change the audit engagement to an engagement that conveys a lower level of assurance. These situations are addressed in Statements on Standards for Accounting and Review Services; thus, including these requirements in GAAS will not affect current practice.

Legal or Regulatory Requirements to the Auditor's Report

Additionally, AU-C section 210 addresses situations in which the law or regulations prescribe the layout or wording of the auditor's report in a form or in terms that are significantly different from the requirements of GAAS. Extant standards require that, in such circumstances, the auditor reword the prescribed form or attach a separate report. AU-C section 210 includes the explicit requirement that if the auditor determines that rewording the prescribed form or attaching a separate report would not be permitted or would not mitigate the risk of users misunderstanding the auditor's report, the auditor should not accept the engagement. Thus, this change in requirement may affect current practice.

AU-C section 210 supersedes paragraphs .05–.10 of AU section 311, *Planning and Supervision* (AICPA, *Professional Standards*), and paragraphs .03, .05–.10, and .14 of AU section 315, *Communications Between Predecessor and Successor Auditors* (AICPA, *Professional Standards*).

F.07 Quality Control for Audit Engagements

AU-C section 220 contains requirements and application material that address specific responsibilities of the auditor regarding quality control procedures for an audit of financial statements. This clarified standard strengthens the requirements of the extant standard by making it easier for auditors to understand and apply those quality control procedures that apply to an audit of financial statements (the extant standards do not contain explicit requirements regarding quality control procedures). However, because these procedures are required by Statement on Quality Control Standards (SQCS) No. 7, *A Firm's System of Quality Control,* they should not affect current practice. SQCS No. 8, *A Firm's System of Quality Control (Redrafted)* (AICPA, *Professional Standards,* QC sec. 10A), superseded SQCS No. 7 on January 1, 2012, and no substantive differences exist between the two standards. One perceived change that may affect many firms is that SQCS No. 8 makes clear that monitoring has to include review of complete engagements; it cannot all come from preissuance reviews.

Quality control systems, policies, and procedures are the responsibility of the audit firm. AU-C section 220 specifies quality control procedures at the engagement level that assist the auditor in achieving the objectives of the quality control standards and addresses requirements for supervision in an audit that are included in the extant standard but have not been included in AU-C section 300, *Planning an Audit* (AICPA, *Professional Standards).*

AU-C section 220 supersedes AU section 161, *The Relationship of Generally Accepted Auditing Standards to Quality Control Standards* (AICPA, *Professional Standards).*

F.08 Using a Service Organization

AU-C section 402, *Audit Considerations Relating to an Entity Using a Service Organization* (AICPA, *Professional Standards),* makes certain changes to the auditor's report, adds new requirements for the auditor to conduct communications with client management about the service organization, and requires the auditor to evaluate the impact of certain matters to his or her audit procedures.

AU-C section 402 changes the extant standard in the following ways:

- A user organization is now known as a user *entity.*

- A user auditor is permitted to make reference to the work of a service auditor in the user auditor's report to explain a modification of the user auditor's opinion. In such circumstances, AU-C section 402 requires the user auditor's report to indicate that such reference does not diminish the user auditor's responsibility for that opinion. (As in the extant standard, the user auditor is prohibited from making reference to the work of a service auditor in a user auditor's report containing an unmodified opinion.)

- AU-C section 402 requires a user auditor to inquire of management of the user entity about whether the service organization has reported to the user entity any fraud, noncompliance with laws and regulations, or uncorrected misstatements. If so, it requires the user auditor to evaluate how such matters affect the nature, timing, and extent of the user auditor's further audit procedures.

- In determining the sufficiency and appropriateness of the audit evidence provided by a service auditor's report, the user auditor should be satisfied regarding the adequacy of the standards under which the service auditor's report was issued.

AU-C section 402 contains guidance only for user auditors. Guidance for service auditors is contained in Statement on Standards for Attestation Engagements No. 16, *Reporting on Controls at a Service Organization* (AICPA, *Professional Standards,* AT sec. 801).

AU-C section 402 supersedes AU section 324, *Service Organizations* (AICPA, *Professional Standards*).

F.09 Audit Evidence-Specific Considerations

AU-C section 501, *Audit Evidence—Specific Considerations for Selected Items* (AICPA, *Professional Standards*), combines the requirements and guidance from extant AU sections 331, *Inventories*; 332, *Auditing Derivative Instruments, Hedging Activities, and Investments in Securities*; and 337, *Inquiry of a Client's Lawyer Concerning Litigation, Claims, and Assessments* (AICPA, *Professional Standards*).[3]

AU-C section 501 takes a more principles-based approach to determining whether to seek direct communication with the entity's lawyers than the extant standard. It requires the auditor to seek direct communication with the entity's external legal counsel (through a letter of inquiry) only if the auditor assesses a risk of material misstatement regarding litigation or claims or when audit procedures performed indicate that material litigation or claims may exist. (Extant AU section 337 states, in part, that "the auditor should request the client's management to send a letter of inquiry to those lawyers with whom management consulted concerning litigation, claims, and assessments.") AU-C section 501 requires the auditor to document the basis for any determination not to seek direct communication with the entity's legal counsel.

Requirements and guidance addressing auditing investments accounted for using the equity method have been excluded from AU-C section 501 because the auditing of equity investees is addressed more broadly by AU-C section 600.

AU-C section 501 supersedes AU sections 331; 332; 337; 337A, *Appendix— Illustrative Audit Inquiry Letter to Legal Counsel*; and 337C, *Exhibit II— American Bar Association Statement of Policy Regarding Lawyers' Responses to Auditors' Requests for Information* (AICPA, *Professional Standards*), and rescinds AU sections 337B, *Exhibit I—Excerpts From Financial Accounting Standards Board* Accounting Standards Codification 450, *Contingencies*, and 901, *Public Warehouses—Controls and Auditing Procedures for Goods Held* (AICPA, *Professional Standards*).

F.10 External Confirmations

AU-C section 505, *External Confirmations* (AICPA, *Professional Standards*), provides additional application material regarding the use of oral responses to confirmation requests as audit evidence. The extant standard notes that an oral confirmation should be documented, implying that it is acceptable to have an oral confirmation. AU-C section 505 requires the auditor to obtain written

---

[3] Many of the requirements of extant AU section 332, *Auditing Derivative Instruments, Hedging Activities and Investments in Securities* (AICPA, *Professional Standards*), are essentially the same as requirements in other clarified standards, primarily AU-C section 540, *Auditing Accounting Estimates, Including Fair Value Accounting Estimates, and Related Disclosures* (AICPA, *Professional Standards*), and the suite of standards known as the risk assessment standards, which includes AU-C sections 501, *Audit Evidence—Specific Considerations for Selected Items*; 320, *Materiality in Planning and Performing an Audit*; 450, *Evaluation of Misstatements Identified During the Audit*; 300, *Planning an Audit*; 315, *Understanding the Entity and Its Environment and Assessing the Risks of Material Misstatement*; and 330, *Performing Audit Procedures in Response to Assessed Risks and Evaluating the Audit Evidence Obtained* (AICPA, *Professional Standards*).

The Auditing Standards Board concluded that the application of those requirements in the other clarified standards to the subject matter addressed by the extant standard is most appropriately addressed as interpretive guidance in the Audit Guide *Auditing Derivative Instruments, Hedging Activities, and Investments in Securities*. Consideration of these requirements and related application guidance will be a specific focus in updating the Audit Guide.

confirmations; additional audit procedures may be necessary in order to meet this requirement. For example, the auditor may need to send additional confirmation follow-ups to avoid additional audit work.

Although AU-C section 505 provides guidance regarding the use of oral responses to confirmation requests as audit evidence, it specifically clarifies that the receipt of an oral response to a confirmation request does not meet the definition of an *external confirmation*. It provides guidance on how the response may be considered part of alternative procedures performed in order to obtain sufficient appropriate audit evidence.

AU-C section 505 also addresses the responsibilities of the auditor when management refuses to allow the auditor to send a confirmation request. These responsibilities include communicating with those charged with governance if the auditor concludes that management's refusal is unreasonable or if the auditor is unable to obtain relevant and reliable audit evidence from alternative audit procedures. These procedures are not required by the extant standard.

In AU-C section 505, the definition of *external confirmation* includes audit evidence obtained by electronic or other medium (for example, through the auditor's direct access to information held by a third party). AU-C section 505 also clarifies the following in regard to such:

- Access to the information must come from the third party.

- Access provided by management to the auditor does not meet the definition of an *external confirmation*.

- Even when audit evidence is received from external sources, the auditor must consider the risk that the electronic confirmation process is not secure or is improperly controlled.

The presumptively mandatory requirement in the extant standard to confirm accounts receivable is included in AU-C section 330, *Performing Audit Procedures in Response to Assessed Risks and Evaluating the Audit Evidence Obtained* (AICPA, *Professional Standards*). The requirement is placed in that clarified standard because it is part of the process of determining the appropriate audit procedures to perform. AU-C section 505 presumes that the auditor has already determined that an external confirmation is the appropriate audit procedure.

AU-C section 505 supersedes AU section 330, *The Confirmation Process* (AICPA, *Professional Standards*).

F.11 Opening Balances on Initial and Reaudit Engagements

AU-C section 510, *Opening Balances—Initial Audit Engagements, Including Reaudit Engagements* (AICPA, *Professional Standards*), strengthens existing standards by making clear that reviewing a predecessor auditor's audit documentation cannot be the only procedure performed to obtain sufficient appropriate audit evidence regarding opening balances, and it clarifies that initial audit engagements include reaudits.

Although the extant standards do not explicitly state that reviewing a predecessor auditor's audit documentation is all that needs to be performed to obtain sufficient appropriate audit evidence regarding opening balances, the ASB felt that this clarification needed to be made because the perception of many auditors is that this procedure alone is sufficient.

AU-C section 510 incorporates guidance from ISA 510, *Initial Audit Engagements—Opening Balances*, which requires the auditor to obtain sufficient appropriate audit evidence about whether

a. opening balances contain misstatements that materially affect the current period's financial statements, and

b. accounting policies reflected in the opening balances have been consistently applied in the current period's financial statements and whether changes in the accounting policies have been properly accounted for and adequately presented and disclosed in accordance with the applicable financial reporting framework.

AU-C section 510 supersedes paragraphs .01–.02, .04, .11–.13, and .15–.23 of AU section 315.

F.12 Using the Work of An Auditor's Specialist

AU-C section 620, *Using the Work of an Auditor's Specialist* (AICPA, *Professional Standards*), is expected to affect current practice because it creates incremental documentation requirements. The extant standard on this topic specifically scopes out from the standard the use of specialists employed by the firm who participate in the audit; however, the clarified standard encompasses these in-house firm specialists.

The extant standard also provides requirements and guidance addressing the use of management's specialist. They have now been included in AU-C section 501 under the view that audit evidence produced by management's experts (internal or external) needs to be evaluated by the auditor for relevance and reliability like any other audit evidence.

AU-C section 620 supersedes AU section 336, *Using the Work of a Specialist* (AICPA, *Professional Standards*).

F.13 Consistency of Financial Statements

AU-C section 708, *Consistency of Financial Statements* (AICPA, *Professional Standards*), requires the auditor to compare and evaluate changes and material reclassifications of prior year financial statements to possible changes in accounting principle or adjustment to correct an error in previously issued financial statements. It also requires the auditor to evaluate a material change in financial statement classification and the related disclosure to determine whether such a change is also either a change in accounting principle or an adjustment to correct a material misstatement in previously issued financial statements. If so, the requirements in the clarified standard apply.

AU-C section 708 also recognizes that the applicable financial reporting framework usually sets forth the method of accounting for accounting changes; therefore, the references to accounting guidance previously included in the extant standard have not been included.

Furthermore, to reflect a more principles-based approach to standard setting, certain requirements that are duplicative of broader requirements in the extant standard are included in the "Application and Other Explanatory Material" section in AU-C section 708.

AU-C section 708 supersedes AU section 420, *Consistency of Application of Generally Accepted Accounting Principles* (AICPA, *Professional Standards*).

F.14 Special Purpose Frameworks

AU-C section 800 replaces *OCBOA* with *special purpose framework* and provides additional requirements for the auditor in addressing special considerations in the application of the standards to an audit of financial statements prepared in accordance with a special purpose framework.

Special purpose frameworks are limited to cash, tax, regulatory, or contractual bases of accounting, commonly referred to as OCBOAs. The term *OCBOA* is replaced with the term *special purpose framework*, which no longer includes a definite set of criteria having substantial support that is applied to all material items appearing in financial statements.

The clarified standard requires

- the auditor to obtain an understanding of the purpose for which the financial statements are prepared, the intended users, and the steps taken by management to determine that the special purpose framework is acceptable in the circumstances.

- the auditor to obtain management's agreement that it acknowledges and understands its responsibility to include all informative disclosures that are appropriate for the special purpose framework used to prepare the financial statements, including, but not limited to, additional disclosures beyond those required by the applicable financial reporting framework that may be necessary to achieve fair presentation, and to evaluate whether such disclosures are necessary.

- the auditor, in the case of special purpose financial statements prepared in accordance with a contractual basis of accounting, to obtain an understanding of any significant interpretations of the contract that management made in the preparation of those financial statements and to evaluate whether the financial statements adequately describe such interpretations.

- the auditor to provide the explanation of management's responsibility for the financial statements in the auditor's report and to make reference to management's responsibility for determining that the applicable financial reporting framework is acceptable in the circumstances when management has a choice of financial reporting frameworks in the preparation of the financial statements.

- the auditor's report, in the case of financial statements prepared in accordance with a regulatory or contractual basis of accounting, to describe the purpose for which the financial statements are prepared or to refer to a note in the special purpose financial statements that contains that information.

- the auditor's report to include an emphasis-of-matter paragraph under an appropriate heading that, among other things, states that the special purpose framework is a basis of accounting other than GAAP.

- the auditor's report to include specific elements if the auditor is required by law or regulation to use a specific layout, form, or wording of the auditor's report.

AU-C section 800 supersedes AU section 544, *Lack of Conformity With Generally Accepted Accounting Principles* (AICPA, *Professional Standards*), and AU section 623, *Special Reports* (AICPA, *Professional Standards*), except paragraphs .19–.21.

F.15 Single Financial Statements and Specific Elements, Accounts, or Items

AU-C section 805, *Special Considerations—Audits of Single Financial Statements and Specific Elements, Accounts, or Items of a Financial Statement* (AICPA, *Professional Standards*), changes certain implicit requirements from the extant standards to explicit requirements, such as determining whether the audit is practicable and whether the auditor is able to perform procedures on interrelated items. It also provides certain new requirements for standalone statements regarding the type of opinion permitted in regard to the opinion issued on the complete set of financial statements.

AU-C section 805 addresses special considerations in the application of GAAS to an audit of a single financial statement or of a specific element, account, or item of a financial statement. It does not apply to a component auditor's report issued as a result of work performed on the financial information of a component at the request of a group engagement team for purposes of an audit of group financial statements. It explains that a single financial statement and specific element include the related notes, which ordinarily comprise a summary of significant accounting policies and other relevant explanatory information.

The clarified standard

- requires the auditor, if the auditor is not also engaged to audit the entity's complete set of financial statements, to determine whether the audit of a single financial statement or specific element is practicable and to determine whether the auditor will be able to perform procedures on interrelated items. In the case of an audit of a specific element that is, or is based upon, the entity's stockholders' equity or net income (or the equivalents thereto), it requires the auditor to perform procedures necessary to obtain sufficient appropriate audit evidence about the financial position or results of operations, respectively.

- requires the auditor to obtain an understanding of the purpose for which the single financial statement or specific element is prepared, the intended users, and the steps taken by management to determine that the application of the applicable financial reporting framework is acceptable in the circumstances.

- requires the auditor to determine the acceptability of the financial reporting framework, including whether its application will result in a presentation that provides adequate disclosures to enable the intended users to understand the information conveyed and the effect of material transactions and events on such information.

- requires the auditor, if the auditor undertakes an engagement to audit a single financial statement or specific element in conjunction with an engagement to audit the complete set of financial statements, to issue a separate auditor's report and express a separate opinion for each engagement.

- requires the auditor, in the report on a specific element, to indicate the date of the auditor's report on the complete set of financial statements and, under an appropriate heading, the nature of the opinion expressed.

- permits, except as otherwise indicated, an audited single financial statement or a specific element to be published together with the audited complete set of financial statements, provided that the presentation of the single financial statement or specific element is sufficiently differentiated from the complete set of financial statements.

- requires the auditor, if the opinion in the auditor's report on the complete set of financial statements is modified, to determine the effect that this may have on the auditor's opinion on a single financial statement or specific element. In the case of an audit of a specific element, if the modified opinion is relevant to the audit of the specific element, it requires the auditor to

  — express an adverse opinion on the specific element when the modification on the complete set of financial statements arises from a material misstatement.

  — disclaim an opinion on the specific element when the modification on the complete set of financial statements arises from an inability to obtain sufficient appropriate audit evidence.

- permits the auditor, when it is necessary to express an adverse opinion or disclaim an opinion on the complete set of financial statements as a whole, but in the context of a separate audit of a specific element, the auditor, nevertheless, considers it appropriate to express an unmodified opinion on that element, to express or disclaim such an opinion only if

  — that opinion is expressed in an auditor's report that is neither published together with, nor otherwise accompanies, the auditor's report containing the adverse opinion or disclaimer of opinion, and

  — the specific element does not constitute a major portion of the complete set of financial statements, or the specific element is not, or is not based upon, the entity's stockholders' equity or net income or the equivalent.

- prohibits the auditor from expressing an unmodified opinion on a single financial statement if the auditor expressed an adverse opinion or disclaimed an opinion on the complete set of financial statements as a whole.

- requires the auditor, if the auditor's report on the complete set of financial statements includes an emphasis-of-matter or other-matter paragraph that is relevant to the audit of the single financial statement or specific element, to include a similar emphasis-of-matter paragraph or other-matter paragraph in the auditor's report on the single financial statement or specific element.

- permits the auditor to report on an incomplete presentation but one that is otherwise in accordance with GAAP by including an emphasis-of-matter paragraph in the auditor's report that states the purpose for which the presentation is prepared; refers to the note that describes the basis of presentation; and indicates that the presentation is not intended to be a complete presentation of the entity's assets, liabilities, revenues, or expenses.

AU-C section 805 supersedes paragraphs .33–.34 of AU section 508 and paragraphs .11–.18 of AU section 623.

F.16 Summary Financial Statements

AU-C section 810, *Engagements to Report on Summary Financial Statements* (AICPA, *Professional Standards*), addresses the auditor's responsibilities when reporting on summary financial statements derived from financial statements audited by that same auditor. This clarified standard puts certain restrictions on auditors for reporting on summary financial statements, including new requirements for the auditor in relation to the use of information issued by other auditors, the use of information provided by management, and obtaining certain representations from management. Additionally, an auditor cannot report on summary financial statements that the auditor has not audited.

AU-C section 810

- eliminates reporting on selected financial data.

- introduces the notion of criteria for preparing summary financial statements and requires the auditor to determine whether the criteria applied by management in the preparation of the summary financial statements are acceptable.

- requires the auditor to obtain management's agreement that it acknowledges and understands its responsibilities for the summary financial statements, including its responsibility to make the audited financial statements readily available to the intended users of the summary financial statements.

- establishes that being available upon request is not considered readily available.

- establishes specific procedures to be performed as the basis for the auditor's opinion on the summary financial statements.

- establishes specific elements of the auditor's report, including management's responsibility and a description of the auditor's procedures.

- requires the auditor to request management to provide, in the form of a representation letter addressed to the auditor, written representations relating to the summary financial statements.

- requires the auditor's opinion to state that the summary financial statements are consistent, in all material respects, with the audited financial statements from which they have been derived, in accordance with the applied criteria, when the auditor has concluded that an unmodified opinion on the summary financial statements is appropriate. The extant standard requires the auditor's opinion to state whether the information set forth in the summary financial statements is fairly presented, in all material respects, in relation to the complete set of financial statements from which it has been derived.

- requires the auditor to withdraw from the engagement, when withdrawal is possible under applicable law or regulation, when the auditor's report on the audited financial statements contains an adverse opinion or a disclaimer of opinion. Otherwise, AU-C section 810 requires the auditor to state in the report that it is inappropriate to express, and the auditor does not express, an opinion on the summary financial statements.

- clarifies the auditor's responsibilities related to subsequent events and subsequently discovered facts when the date of the auditor's report on the summary financial statements is later than the date of the auditor's report on the audited financial statements.

- includes specific requirements relating to comparatives, unaudited information presented with summary financial statements, and other information included in a document containing the summary financial statements and related auditor's report.

- addresses the auditor's responsibilities as they relate to the auditor's association with summary financial statements.

AU-C section 810 supersedes AU section 552, *Reporting on Condensed Financial Statements and Selected Financial Data* (AICPA, *Professional Standards*).

F.17 Restricted-Use Alert

AU-C section 905, *Alert That Restricts the Use of the Auditor's Written Communication* (AICPA, *Professional Standards*), applies to auditor's reports and other written communications (hereinafter referred to as *written communications*) issued in connection with an engagement conducted in accordance with GAAS.

It establishes an umbrella requirement to include an alert that restricts the use of the auditor's written communication when the subject matter of that communication is based on

- measurement or disclosure criteria that are determined by the auditor to be suitable only for a limited number of users who can be presumed to have an adequate understanding of the criteria,

- measurement or disclosure criteria that are available only to the specified parties, or

- matters identified or communicated by the auditor during the course of the engagement that are not the primary objective of the engagement (commonly referred to as a *by-product of the audit*).

The appendix to AU-C section 905 lists other standards that contain requirements for such an alert in accordance with the aforementioned umbrella requirements.

The alert language in AU-C section 905, which indicates that the communication is solely for the information and use of the specified parties, is consistent with the extant standard, except when the engagement is also performed in accordance with *Government Auditing Standards*, and the written communication pursuant to that engagement is required by law or regulation to be made publicly available. In this circumstance, the alert language describes the purpose of the communication and states that the communication is not intended to be and should not be used for any other purpose. No specified parties are identified in this type of alert.

AU-C section 905 also modifies the guidance pertaining to single combined reports covering both communications that are required to include an alert regarding the intended use and communications that are for general use, which do not ordinarily include such an alert. The extant standard states that if an auditor issues a single combined report, the use of a single combined report should be restricted to the specified parties. AU-C section 905, however, indicates that the alert regarding the intended use pertains only to the communications required to include such an alert. Accordingly, the intended use of the communications that are for general use is not affected by this alert.

AU-C section 905 does not include a requirement, as required by the extant standard, for the auditor to consider informing his or her client that restricted-use reports are not intended for distribution to nonspecified parties, and it makes clear that an auditor is not responsible for controlling the distribution of the written communication. The alert required by AU-C section 905 is designed to avoid misunderstandings related to the use of the written communication, particularly when taken out of the context in which it is intended to be used. An auditor may consider informing the entity that the written communication is not intended for distribution to parties other than those specified in the written communication.

AU-C section 905 supersedes AU section 532, *Restricting the Use of an Auditor's Report* (AICPA, *Professional Standards*).

F.18 Financial Reporting Framework Accepted in Another Country

AU-C section 910, *Financial Statements Prepared in Accordance With a Financial Reporting Framework Generally Accepted in Another Country* (AICPA, *Professional Standards*), requires the auditor to obtain an understanding of a relevant financial reporting framework generally accepted in another country and relevant auditing standards other than GAAS. The extant standard indicates that the auditor should consider consulting with persons having expertise in auditing and accounting standards of another country. The ASB believes that the consideration of consulting with persons having expertise in auditing and accounting standards should not be a requirement; therefore, this extant standard requirement has been converted to application material in the clarified standard.

AU-C section 910 eliminates the concept of limited use and, in instances when a report that is to be used in the United States is prepared in accordance with a financial reporting framework generally accepted in another country, requires the auditor to include an emphasis-of-matter paragraph highlighting the foreign financial reporting framework and permits the auditor to express an unqualified opinion. The extant standard requires the auditor to report using the U.S. form of report, modified as appropriate (qualified or adverse), because of departures from U.S. GAAP, if financial statements prepared in accordance with a financial reporting framework generally accepted in another country would have more than limited use in the United States. The extant standard further requires that when the financial statements would not have more than limited use in the United States, the auditor's report may include, as appropriate, an opinion only with respect to the financial reporting framework generally accepted in the other country (and no opinion relative to U.S. GAAP).

AU-C section 910 supersedes AU section 534, *Reporting on Financial Statements Prepared for Use in Other Countries* (AICPA, *Professional Standards*).

Appendix G

Mapping and Summarization of Changes— Clarified Auditing Standards

This appendix maps the extant[1] AU sections to the clarified AU-C sections. As a result of the Auditing Standards Board's (ASB's) Clarity Project, all extant AU sections have been modified. In some cases, individual AU sections have been revised into individual clarified standards. In other cases, some AU sections have been grouped together and revised as one or more clarified standards. In addition, the ASB revised the AU section number order established by Statement on Auditing Standards No. 1, *Responsibilities and Functions of the Independent Auditor* (AICPA, *Professional Standards*, AU sec. 110), to follow the same number order used in International Standards on Auditing (ISAs) for all clarified AU sections for which there are comparable ISAs. The clarified standards are effective for periods ending on or after December 15, 2012. Early adoption is not permitted.

Although the Clarity Project was not intended to create additional requirements, some revisions have resulted in changes that may require auditors to make adjustments in their practices. To assist auditors in the transition process, these changes have been organized into the following four types:

- Substantive changes
- Primarily clarifying changes
- Primarily formatting changes
- Standards not yet issued in the Clarity Project

This appendix identifies those AU-C sections associated with these four types of changes.

Substantive Changes

Substantive changes are considered likely to affect the firms' audit methodology and engagements because they contain *substantive* or *other changes*, defined as having one or both of the following characteristics:

- A change or changes to an audit methodology that may require effort to implement
- A number of small changes that, although not individually significant, may affect audit engagements

Primarily Clarifying Changes

Primarily clarifying changes are intended to explicitly state what may have been implicit in the extant standards, which, over time, resulted in diversity in practice.

(continued)

---

[1] The term *extant* is used throughout this appendix in reference to the standards that are superseded by the clarified standards.

Primarily Formatting Changes

Primarily formatting changes from the extant standards do not contain changes that expand the extant sections in any significant way and may not require adjustments to current practice.

Standards Not Yet Issued in the Clarity Project

Standards not yet issued in the Clarity Project contain the remaining sections that are in exposure or have not yet been reworked.

The preface of this guide and the Financial Reporting Center at www.aicpa.org/InterestAreas/FRC/Pages/FRC.aspx provide more information about the Clarity Project. You can also visit www.aicpa.org/InterestAreas/FRC/AuditAttest/Pages/ImprovingClarityASBStandards.aspx.

Extant AU Sections Mapped to the Clarified AU-C Sections

Extant AU Section		AU Section Super- seded	New AU-C Section		Type of Change
110	Responsibilities and Functions of the Independent Auditor	All	200	Overall Objectives of the Independent Auditor and the Conduct of an Audit in Accordance With Generally Accepted Auditing Standards [1]	Primarily formatting changes
120	Defining Professional Requirements in Statements on Auditing Standards	All			
150	Generally Accepted Auditing Standards	All			
161	The Relationship of Generally Accepted Auditing Standards to Quality Control Standards	All	220	Quality Control for an Engagement Conducted in Accordance With Generally Accepted Auditing Standards	Primarily clarifying changes
201	Nature of the General Standards	All	200	Overall Objectives of the Independent Auditor and the Conduct of an Audit in Accordance With Generally Accepted Auditing Standards [1]	Primarily formatting changes
210	Training and Proficiency of the Independent Auditor	All			
220	Independence	All			
230	Due Professional Care in the Performance of Work	All			
311	Planning and Supervision	All except para- graphs .08–.10	300	Planning an Audit	Primarily formatting changes
		Para- graphs .08–.10	210	Terms of Engagement	Primarily clarifying changes

(continued)

Extant AU Section		AU Section Super-seded	New AU-C Section		Type of Change
312	Audit Risk and Materiality in Conducting an Audit	All	320	Materiality in Planning and Performing an Audit	Primarily formatting changes
			450	Evaluation of Misstatements Identified During the Audit	Primarily formatting changes
314	Understanding the Entity and Its Environment and Assessing the Risks of Material Misstatement	All	315	Understanding the Entity and Its Environment and Assessing the Risks of Material Misstatement	Primarily formatting changes
315	Communications Between Predecessor and Successor Auditors	All except paragraphs .03–.10 and .14	510	Opening Balances— Initial Audit Engagements, Including Reaudit Engagements	Primarily clarifying changes
		Paragraphs .03–.10 and .14	210	Terms of Engagement	Primarily clarifying changes
316	Consideration of Fraud in a Financial Statement Audit	All	240	Consideration of Fraud in a Financial Statement Audit	Primarily formatting changes
317	Illegal Acts by Clients	All	250	Consideration of Laws and Regulations in an Audit of Financial Statements	Substantive changes
318	Performing Audit Procedures in Response to Assessed Risks and Evaluating the Audit Evidence Obtained	All	330	Performing Audit Procedures in Response to Assessed Risks and Evaluating the Audit Evidence Obtained	Primarily formatting changes

Extant AU Section	AU Section Super-seded	New AU-C Section		Type of Change
322	The Auditor's Consideration of the Internal Audit Function in an Audit of Financial Statements	All	Planned to be issued as AU-C section 610	The Auditor's Consideration of the Internal Audit Function in an Audit of Financial Statements	Standards not yet issued in the Clarity Project
324	Service Organizations	All	402	Audit Considerations Relating to an Entity Using a Service Organization	Primarily clarifying changes
325	Communicating Internal Control Related Matters Identified in an Audit	All	265	Communicating Internal Control Related Matters Identified in an Audit	Substantive changes
326	Audit Evidence	All	500	Audit Evidence	Primarily formatting changes
328	Auditing Fair Value Measurements and Disclosures	All	540	Auditing Accounting Estimates, Including Fair Value Accounting Estimates, and Related Disclosures [2]	Primarily formatting changes
329	Analytical Procedures	All	520	Analytical Procedures	Primarily formatting changes
330	The Confirmation Process	All	505	External Confirmations	Primarily clarifying changes
331	Inventories	All	501	Audit Evidence—Specific Considerations for Selected Items [3]	Primarily clarifying changes
332	Auditing Derivative Instruments, Hedging Activities, and Investments in Securities	All	501	Audit Evidence—Specific Considerations for Selected Items [3]	Primarily clarifying changes

(continued)

Extant AU Section		AU Section Super- seded	New AU-C Section		Type of Change
333	Management Representations	All	580	Written Representations	Primarily formatting changes
334	Related Parties	All	550	Related Parties	Substantive changes
336	Using the Work of a Specialist	All	620	Using the Work of an Auditor's Specialist	Primarily Clarifying Changes
337	Inquiry of a Client's Lawyer Concerning Litigation, Claims, and Assessments	All	501	Audit Evidence— Specific Considerations for Selected Items [3]	Primarily clarifying changes
339	Audit Documentation	All	230	Audit Documentation	Primarily formatting changes
341	The Auditor's Consideration of an Entity's Ability to Continue as a Going Concern	All	Planned to be issued as AU-C section 570	Going Concern (in exposure)	Standards not yet issued in the Clarity Project
342	Auditing Accounting Estimates	All	540	Auditing Accounting Estimates, Including Fair Value Accounting Estimates, and Related Disclosures [2]	Primarily formatting changes
350	Audit Sampling	All	530	Audit Sampling	Primarily formatting changes
380	The Auditor's Communication With Those Charged With Governance	All	260	The Auditor's Communication With Those Charged With Governance	Primarily formatting changes
390	Consideration of Omitted Procedures After the Report Date	All	585	Consideration of Omitted Procedures After the Report Release Date	Primarily formatting changes

Extant AU Section		AU Section Super-seded	New AU-C Section		Type of Change
410	Adherence to Generally Accepted Accounting Principles	All	700	Forming an Opinion and Reporting on Financial Statements [4]	Substantive changes
420	Consistency of Application of Generally Accepted Accounting Principles	All	708	Consistency of Financial Statements	Primarily clarifying changes
431	Adequacy of Disclosure in Financial Statements	All	705	Modifications to the Opinion in the Independent Auditor's Report [5]	Primarily formatting changes
504	Association With Financial Statements	All	N/A	Withdrawn	

(continued)

Extant AU Section	AU Section Super-seded	New AU-C Section	Type of Change
508 Reports on Audited Financial Statements	Paragraphs .01–.11, .14–.15, .19–.32, .35–.52, .58–.70, and .74–.76	700 Forming an Opinion and Reporting on Financial Statements [4]	Substantive changes
		705 Modifications to the Opinion in the Independent Auditor's Report [5]	Primarily formatting changes
		706 Emphasis-of-Matter Paragraphs and Other-Matter Paragraphs in the Independent Auditor's Report [6]	Substantive changes
	Paragraphs .12–.13	600 Special Considerations—Audits of Group Financial Statements (Including the Work of Component Auditors)	Substantive changes
	Paragraphs .16–.18 and .53–.57	708 Consistency of Financial Statements	Primarily clarifying changes
	Paragraphs .33–.34	805 Special Considerations—Audits of Single Financial Statements and Specific Elements, Accounts, or Items of a Financial Statement	Primarily clarifying changes
	Paragraphs .71–.73	560 Subsequent Events and Subsequently Discovered Facts [7]	Primarily formatting changes

Extant AU Section		AU Section Super- seded	New AU-C Section		Type of Change
530	Dating of the Independent Auditor's Report	Para- graphs .01–.02	700	Forming an Opinion and Reporting on Financial Statements [4]	Substantive changes
		Para- graphs .03–.08	560	Subsequent Events and Subsequently Discovered Facts [7]	Primarily formatting changes
532	Restricting the Use of an Auditor's Report	All	905	Alert That Restricts the Use of the Auditor's Written Communication	Primarily clarifying changes
534	Reporting on Financial Statements Prepared for Use in Other Countries	All	910	Financial Statements Prepared in Accordance With a Financial Reporting Framework Generally Accepted in Another Country	Primarily clarifying changes
543	Part of Audit Performed by Other Independent Auditors	All	600	Special Considerations— Audits of Group Financial Statements (Including the Work of Component Auditors)	Substantive changes
544	Lack of Conformity With Generally Accepted Accounting Principles	All	800	Special Considerations— Audits of Financial Statements Prepared in Accordance With Special Purpose Frameworks [8]	Primarily clarifying changes
550	Other Information in Documents Containing Audited Financial Statements	All	720	Other Information in Documents Containing Audited Financial Statements	Primarily formatting changes

(continued)

AAG-SOP APP G

Extant AU Section		AU Section Super- seded	New AU-C Section		Type of Change
551	Supplementary Information in Relation to the Financial Statements as a Whole	All	725	Supplementary Information in Relation to the Financial Statements as a Whole	Primarily formatting changes
552	Reporting on Condensed Financial Statements and Selected Financial Data	All	810	Engagements to Report on Summary Financial Statements	Primarily clarifying changes
558	Required Supplementary Information	All	730	Required Supplementary Information	Primarily formatting changes
560	Subsequent Events	All	560	Subsequent Events and Subsequently Discovered Facts [7]	Primarily formatting changes
561	Subsequent Discovery of Facts Existing at the Date of the Auditor's Report	All			

Extant AU Section		AU Section Super- seded	New AU-C Section		Type of Change
623	Special Reports	Para- graphs .19–.21	806	Reporting on Compliance With Aspects of Contractual Agreements or Regulatory Requirements in Connection With Audited Financial Statements	Primarily formatting changes
		Para- graphs .01–.10 and .22–.34	800	Special Considerations— Audits of Financial Statements Prepared in Accordance With Special Purpose Frameworks [8]	Primarily clarifying changes
		Para- graphs .11–.18	805	Special Considerations— Audits of Single Financial Statements and Specific Elements, Accounts, or Items of a Financial Statement	Primarily clarifying changes
625	Reports on the Application of Accounting Principles	All	915	Reports on Application of Requirements of an Applicable Financial Reporting Framework	Primarily formatting changes
634	Letters for Underwriters and Certain Other Requesting Parties	All	920	Letters for Underwriters and Certain Other Requesting Parties	Primarily formatting changes
711	Filings Under Federal Securities Statutes	All	925	Filings With the U.S. Securities and Exchange Commission Under the Securities Act of 1933	Primarily formatting changes

(continued)

Extant AU Section		AU Section Super-seded	New AU-C Section		Type of Change
722	Interim Financial Information	All	930	Interim Financial Information	Primarily formatting changes
801	Compliance Audits	All	935	Compliance Audits	Primarily formatting changes
901	Public Warehouses—Controls and Auditing Procedures for Goods Held	All	501	Audit Evidence—Specific Considerations for Selected Items [3]	Primarily clarifying changes

Legend:

[n] Bracketed number indicates a clarity standard that supersedes more than one extant AU section.

The AICPA has developed an Audit Risk Alert to assist auditors and members in practice prepare for the transition to the clarified standards. It has been organized to give you the background information on the development of the clarified standards and to identify the new requirements and changes from the extant standards. Check out the Audit Risk Alert *Understanding the Clarified Auditing Standards* (product no. ARACLA12P), which is available in the AICPA store on www.cpa2biz.com.

Appendix H
Definitions

For purposes of this guide, the following terms have the meanings attributed as follows:

Applicable trust services criteria. The criteria in TSP section 100, *Trust Services Principles, Criteria, and Illustrations for Security, Availability, Processing Integrity, Confidentiality, and Privacy* (AICPA, *Technical Practice Aids*), that are applicable to the principle(s) being reported on.

Boundaries of the system. The boundaries of a system are the specific aspects of a service organization's infrastructure, software, people, procedures, and data necessary to provide its services. When the systems for multiple services share aspects, infrastructure, software, people, procedures, and data, the systems will overlap, but the boundaries of each service's system will differ. In a SOC 2^{SM} engagement that addresses the privacy principle, the system boundaries cover, at a minimum, all the system components as they relate to the personal information life cycle within well-defined processes and informal ad-hoc procedures.

Carve-out method. Method of addressing the services provided by a subservice organization whereby management's description of the service organization's system identifies the nature of the services performed by the subservice organization and excludes from the description and scope of the service auditor's engagement the subservice organization's controls to meet the applicable trust services criteria. The description of the service organization's system and the scope of the engagement include controls at the service organization that monitor the effectiveness of controls at the subservice organization, which may include the service organization's review of a servicer auditor's report on controls at the subservice organization.

Complementary user-entity controls. Controls that management assumes, in the design of the service provided by the service organization, will be implemented by user entities and that, if necessary to achieve the applicable trust services criteria, are identified as such in that description.

Controls at a service organization. The policies and procedures at a service organization that are likely to be relevant to user entities' internal control, as they relate to meeting the applicable trust services criteria. These policies and procedures are designed, implemented, and documented by the service organization to provide reasonable assurance about meeting the applicable trust services criteria.

Controls at a subservice organization. The policies and procedures at a subservice organization that are likely to be relevant to user entities of the service organization, as they relate to meeting the applicable trust services criteria. These policies and procedures are designed, implemented, and documented by the subservice organization to provide reasonable assurance about meeting the applicable trust services criteria.

Criteria. The standards or benchmarks used to measure and present the subject matter and against which the practitioner evaluates the subject matter.

Data subjects. The individuals about whom personal information is collected.

Inclusive method. Method of addressing the services provided by a subservice organization whereby the service organization's description of its system includes a description of the nature of the services provided by the subservice organization, as well as the subservice organization's controls to meet the applicable trust services criteria.

Management's assertion. A written assertion by management of a service organization or management of a subservice organization, if applicable, about the matters referred to in paragraph 1.17a(ii)(1)–(4) of this guide for a type 2 report and the matters referred to in paragraph 1.17b(ii)(1)–(2)of this guide for a type 1 report.

Personal information life cycle. The collection, use, retention, disclosure, disposal, or anonymization of personal information within well-defined processes and informal ad hoc procedures.

Privacy notice. A written communication by entities that collect personal information to the individuals about whom personal information is collected about the entity's (a) policies regarding the nature of the information that they will collect and how that information will be used, retained, disclosed, and disposed of or anonymized and (b) the entity's commitment to adhere to those policies. A privacy notice also includes information about such matters as the purpose of collecting the information, the choices that individuals have related to their personal information, the security of such information, and how individuals can contact the entity with inquiries, complaints, and disputes related to their personal information. When a user entity collects personal information from individuals, it typically provides a privacy notice to those individuals.

Service auditor. A CPA who reports on the fairness of the presentation of a service organization's description of its system; the suitability of the design of controls included in the description; and in a type 2 report, the operating effectiveness of those controls to meet the applicable trust services criteria. When the report addresses the privacy principle, the service auditor also reports on the service organization's compliance with the commitments in its statement of privacy practices.

Service organization. An organization or segment of an organization that provides services to user entities related to the applicable trust services criteria.

Statement of privacy practices. A written communication by the service organization to the user entities that includes the same types of privacy policies and commitments that are included in a privacy notice (see the definition of **privacy notice**). It is written from the perspective of the service organization and is provided to the user entities when the service organization is involved in any of the phases of the personal information life cycle, and the user entity, rather than the service organization, is responsible for providing the privacy notice. A statement of privacy practices provides a basis for the user entities to prepare a privacy notice to be sent to individuals or for ensuring that the service organization has appropriate practices for meeting the existing privacy commitments of user entities. The criteria for the content of a statement of privacy practices are set forth in TSP section 100.

Subservice organization. A service organization used by another service organization to perform services related to the applicable trust services criteria.

Tests of compliance with commitments in the statement of privacy practices. Procedures designed to help provide reasonable assurance of detecting material noncompliance with the service organization's commitments related to privacy.

Test of controls. A procedure designed to evaluate the operating effectiveness of controls in meeting the applicable trust services criteria.

User entity. An entity that uses a service organization.

Appendix I

Schedule of Changes Made to the Text From the Previous Edition

As of March 1, 2012

This schedule of changes identifies areas in the text and footnotes of this guide that have changed since the previous edition. Entries in the following table reflect current numbering, lettering (including that in appendix names), and character designations that resulted from the renumbering or reordering that occurred in the updating of this guide.

Reference	Change
Preface	Updated.
Paragraphs 1.01 and 1.04	Revised for clarification.
Paragraph 1.05	Deleted for clarification.
Paragraph 1.07	Added for clarification.
Paragraph 1.08 and preceding heading, heading before paragraph 1.09, footnote 6 in paragraph 1.09, paragraph 1.10 and preceding heading, heading before paragraph 1.11, and paragraph 1.12	Revised for clarification.
Paragraph 1.13	Added for clarification.
Paragraphs 1.14–.15, heading before paragraph 1.17, paragraph 1.18	Revised for clarification.
Former footnote 13 in paragraph 1.18	Deleted.
Paragraph 1.19	Revised for clarification.
Paragraph 1.20	Revised for clarification.
Footnote 14 in paragraph 1.20	Added for clarification.
Paragraphs 1.25, 3.16, 3.18, 3.39, 3.68, 3.72, 3.84, 3.90, 3.101, 4.12–.14, 4.19, 4.25, 4.27, and 4.29	Revised for clarification.

(continued)

Reference	Change
Heading before paragraph 4.30	Added for clarification.
Paragraphs 4.30, 4.32–.34, 4.36– .37, 4.40, and 4.42	Revised for clarification.
Paragraph 4.47	Added for clarification.
Appendix A	Revised for clarification.
Appendix C	Revised for clarification.
Appendix D	Added.
Former Appendix E	Deleted.
Appendix E	Added.
Appendix F	Added.
Appendix G	Added.
Appendix H	Revised for clarification.
Index	Updated.

Index

AICPA) Online Professional Library

Powerful Online Research Tools

The AICPA Online Professional Library offers the most current access to comprehensive accounting and auditing literature, as well business and practice management information, combined with the power and speed of the Web. Through your online subscription, you'll get:

- Cross-references within and between titles — smart links give you quick access to related information and relevant materials
- First available updates — no other research tool offers access to new AICPA standards and conforming changes more quickly, guaranteeing that you are always current with all of the authoritative guidance!
- Robust search engine — helps you narrow down your research to find your results quickly
- And much more…

Choose from two comprehensive libraries or select only the titles you need!

With the *Essential A&A Research Collection*, you gain access to the following:
- AICPA Professional Standards
- AICPA Technical Practice Aids
- PCAOB Standards & Related Rules
- Accounting Trends & Techniques
- All current AICPA Audit and Accounting Guides
- All current Audit Risk Alerts
One-year individual online subscription
Item # ORS-XX

OR

***Premium A&A Research Collection* and get everything from the *Essential A&A Research Collection* plus:**
- AICPA Audit & Accounting Manual
- All current Checklists & Illustrative Financial Statements
- eXacct: Financial Reporting Tools & Techniques
- IFRS Accounting Trends & Techniques
One-year individual online subscription
Item # WAL-BY

You can also add the FASB *Accounting Standards Codification*™ and the GASB Library to either collection.

Take advantage of a 30-day free trial!
See for yourself how these powerful online libraries can improve your productivity and simplify your accounting research.

Visit **cpa2biz.com/library** for details or to subscribe.